THE NECESSARY APTITUDE

THE NECESSARY APTITUDE

A Memoir

Pam Ayres

WINDSOR
PARAGON

AYR

First published 2011
by Ebury Press
This Large Print edition published 2012
by AudioGO Ltd
by arrangement with
Ebury Publishing

Hardcover ISBN: 978 1 445 87795 2
Softcover ISBN: 978 1 445 87796 9

Copyright © Pam Ayres 2011
Illustration on page x © Bill Grant

British Library Cataloguing in Publication Data available

Printed and bound in Great Britain by
MPG Books Group Limited

*For Dudley, William and James,
and for all my family, especially Tony, Jeff,
Roger, Allan and Jeannie*

CONTENTS

Part One

Part Two

Whiles' lawn, with the Campdene houses beyond

PART ONE

OUR FAMILY

I was born in March 1947 into a time of great hardship for the population of Britain. The snowiest winter of the twentieth century was drawing to a close and would be followed by a colossal and devastating thaw. The country was mired in the aftermath of war, all essential items were rationed and I wonder how much enthusiasm Mum was able to muster when presented with a sixth child to join the swelling ranks of the Ayreses.

Nurse Speed was our local midwife; she drove a smoke-grey Morris Minor and had struggled through ferocious weather to reach Mum for the birth. Although her manner seemed terse and clipped, the mothers of the village regarded her very highly. Nurse Speed saw the true lot of the village wives, the unalleviated pain of their childbirth, the huge, exhausting families.

Mum's name was Phyllis Evelyn Ayres; she was dark-haired, slim, attractive and unassuming. We could not have had a better mother; she defended us, comforted us and was always on our side. Hers was a difficult marriage but she said, 'The kids made up for all that.'

She was born in the hamlet of Baulking, then in Berkshire. It was a quiet, out-of-the-way place, made up of farms and cottages encircling a huge green. Mum grew up there in a stone cottage with her four brothers and widowed mother Florence. In later years, by shocking contrast, fuller's earth was discovered under the ground and a vast opencast mine yawned across the green fields.

Mum was clever at school, particularly at English, and received the offer of a scholarship to the local grammar school. Family circumstances made the notion laughable. She was a clear-sighted, ambitious person who saved up diligently for one of the new bikes then appearing on the roads and byways. Later she worked as a domestic servant in Cromwell Road, London, a setting as removed from Baulking as the far side of the moon. Her independence was cut short when she became pregnant by my father and was hastily married in a sad, anonymous church in Oxford. The attaching shame at that time was such that in our home their wedding anniversary was never mentioned or celebrated in any way. Thus, the six of us acquired our marvellous mother, and we all loved her dearly.

My father was Stanley William Ayres, the only son of Ada and William Ayres of The Common, Uffington. They also had a daughter, Dorothy, who sported an abundance of beautiful fair hair. The family lived in a thatched cottage with a red-brick path, and alongside it in a blaze of orange grew the spotty fat-lipped flowers my granny called monkey musk.

Dad was a treasured son and, in surviving baby photographs, he is exquisitely dressed in the bonnets and sailor suits of the time. He looks like a royal baby.

As a youth, by claiming to be older than his years, he joined the Grenadier Guards and in time became a sergeant. Nicknamed Lew after the American film star Lew Ayres, who appeared in *All Quiet on the Western Front*, Dad saw years of heavy conflict. After evacuation from Dunkirk, he fought

4

in Belgium, France and Germany and finally was sent to Nuremburg during the war trials of 1945–6, which he detested. He held Winston Churchill in the highest esteem.

Dad was a tall man with startlingly blue eyes and fantastic tattoos on his shoulders and upper arms. I found the inky, red-and-blue decorations fascinating. He had several, including a stylised exploding grenade, a dagger, the head of a bearskin-clad grenadier and a pennant bearing the word *Mother*. He always maintained a stark army haircut and narrow moustache. Though immensely strong, hard and tough, on the day our dog was run over he turned away from me to conceal his tears. After leaving the army, he worked for over forty years as a linesman for the Southern Electricity Board, and his working attire never varied from navy blue overalls and a dark beret narrowly hemmed with black leather. Possessed of a dry, outstanding sense of humour he also had a terrifying, explosive temper.

I had four brothers and a sister; there were approximately two years between all of us in age. The boys were Tony, Jeff, Roger and Allan. Tony was tall and dark-haired, Jeff was shorter with a shock of black hair, Roger had brown hair and was slighter, and Allan was fair with National Health spectacles and a wide, endearing grin.

Tony and Jeff were in the church choir. This was not so much due to an irresistible desire on their part to sing, but was more a reflection of their interest in the fact that the choir went on an annual holiday to Rhyl. One evening at choir practice in Stanford vicarage the reverend, weary from a long day, was doing his best to teach the boys a difficult descant, which was to be performed during the imminent visit of a bishop. The boys were in a wild mood and mucked about throughout. In the end the vicar's patience snapped. 'Get out!' he bellowed, 'GET OUT!' Disconcerted by this unusual reaction, the boys stampeded for the door with such speed that there was a temporary jam before they burst through. Tony was one of the last out. He remains the only member of our family to have been kicked up the arse by a man of the cloth.

The two young brothers did indeed go on the holiday to Rhyl. Mum had instructed Tony, as the eldest, to carry Jeff's suitcase and look after him. On the return rail journey Tony was stunned by the near-immoveable weight of his brother's case as he heaved it along various platforms. The reason for this was revealed upon arriving home, when Jeff excitedly unpacked from his suitcase a collection of large rocks still damp from Rhyl beach.

My sister was Georgina, always known as Jean. Taller and slimmer than I was, she had creamy skin and beautiful blonde hair. As a small girl, she had a gap between her front teeth and the dentist made her wear a tiny, tight rubber band to draw them together. It used to wheedle its way upwards and disappear painfully into the gum.

I was no particular beauty, but somewhat chunky and given to glowering. Like my brother Jeff, I had masses of thick hair but unlike him, I was heavily freckled. From time to time, Mum inexpertly cut my hair into a futuristic style. I loved animals and assembled a large assortment of them around me as soon as I could.

I was very happy and secure with my family in our crowded home, except when arguments broke out between Mum and Dad. These were

6

intolerable and struck like a storm. I loved Dad very much; he was strong and funny, brave and industrious. I believe his wartime experiences damaged and disturbed him in ways that could not be seen. Stress counselling was unknown; people were on their own. His insane, unprovoked rages terrified us all. It was unbearable that we could not protect Mum; she would disappear and cry and we couldn't help her. There was no physical violence but plenty of harm was done by vicious bawling words. Then, for many days afterwards Dad became morose and spoke to no one. A poisonous, draining silence filled our home and killed all happiness. In between, there were long sunny times when all was well, but for Jean and me, and I suspect for all my brothers, fear of the next time ran coldly in the gut.

2

OUR HOME

My delivery by Nurse Speed took place at 9pm on 14 March 1947 in the front bedroom of our house at No. 2 Campdene, Stanford in the Vale, then in Berkshire. I was the only member of our family to be born there; the others were all born in a thatched cottage in a row named Southdown, which stood opposite the school. It had a communal washhouse and a dark, square well covered by a lid of wooden planks.

At Campdene, Mum missed the companionship of the little Southdown community, and occasionally we would go to visit a former neighbour Mrs Howse, who owned a golden Labrador. I was tiny then but I remember kindly Mrs Howse giving me a digestive biscuit to feed to her dog. This was a breathtaking experience for me as I had never met a dog before and he was a nice one. And fat. On the other hand, digestive biscuits were a rare sight in our house and I would have liked to eat it myself. It was one of my early dilemmas. Feeling the weight of expectation upon me, however, I gave the biscuit to the dog.

Mum said that only intolerable overcrowding forced them to move from Southdown; she never wanted to go to Campdene right out at the far end of the village. She had heard that it was regarded by the council as a dumping ground for rough families and awkward types, and she didn't wish to be tarred with the same brush. 'People looks down on you if you got a crowd of kids,' she said.

Certainly, the architecture was no great shakes. Planted along the back of the less revered of our two village greens were four grey, block-like houses. Named after Roger Campdene, a long-forgotten former village priest, these formed eight semi-detached council homes. Ours was second from the left.

Mum disliked the new home for several reasons. One major source of unease was the front path, which was narrow, unfenced, and shared with our neighbours Tom and Hilda Parsons. They had one quiet daughter and a garden filled with prized dahlia and gladioli tied tenderly to supporting canes. Our family was made up of six large, energetic children fond of pushing, shoving, horseplay and loud arguments. More often than not, they would also be travelling at speed on numerous assorted bikes, scooters, homemade

8

buggies with calamitous steering, cocoa-tin stilts or in my case a stagecoach drawn by chickens. All these in close proximity to Mr Parson's garden, or indeed our own, were not a harmonious combination. Invariably the mean, narrow path was overstepped, bikes and buggies careered over and damaged affectionately regarded plants, and this caused friction all round. Mum raged against the shared path on a daily basis.

Our house had two rooms downstairs and three up, no bathroom, no hot water and a lavatory comprised of a wooden seat over a large galvanised bucket with a flared top. The lavatory was situated immediately next to the kitchen, ensuring that we ate all our meals within an exceedingly short distance of a heaped bucketful of sewage, and this inspired design was another reason why Mum detested the house. She fought a constant, vengeful battle against flies with the only tool then available, a useless, leaking contraption known as a Flit gun. This shot creamy-coloured jets of noxious insecticide guaranteed to miss the fly. There was also a depressing, sticky brown flypaper spiralling down from the ceiling, on which flies writhed at all times.

The back door faced north and opened directly on to the kitchen, which meant that in winter any heat generated in the room was immediately dissipated when someone came into or went out of the house. Such movements were accompanied by howls of dismay and threatening bawls of 'Shut that door!' as an icy blast swirled round the room. During snowstorms, great gusts of snowflakes blew in like a corny comic sketch, and at all times a barricade of coats lay along the bottom of the door in a hopeless attempt to keep out the draught.

The kitchen was distempered green and very small, certainly for a family of eight. It had little storage space. A row of brass clothes hooks took up all of one wall and these must have been of colossal strength to endure the massive weight of coats that bulged out into the room. Heaped below was a dusty graveyard of footwear. Enormous quantities of plimsolls, wellingtons, nailed boots, football boots, low shoes, court shoes, sandals and gaiters spilled out into the room, and were regularly ransacked by frantic persons holding one shoe while searching for the other.

On the opposite side of the room was a kitchen range with a fireplace and ovens, which, as we had an electric cooker, was seldom used. Below the window was a large Belfast-type sink with a revoltingly soft, rotting wooden draining board. At this sink, everyone washed and performed their daily ablutions. Ranged along the windowsill was evidence of this in numerous round tins of pink Gibbs toothpaste, ancient shattered toothbrushes, razors, shaving soap, bald shaving brushes and pots of Brylcreem. There were bottles of bay rum and liquid paraffin, world-weary grey face flannels and a great pink brick of Lifebuoy soap. Later, exotic additions such as Old Spice aftershave lotion appeared in the line-up.

Our kitchen furniture consisted of odd wooden chairs with a bigger, carver type for Dad placed beside the cheerlessly cold kitchen range. On the floor was an item to be seen everywhere at that time, the rag rug. Crafted by hand from cut-up old clothes and a length of sacking, they were mostly made by men. Holes were poked in the hessian with a special tool, and a loop of cloth was pushed in and threaded back through itself. Done enough times, this produced a shaggy floor covering, warm to the feet and capable of attracting monumental quantities of dust. Women shaking them out of the back doors risked death by choking, so impressive were the engulfing clouds of dust that rose up. Mum hated the rugs; they were so gloomy-looking, formed from worn-out drab clothing, the flooring of the poor.

Opposite the window stood a kitchen table, which was never out of use. Upon it stood the suitcase-like bulk of our brown wooden wireless, and here every day Mum worked on a vast variety of household chores. She rolled out great grey boulders of pastry, stirred up gargantuan one-egg currant cakes, bottled fruit into Kilner jars and sealed down innumerable pots of homemade jam as dark protective jewels for the winter. At this table, she dished up colossal meals every day and, at night, before she went to bed, she used it to saw up more loaves to make packed lunches for the men to take to work in the morning. She never stopped working and I am sorry to say that I took her entirely for granted. I was used to seeing her stagger across the kitchen with great wrist-cracking brown saucepans full of cooked vegetables, shouting warningly: 'Boiling water! Boiling water!' Every day I watched her back out of the stiflingly hot cupboard where she fried, roasted, baked and boiled on our bandy-legged Jackson electric cooker. She would be drenched in sweat and red in the face, her dark hair tied up in a scarf because she so hated it to smell of fat. Most mornings she would pedal off down to the village shops on her bike, returning unsteadily with heavy bags crowded on to the handlebars. On Mondays, she would be wrestling the hard flapping sheets on and off the clothes line, buckets of grey water and bowls of soaking garments cluttered the kitchen floor, and the whole scene would be permeated by the immediately recognisable and unlovely smell of washday. At any other time she might be energetically mashing up food for the chickens, cleaning windows, top-and-tailing gooseberries, knitting jumpers, peeling heaps of apples and mud-caked potatoes, or making beds with one hand wrenching back the sheets and the other clutching a bar of soap for pouncing on fleas. I never expected her to be ill and she never was, apart from once. I watched her work year in, year out, doing the endless round of chores and it never once occurred to me that she might have wanted some other life, some tiny bit of freedom for herself.

Next to the kitchen where Mum laboured was our front room. This contained a sofa, which by the use of brute force could be transformed into a chaise-longue, together with various chairs, a large cherry-wood drum table and a sideboard with dangly metal door handles that rattled if poked. Done continuously this could irritate people in a satisfying way.

Heating was by an open fire around which all the family gathered on winter evenings. A forest of legs stretched out gratefully towards the flames and my clear recollection is of having a hot front and cold back. Sometimes we played Ludo, Snakes and Ladders or cards. We had a bagatelle where a sprung bolt shot metal balls noisily round a shallow, tray-like board, and we played shove ha'penny on a home-made board with a rounded top like a church window.

When too many startling and unwelcome clods

of fiery soot fell down into the fireplace of an evening, money would have to be spent on the chimney-sweeping service provided by Harry Belcher of Joyce's Road. He would arrive with brushes, lengths of sacking and a blackened nephew. A ribald crowd would then assemble outside on the green and enthusiastically cheer the appearance of Harry's brush as it was suggestively thrust far up out of the chimney more times than were strictly necessary.

Resident in the front room was Mum's budgerigar Joey who was bright green. He lived in a cage where boredom was not an option. In addition to a seed dish and water container, he fought his way through a combined hanging mirror and bell, a small swing, a thicket of millet chunks, a whole cuttlefish and a life-sized, weighted, green plastic effigy of himself, the whole underslung by an elasticated shower-hat arrangement to catch debris. He was a nice, cheery little bird who would hop on to a proffered finger and emerge for a fly round the room once all windows and doors were sealed shut. In later years, it was Mum's proud achievement that she taught Joey to say, 'Where's Jeannie? Where's Pam? Gone-a-school!' Joey would pose and answer the question far into the night unless shrouded by a tea towel.

At bedtime, the family retired upstairs. Mum and Dad slept in the front bedroom, which had a lovely view over the green and down into the village. When we were very little Jean and I also slept in our parents' bedroom, Jean in a single bed and me in a cot. Mum and I had an arrangement. If I woke up during the night, on feeling along the mantelpiece beside me I would find a treat. It was always the same; a long wedge-shaped corner cut

13

off a loaf of bread, buttered and dipped in sugar. I would settle back down quietly with my prize. This worked a treat for both parties and is no doubt the reason why my front teeth are now held together by colossal fillings.

One night in my cot, I remember being woken by energetic movement and stifled gasps issuing from the bed beside me. I enquired loudly into the darkness as to whether Mum was all right. All activity froze, there was an embarrassed mumbling and within a day or so Jean and I were whipped out of that bedroom and installed into one at the back of the house. All four brothers were somehow shoehorned into the third and last bedroom. Thus, the family settled down to sleep.

At night, it was unthinkable to have to go outside to answer the call of nature so alternative arrangements were provided. There was a squat white chamber pot or 'po' beneath some of the beds but for a man-sized piddle an enamel bucket stood ready on the landing. Here, Father, home from the pub, would stand to urinate thunderously like a horse. It was not unusual in the morning to see a fine head of foam in the bucket, like Guinness. The stench must have been ruinous but I never noticed it, not once. It was a tall bucket with a wire handle and wooden grip, all in a pleasant shade of aqua. In the morning, the various receptacles were brought down and the contents poured gingerly into the lavatory bucket.

This bucket needed to be emptied at frequent intervals. Dad would nominate a volunteer to assist him in the detested task and the chosen son would approach his side of the bucket with revulsion. Using gloved hands the two operatives would grasp its stout handles, lift it carefully forth from

14

under the wooden seat and shakily convey its considerable weight up the garden. Here a large gaping hole had been dug and the contents were poured splashily in. Grass grew spectacularly soft and lush in the area, but the marshy ground was never used or cultivated in any way.

3

THE IMMEDIATE VICINITY

Opposite the back door of our house were two things of interest to me as a child, and the first of these was Dad's shed. Creosoted black and of unpromising ramshackle appearance, it scowled from beneath a mean slit window covered in chicken wire. Once the hasp and staple fastening was released and the door flung back, however, a great cornucopia of goods was revealed, much of it the paraphernalia of war and death. There was a wooden-lidded copper for boiling the washing, and tightly packed all round it was an intricate, interlocked mass made up of bicycles, bicycle parts, a boot-repairing last, strings of onions, sacks of potatoes and a vast quantity of gardening tools. There was the apparatus for catching and killing countless small animals: rabbit nets, wires and snares, rods for catching fish and priests for coshing them senseless. There were gormless-looking pigeon and duck decoys and, for luring the birds to their deaths, a strange croaking duck whistle, which sounded like no duck I had ever heard. For the maiming of defecating cats there was a supply of small round potatoes and a great black homemade catapult. Rising haphazardly beyond were assorted pumps, metal ammunition boxes, army-type crates with stencilled numbers, wire, rope, coal, wheat, grit, mouse traps, rat traps, gin traps, mole traps, eel traps, gaffes, a harpoon, a brass knuckleduster, a crossbow, a bayonet, further old weaponry of various types and, like a cherry on the top, a dust-encrusted Jerry helmet. It was a stupefying sight.

Apart from the shed, the other item of considerable interest to me was a water pump. Along the backs of the Campdene houses ran a path that linked them all, and evenly spaced along it were several hand pumps. The water drawn up had originally been Campdene's only supply, but when tested it was found to be contaminated. This came as a surprise to no one, considering the vast quantity of lavatory buckets upended cheerfully into nearby holes in the ground, but mains water was greeted with relief when it arrived and the redundant pumps fell into disuse. Ours was important-looking, raised aloft on a concrete cube with steps leading up as if to a throne. The curvaceous handle, when energetically pumped, first produced a remote subterranean clanking from the failing mechanism, then puffs and belches of air laden with a peculiar metallic smell, and finally a coughing and spewing of rusty water, which shot forth and flowed thrillingly down the dry steps like a waterfall. When the pump finally despaired of receiving no maintenance and gave up, I was aghast, heartbroken. The water had been such a great plaything. With it, I could command the seas; I could call up the flood.

Hanging on the back wall of our house were two tin baths, and next to them was a broken-down

16

mangle with cracked rollers like the chapped lips of a mouth. The tin baths, one large and one small, had given at the seams and been much repaired, using rubbed-in daubs of pink Lifebuoy soap. On a fairly infrequent basis, they were brought indoors and the family bathed in front of the fire. As each new person got in, the water was warmed up and the silt diluted by the perilous addition of boiling water from a kettle. Modesty was of great importance to Mum. Long before any male family members thought about undressing, she would swathe Jean and me in our warmed-on-the-fender winceyette nightdresses, and hurry us up to bed.

4

OUR GARDEN

Each house at Campdene was provided with a generously long strip of garden at the back. These were highly productive and cultivated all year round for the growing of food. Lush and richly green, they contained all the basic vegetables planted in wide flourishing stripes. Sturdy rows of runner beans stood fast against the wind, spiralling up hazel poles chopped from the hedgerows. Dangling from leafy bushes were strings of jewel-like blackcurrants and sweet, thin-skinned gooseberries safe amid their thorns. Fruit trees rose up over rampant clumps of mint trapped in half-buried rusty buckets, and close by the back doors in soft rounded cushions grew sage, used to perfume countless stuffings and rabbit stews.

Dad was an exceedingly good vegetable

gardener and very competitive. All that separated the long individual gardens from each other were narrow grass paths, so the effect was more that of a burgeoning field dotted with men bent over their labours. It was easy to look across to see what neighbours were growing and observe their methods. Dad was highly critical of those who rushed to plant their seeds too early in the season when the ground was cold and wet. 'They be in too much of a hurry,' he would scoff, 'they don't gain a thing.' It was always on 21 April that he planted his seeds each year because, he said, 'they don't get checked'. The range and quantity of food he grew was awesome. Potatoes, carrots, onions, massive parsnips, runner beans, broad beans, peas, celery and a wealth of other staples besides.

Feared like a pox was the Colorado beetle, a thumb-sized, striped job that represented a dire threat to potatoes. This substantial insect was much publicised and notorious throughout the war years as an ever-present, cataclysmic threat to the home potato crop. Our potatoes were closely scrutinised for the pest and Dad was constantly vigilant in case one scuttled out of the shed.

Additionally, he grew brassica plants to sell. While most of the front gardens at Campdene sported flowers, ours was finely raked and meticulously planted with all members of the cabbage tribe. Curly kale, Brussels sprouts, January king and Savoys flourished there in ruler-straight rows, and in spring a succession of old gents and gaffers made their way across the village green to buy their plants for the season ahead. Pulled fresh, they scented the air with the smell of exposed earth clinging to their roots. Wrapped in a band of newspaper and tied with string, they were

18

cordially exchanged for the sum of two bob, and the old gaffers would pedal off on their bikes to reappear at the same time next year.

Not only did Dad cultivate the long garden at Campdene, he also meticulously kept two large allotments at Holywell on the south side of the village. This represented a massive amount of work and my brothers were made to help him. After he had eaten his tea at night, he would tie a garden spade, rake or 'prong' on the crossbar of his bike and go 'down Holywell'. Occasionally I went with him although I was bored by all gardening. There was a dark pond fringed with trees and populated by frogs. Decades later, long after it was filled in, I realised that this had probably once been the Holy Well the place was named after.

Less holy were the attitudes that prevailed towards fellow creatures. Gardening was different then. Nobody cultivated their ground as some sort of optional relaxing recreation. It was gruelling work undertaken to feed the family, for survival. You did it or you went hungry. When I was little, food was still rationed and an abhorrence of waste and a dread of hunger and shortages still burned bright in my parents' generation. Garden produce was fiercely watched over and protected, and this meant the wholesale and detestable slaughter of countless small creatures. Pests were not tolerated in the garden, butterflies were killed in their thousands and, with cold indifference, salt was pinched on to slugs so that their skins rolled up grotesquely. Kettles of boiling water were routinely poured over colonies of ants doing no harm at all, and in the foreign light of day soft velvet moles were left to die in uprooted mole traps left on the garden path. The memory of their blind faces and anguished open mouths, their perfect pink hands flailing in agony, always haunted me.

Every household kept poultry for fresh eggs, and because they gave a useful return for table scraps. Three types of bird were commonly available, the Rhode Island Red, the Light Sussex or a popular cross between the two, advertised by sellers as RIR x LS. At the top end of the Campdene gardens all the tenants had created homes for their laying hens, some with more flair than others. A line of chicken runs and henhouses in various architectural styles from the admirably practical to the pitiful collapsing formed a ragged boundary across the horizon. Our henhouse bore the trademarks of having been crafted by Dad. Soaked and pungent with creosote, it had chicken-wire windows, a roof of corrugated iron and a leather hasp made out of an old boot. A terrace of similarly creosoted hutches ran alongside it and, in these, insensitively placed side by side, lived Dad's ferrets and my pet rabbits, one lot being by nature the hunter and the other the terrified prey. There was also an enclosure for Roger's collection of beautiful white fantail pigeons, and a straggle of greengage trees, which seldom fruited.

Mysteriously, despite the all-enveloping creosote, our henhouse still teemed with red mite, a common parasite of poultry. Nonetheless I spent many hours crouched inside, peering out of the narrow wire mesh window in order to catch birds. This inconvenienced them but was not sinister in any way. They were marvellous to me. I liked to inspect them fondly, stroke their downy heads and let them go. The trapping equipment was easily scavenged; a short stick, a length of string, Mum's washing-up bowl and a handful of wheat. The bowl

20

was placed over the wheat and propped up on one side by the stick. String tied to the stick was threaded up through the chicken-house window into the sweaty hand of the trapper. Several nail-biting hours would then elapse during which time things could go seriously wrong. A chicken could stick its head under the bowl to pinch the grain, causing the collapse of the finely-balanced device, or a strong wind might whirl the bowl away. Usually though, after half a day or so, a peckish sparrow would hop underneath, the stick would be wrenched excitedly forth, the chicken-house door would be kicked open and a triumphant red mite-speckled figure bent double with cramp would emerge to claim the prize.

Beyond the erratic roofline of poultry houses was a market garden belonging to Brigadier Kellie, a short, peppery ex-army officer with a bristly moustache. He seemed of a somewhat frosty disposition towards us. In his brown warehouse-man's coat he could be seen supervising the running of the business. The place was smartly immaculate; long greenhouses flashed in the sun and, in the fields, fragile glass cloches stood in carefully placed rows. Expensive, luxurious asparagus flourished in ferny abandon and beyond it were rows of blackcurrants, which village women were paid to pick in high summer. Sometimes I went with Mum but it was hot, boring work that I and the other kids enlivened by placing stones in the bottom of our punnets to increase the weight. Brigadier Kellie soon cottoned on to this, however, and, to our horror, took to upending the punnets into the large metal dish of a weighing scale. The stones were revealed, shamefully exposing us as cheats.

5

OUR FOOD

At mealtimes, our family devoured mountainous heaps of vegetables and limited meat, which in reality was a perfect diet. We had little in the way of apple trees but a neighbouring farmer Mr Harold Sharps sold good apples by the bushel basket; we bought those if we could afford it. Gold-coloured Blenheims were much prized as excellent keepers, and we would still be eating them after Christmas though their skins were soft and latticed with wrinkles like the cheeks of a favourite granny.

Dad owned a number of guns, kept in an understairs cupboard, which we were not allowed to open. My impression was that some were legally held and some were not. At any rate, he used them to poach pheasants. We ate a lot of pheasant and every feather was scrupulously burned. We were always told to say we had eaten pigeon, even for our Christmas dinner, but in reality it was pheasant or partridge.

Dad used to go out on windy nights, and under his coat was a big square canvas bag on a leather strap running diagonally across his chest. A gun was broken and concealed in the layers of clothing. Hours later, he would come home with bleeding scratches on his face, and slyly show us a glimpse of the canvas bag grown plump, with long tail feathers extending from it. In later years, he took one or other of my brothers with him. Mum was uneasy, afraid they would be caught and prosecuted, but there was a feeling that any pheasants coming into our house carried with them a sense of redressing the balance, of taking a little from those who had a lot.

Rabbits were different, and plentiful. It was easier to get permission to go on a farmer's land to catch rabbits because they laid crops to waste. Dad made hundreds of snares comprised of a wooden peg and running noose of wire. These were cruel, and killed rabbits by strangulation. The positioning was crucial; much attention was paid to the placement of the lethal loop precisely between the rabbit's regular footprints, to catch him as he bounced up in mid-stride, bring him down and choke him as he struggled. Rabbits were also netted, with a long net fixed along the hedgerow to entangle them as they sprinted back to their burrows in alarm.

A rabbit once caught would have to be 'done'. This involved paunching, the stinking removal of its guts, and then skinning, when its furry coat was pulled up and over the head like a jumper. This beautiful free meat, either roasted or jointed up in rich, herby stews, sustained innumerable families. The pelts also sold cheaply for a few pence and were used in the clothing trade for trimming and warm linings.

Apart from vegetables, fruit, rabbits and other people's game birds, we ate a certain amount of cheaper meats from the butcher. Mum had a strong sense of fairness and was outraged by the practice in our butchers' shop of serving the rich first. Thus if she was standing in the queue and someone from a wealthy family came in behind her, even though she might be at the very front, it was the habit of those serving to look straight over her head, and oblige the moneyed person first. Mother would come home blazing. Sadly, there was no other butchers' shop in the village so she couldn't protest by going elsewhere. Our purchases tended to be modest anyway, suet for pastry, shin of beef for stews, hunks of fat bacon for slicing, and pale boiled pig's trotters, which Dad gripped with both hands and sucked picturesquely at suppertime.

Fish was a different matter. It was abundant and dirt cheap. On the cold marble shelves of Taylor's the fishmonger in Faringdon, cod and haddock were heaped in profusion with sprats, kippers and herrings. As a food it didn't seem to be much valued for its own sake, but was seen more as a second-best choice when no money was available for meat.

An ungainly, murky blue fish-and-chip van visited the green every Thursday evening, looking faintly sinister with an angular chimney sticking out of the top. The hatch remained firmly shut for an agonisingly long time as the fish was fried and, in the meantime, wisps and vapours of the tantalising fragrance escaped to madden the queue. Finally, the hatch was raised up to reveal a moustachioed gent of surly demeanour wielding a large metal scoop. Mum and Dad allowed us four penn'orth of chips each and we would plead with the man for the crispy bits of batter that had fallen off the fish. Stony-hearted, he seldom shovelled any our way. As a sweet treat he sold a kind of honeycomb like Crunchie bars, only nastier. It came in massive orange lumps coated in cheap, soapy chocolate. Gnawing on a boulder with both hands plastered in melting chocolate was the ultimate culinary joy to us, though an alarming sight to the fastidious. I think the unsmiling proprietor was an ex-serviceman who had set up a little business after the war.

Fish, however, could also be caught. All along the eastern edge of Stanford flows the modest River Ock. In addition to being a wondrous if potentially lethal playground, a startling variety of edible creatures could be extracted from it by skill or treachery. Small rainbow trout were one, along with red-finned roach and slim silver dace. Eels could be caught on the rare moonlit nights when they were mysteriously 'on the move', but most fascinating of all were the teeming crayfish that lived in the unpolluted water.

My brothers would craft a ramshackle trap from a bicycle wheel underslung by netting. Attached to a long pole by ropes, the trap would be lowered into the unpromising-looking water, having first been baited with a foul tangle of rabbit guts wired to the hub. The water closed over the trap and a shortish wait ensued before it was hauled out again. In no time an astonishing change had taken place. Now it was heaped with olive-green, whiskery crayfish, their shells clattering together as they grappled over each other to reach the overripe rabbit intestines. Streaming clusters of the creatures dangled from the wheel, flapping their tails like little lobsters as they were lifted up out of the water, shaken into a hessian sack and borne back to Campdene to a gruesome fate. There the smaller of the tin baths was taken down, filled with water and placed over a bonfire to heat. When the water was boiling, the crayfish were tipped in, disappearing into the billowing steam and forced under with sticks. I hated it and could not watch the unbearable scene. Mum felt the same but was more resigned, having seen many seasonal repetitions of the procedure. Still, she went out until it was over.

When the crayfish were cooked and cooled, however, when the vivid brightness of their red bodies was tipped in a slithering heap on to the kitchen table, it was different. Then they would be cracked open and from their shells and claws the delicious white meat would be levered out and devoured with chunks of freshly buttered bread. It was not so difficult then to draw a veil over their suffering, to reach out for more.

Some fish were a lot more prized than others. Chub were looked down upon and dismissed as 'muddy' in flavour. Dead, beak-faced pike were laid out on the kitchen table for family inspection with the kind of grudging respect that might be accorded to a wolf. Their needle-sharp, backward facing teeth were exposed and touched with tentative fingers. They were mean looking and feared. Large numbers of them cruised watchfully along the Ock.

All these, then, were our sources of protein, supplemented by an abundance of vegetables. Thereafter it was a question of stodge. 'Aha!' Mother would exclaim as she rolled up a great suet duff. 'This'll stick to their ribs!' After every meal, we waited for the pudding to appear. Most of these involved large, leg-shaped duffs of shiny grey suet pastry. We had jam roly-poly, spotted dick, apple duff with cloves, or plain duff sliced up and soaked with overwhelmingly sweet golden syrup. Apart from the weighty duffs, monumental rice puddings were a regular sight. Mum made them with what she called 'liquid milk', which was the canned Carnation type, and they simmered for hours topped with a torn, brown, nutmeg-sprinkled skin. Much home-produced fruit was used in golden-topped apple crumbles and plate pies, or in tarts filled with rhubarb, gooseberries or blackberry-and-apple. We had fruit jellies, milk jellies, plain jellies and on Sundays, as a treat, tinned sliced peaches with Bird's custard.

Our baker was a broad man named Arthur Shepherd, rumoured to have an eye for the ladies. His bakery was in the nearby hamlet of Hatford and he started work in the small hours of the morning. As a sideline, he was a kind of bookie's runner, obliging customers who wanted to back racehorses. Father, despite marital friction, was one of those obliged. The creaking of Arthur's massive basket announced his coming long before he strode round to our back door. He sold large 'tin' loaves of bread, currant buns, jam tarts, Swiss rolls and lardy cakes. That was the entire range. The lardy cakes came in a special bag with greaseproof paper underneath and transparent cellophane on top, thus it could be admired in all its currant-speckled greasiness from above, while copious amounts of lard seeped through below. I never liked lardy cake, its cold fattiness, the hard bits of citrus peel and the way it coated your mouth with grease. It was the only bought cake that came into our house, apart from an occasional luxurious ginger cake for Dad when times were rosy.

There were two sweet shops in the village, the closest one to us owned by Mrs Miles. I remember one day pushing our ration book over the counter for her to cut out the coupon with scissors as usual, and her giving it back to me, saying kindly, 'We don't need this any more Pammie.' It was 1953, the year that sweet rationing ended. I was six.

My favourite sweets in Mrs Miles's sweet shop were chocolate drops. You could get white ones or brown ones, sprinkled with coloured hundreds-and-thousands. I also liked the pink prawns made out of some kind of edible foam, and coconut macaroons that were shaped like mushrooms, with white stalks, chocolate-coloured caps and a good overall flouring of desiccated coconut. With my pocket money, I also bought Fry's Five Centre bars, Fry's Peppermint Cream bars and Bounty bars, which were then large and chunky. Later, they shrank. I liked sherbet; you could buy it as a Dab containing a lolly to stick in it, or in Barratt's yellow paper tubes complete with a liquorice 'straw' to suck it up with, which frequently clogged. Either that, or after too enthusiastic a suck, a great nugget of sherbet shot up the straw and paralysed the nostrils.

Of all the jars lined up in the little shop, the one filled with peanut sweets was the most tantalising to me. These were caramel coloured, and shaped into the exact size, shape and texture of a peanut in its shell. After diligent sucking, the outer covering dissolved to expose a centre of sweetened, roasted peanut fragments. Mum used to like Mars bars, and ate them with great restraint after tea at night. She sliced them up like a loaf and shared them with us.

Mrs Evelyn Norton was our neighbour and lived with her family on our left-hand side. She was a Welsh lady, and very kind indeed. She used to make a marvellous treat out of Puffed Wheat and boiled sugar. When finished, it was a great ball of glistening, sugared crunchiness, which needed both hands to hold. These marvels would come over the fence to me with a smile and a lovely feeling of affection and warmth. She was a special, thoughtful lady, and when her eldest daughter Jean began going out with an American GI, Mrs Norton invited me in to see Jean's new dress bought for a special dance. It was a ball gown in dull gold silk, gathered at the bodice in typically Fifties style. It had been laid tenderly over the sofa and I remember how it gleamed in their modest house, lavish among the humble furnishings. As she had thoughtfully anticipated, the dress was a marvel, a thing of undreamed-of splendour to me. Jean eventually married her GI and went away to America to live. Sadly, the Norton family also moved away, and into the vacant house came a postman called Mr Howard who kept himself to himself. With hindsight this was probably out of a healthy respect for Dad's explosive temper. I forgave him anyway because he brought to Campdene a friendly dog called Judy who had a pleasant doggy smell. She used to come round and share my profound thoughts in Dad's shed.

Mr and Mrs Parsons, our neighbours on the other side, had one daughter named Margaret. She was tall and nice, with plaited hair like mine. We three girls used to play together. This was fine except that I, being the youngest, always came last in the queue for everything. The chant was always 'Jeannie first, Margaret second, Pammie last', which I hotly resented but couldn't do anything about. Jean and I were indispensable to each other, but still enjoyed a fairly explosive relationship. We squabbled a lot and to Mum's great annoyance were fond of bashing one another. 'Stoppit!' she would shout, 'You're just like a couple of cats!'

One Easter, Mum gave Jean and me Easter eggs

made out of white sugar with a scalloped edge. We were delighted and went out on the front step to eat them. Sitting on the step next door was Margaret, the only child, who had a luxurious chocolate egg with edible flowers and a flamboyant box. She was sitting on her step holding the mighty egg, nibbling the flower petals. Mum must have looked out of an upstairs window and seen the disparity between the two types of egg, one so expensive and one so modest. To us she seemed bafflingly upset. I think it tormented her that she couldn't afford better ones for us. It would have comforted her to know that Jean and I made no such comparisons. Margaret had an Easter egg and so did we. We were happy.

*   *   *

I remember Christmas at Campdene in a series of little scenes. There was always somebody dolefully saying, 'Well, it don't feel a bit like Christmas to *me*,' which I hated because I *wanted* it to feel like Christmas, to have the magic it was supposed to have. However, I have since found that no Christmas ever goes by without this unwelcome utterance from somebody or other.

Nice preparatory signs appeared beforehand in the form of a bottle of Stone's ginger wine, a bottle of port and a dish of nuts on the sideboard. From Mr Milne the grocer you could buy strips of coloured paper in a pack. Gummed at one end, these could be linked together to form homely festive decorations. Making these up with Mum and Jean in the front room, exclaiming excitedly on the length of the chain as it grew, was such a laughably simple occupation yet also a lovely beacon of affectionate and conspiratorial closeness, making something together that was going to surprise the others.

One year the brothers made a foray to Hatford Warren and sawed the top out of a fir tree. While this could be seen on the one hand as a despicable act of theft, the joy it brought their two small sisters was unimaginable. It was the first Christmas tree we had ever had. Mum bought a hard, blue-wrapped baton of cotton wool from the chemist and we rolled it into balls for snow, dotting them over the branches with cut-up strips of silver paper. It was a gigantic tree, which filled the kitchen with both its presence and its strong, resinous smell.

We were always given exciting presents though money was tight. Mum's present-wrapping understandably lacked finesse because she had a staggering amount of other work to do. Her gifts were encased in Christmas paper with screwed-up ends, like a boiled sweet. One year I received a small yellow lorry with a length of string attached, so it could be pulled alongside as you walked. Although it lacked a certain femininity, I loved it and undertook important haulage jobs up the garden with consignments of wheat for the chickens.

Jean and I also normally received a pair of plaid slippers with a turned-down collar and extravagant red pom-pom, a *Rupert* annual and a box of Cadbury's Milk Tray chocolates that we regularly scoffed in its entirety before breakfast, except for the orange-flavoured ones, which we tried to fob off on someone else. I also loved Maltesers and would sometimes joyfully unwrap a whole rattling box.

At midday, we had our Christmas dinner made

up of somebody else's pheasant. The delicious smell, both of the roasting meat and rich, sage-laden stuffing, was mouth-watering. Afterwards there was homemade Christmas pudding with threepenny bits and sixpences to be discovered loose inside if you hadn't already bitten on one and cracked a tooth. Dad always had a drop of rum during the festive season and Mum would watch dubiously as he filled a glass and the pungent smell reached her nostrils. 'He don't get on with it,' she would say darkly, but would not elaborate.

One particular Christmas when money could not have been so tight, Jean and I were each given a large, beautiful doll. Jean's was named Anne; she was dark-haired, cherubic and reminded me of Queen Elizabeth the Queen Mother because of her hairstyle. My doll was called Lucy, and was tall and blonde. They were the best and only real dolls we ever had. Jean still has Anne in a well-loved but admirable condition. I was rougher with Lucy; her hair came off, she looked dishevelled. I went on without her.

Disturbingly, Jean and I had a doll we always hated and blamed for everything. Her name was Greta; she may have come home in Dad's kitbag from war-torn Germany. She had no luxuriant wig, only sculpted-on hair, and a cloth body with china head and limbs. Jean and I detested her; she was an outcast and had no place amongst our other well-loved toys. Anything that went wrong was Greta's fault; she would be angrily flung across the room and taught a lesson. We were cruel and hostile to Greta; she had a horrible life.

THE SOUNDS OF THE VILLAGE

Beside our front step grew two types of flower. One was a white Shasta daisy that Dad called Estereets, and years elapsed before it dawned on me that this translated as 'Esther Reed', a popular type. The other flower was the beautiful, coarsely hairy Canterbury bells. As a child, it was my habit to sit on the step beside these flowers for long periods, and to consider the sights and sounds of the village.

Stanford was a quiet place then, with very few cars. The sleepy silence was broken only by the daily arrival of a milk lorry from Faringdon, calling to collect the few churns from their wooden platform outside the Sharps' farm on the far side of the green. Occasional glimpses might also be caught of Mr Harold Sharps himself, driving a shooting brake with elaborate planked sides. He was tremendously courteous, raising his hat respectfully to the women of the village. Mum liked him for his gentlemanly ways, and although often taxed and tired by the raising of her own six children, pitied the childless Mrs Sharps, a plump, solitary figure who walked round the village leading a host of dachshunds. Mum used to look at her sadly and at their big house shielded by lime trees with farmland rising beyond. 'They got all that,' she would say, 'and they can't have any kids.'

Opposite Campdene was another farm, a small, pleasant place owned by Johnny Fowles who wore a trilby hat. A group of spotty-feathered guinea fowl trundled around the fields, hayricks, stables and large wooden barn in a never-ending search for food. There was a dreadful yard where cattle were kept in winter. The waste built up until they stood wretchedly in wet ordure up to their bellies. When spring finally brought relief, they tottered out on their poor mired legs, and cantered into the daisy-sprinkled fields.

I was afraid of the beer lorry that came from time to time to replenish the cellars of our nearby pub The Cottage of Content. The squat, black vehicle seemed deeply sinister, parked on the forecourt with its engine running. Somehow, the dark, shuddering bulk of the lorry and the glassy trembling of a thousand bottles of beer filled me with unease, as if the whole thing might suddenly rise up on its back wheels and lurch towards me.

Except for the milk lorry, beer wagon and an occasional vehicle emerging from Emblings the seed merchant, the pale road running through the village was not much used. Large flocks of chirruping sparrows settled upon it and fluffed their feathers in the dust. Occasionally a raw, grinding sound would well up out of the silence, and a sweating apprentice would appear pushing a loaded handcart from one of the two builder's yards in the village. These carts, painted red for Pendell & Spinage or orange for Knapps, were of a curious design, very high off the ground and set upon iron-rimmed wheels of prodigious tallness. The height of the contraption had the effect of dwarfing the pusher. He walked awkwardly, half-crucified, bent forward from the waist with arms outstretched. His grating progress could be heard long before he materialised, or had passed from view.

Tractors had also appeared during these early years of the Fifties. Some farmers chose the extraordinary Field Marshall, which needed the subtlety of a mighty hammer blow on a cartridge to start it, but mostly we saw the big red and blue Fordsons, which roared through the village, flinging up a halo of mud from their massive tyres.

Of particular interest to us children were their trailer-loads of mud-caked sugar beet. Sometimes a weighty beet the size of a human head would roll down and bounce ponderously along the road like a flying bomb. Though frequently disappointed before, we were ever hopeful that this time would be different as, inflamed by the magic word *sugar*, we would race off in pursuit, catch it with both hands and start gnawing it after only the most perfunctory wipe with a sleeve. Shouts of disappointment and disgust would then go up as once more we discovered only a gritty, acrid juice with no trace of sweetness at all.

Sometimes a horse and rider clopped past. Although on many farms the cobbled stables of the heavy working horses now stood empty and silent, many owners and well-to-do families continued to keep horses and ponies to hunt and ride for pleasure. When I saw those riders pass I felt envious. From a very early age, I craved a horse and the lifestyle it stood for, and it was my custom to glare particularly hard at a woman called Mrs Bean. I did not know her or much about her, only that she lived in one of the grander houses at the other end of the village. Mrs Bean, haughty, straight backed and remote, would ride past on a comely horse, leading another alongside. She wore a fitted navy jacket with cream jodhpurs and fine leather boots. Rounded by a net, her yellow hair bulged below the back of her riding hat. Two sleek Labradors scampered on the wide grass verge beside her; a murmur from Mrs Bean would bring them to heel. From my clump of Canterbury bells I watched her as she passed our green and, although she never glanced at me, a village child with home-cut hair, she gave me a feeling that I did not like: of being a nobody, at the bottom of the heap. I had never heard of the class system, but I could feel the gulf between Mrs Bean and me. She made me feel that I didn't want to be the sixth kid in a big hard-up family from a council house. I wanted to be like her. I wanted what she had.

On Sundays, it was the bells of the parish church of St Denys that rang out over the village of Stanford, shattering the silence and bossily summoning the faithful to prayer. We never went. Mum, who every Sunday of her own childhood had been made to attend three church services, had no intention of attending any more. She restricted her churchgoing to village weddings, because she liked the finery and the optimism. Then she would go along and stand in the crowd outside the church 'just to see her come out'.

I never once attended a Sunday morning church service in Stanford. There was always the feeling that they weren't aimed at families like ours, and if I happened to be sauntering past at the time I would look at the churchgoers as if they were a foreign species. The pious seemed different, consisting mainly of landowners and gentry. They had cars, wore different, immaculate clothes and their ringing speech was nothing like our own. They were regarded coldly from the council houses; their wealth and comfortable circumstances were envied. From an early age I

36

heard them referred to as *The Nobs* and was given to understand various less than complimentary facts. They were *Hypocrites*. They were *tight*, they *didn't give much away*, and they *lived off the fat of the land*. I absorbed all this and concluded that there must therefore be two sorts of people; The Nobs and People Like Ourselves. The feeling seemed to be fairly deep-seated in the village, this envy of the few who seemed to have everything, by the majority who, as Dad would prosaically observe, had bugger all.

From the front step, I could always hear the endearing low murmur of countless English elms. They flourished all round us at that time, long before Dutch elm disease came and laid them all to waste. They were a massive, stately presence, never still or silent, whispering pleasantly to themselves in a light breeze, but roaring and thrashing monstrously when storms came. A beautiful, gigantic elm stood right behind our house. We had hours of soaring joy on a swing, which Dad roped to one of its muscular lower branches, and every year the tree released a tremendous confetti of papery, pink-hearted seeds, which gathered in drifts, and sprinkled themselves over No. 2 Campdene.

7

FEMININE BEAUTY

Mum was always busy but still found the time to dress us lovingly and well on an exceedingly tight budget. Mrs Marshall, a clever seamstress in the village, made us matching dresses with little gathered sleeves and Peter Pan collars. We wore whatever hand-me-downs fleetingly fitted us as we shot upwards, and Mum patronised a dimly-lit shop called Goddards in Faringdon for our other clothing. 'How much do they run?' she would ask anxiously when shown new vests or liberty bodices. Goddards operated a tallyman service whereby goods could be bought with an early form of hire purchase, and the payments collected each week by their employees. There were two, Mr Golf and Mr Clistle, smartly suited and unfailingly polite to Mum as they appeared with their notebooks and ledgers at the back door.

*   *   *

On rare occasions, an exotic and extraordinary vendor of clothing would turn up in the form of a pedlar. His skin was fascinatingly brown but as to his nationality we had no clue, other than that he was foreign. He arrived on a bike bearing a mighty suitcase on a rack over the back wheel. Given half a chance, he would stagger into our kitchen with it, raise the lid and expose the alluring contents. He was soft-spoken, infinitely polite and gently flattering. One day he drew out of the suitcase a cardigan more ornate than anything we had ever seen, with entwined flowers worked vertically on either side of the front fastening. Our own woollens were all plain and hastily hand-knitted; by contrast, this was a bird of Paradise. He respectfully gave the cardigan to Mum to hold. Jean and I frantically urged her to buy it; we wanted her to have the lovely thing, but she only looked wistfully at it and handed it back. We

38

couldn't afford or justify such luxuries.

I learned later that beneath the soft layers of clothing the pedlar also stocked a plentiful supply of condoms, mystifyingly known at that time by the whispered euphemism of French letters, and that he did discreet deals over the suitcase with the menfolk of the village before pedalling off to his unknown home.

Sometimes brown-faced gypsies called, broad women bound with shawls, carrying baskets of homemade wood-and-tin clothes pegs and small beribboned bunches of unfamiliar heather. If Dad saw them, he snarled as if they were dogs and the ladies just ducked, spun on their heel and scuttled away in an awful manner, as if they were used to it and it was a way of life.

The first time this happened, I was very shocked. For most of the time, Dad was a kind man and I couldn't believe this swift, horrible, driving away of a woman he didn't even know. I now suspect it was done simply out of fear. Families such as his who lived for generations in remote country hamlets did not dismiss the power of gypsies to bring down curses; they were deeply, unquestioningly superstitious and lived by an old lore. My brother Tony would go out with Grampy Ayres shooting rabbits at Uffington. If a magpie crossed their path Grampy would say 'We shan't do no good today boy' and unhesitatingly turn for home.

*   *   *

Mum was particular about the appearance of her daughters. For some reason when she looked at Jean and me, she could not abide the sight of our

39

straight hair and so arranged to have it permed by a village lady called Mrs Pearl Frost who was good at hairdressing. We would be dispatched off to her house clutching a box containing one Twink home perm between us, which Mrs Pearl Frost found parsimonious. At a tender age, we would sit in Mrs Frost's cold kitchen and wait for the unpleasant ritual to be over. We received half the perm each. Our hair was enclosed in papers, rolled up teeth-grittingly tightly on turquoise curlers and drenched with reeking perm lotion. After an age, it was neutralised and robustly towelled. We went gratefully home, our hair damp, ammonia-laden and duly frizzied up. As we trooped indoors, Mum eyed Mrs Pearl Frost's handiwork with satisfaction.

Mrs Frost and her husband Chas had a son named Derek. He was the same age as me and we were friends. As a young boy, he had an extraordinary religious faith, and could be seen alone every Sunday carrying his bible, crossing the village green to go to church. He tolerated the teasing and ridicule he received for being different, for being perceived as a hymn-singing softie, and never once wavered from his course. He went on to be ordained and became an inspiring and hugely popular priest.

I wanted to be a ballerina when I was very young. This baffles me now, because I can't think where I would have seen one to want to emulate. No ballerinas chose to reside at Campdene; we had no television and were hardly frequenters of the ballet. Nevertheless my sister Jean did her best to further my ambition by standing me on the kitchen table and crafting me a tutu from our regular Sunday newspapers, *The People* and *The News of the World*. Had I been able to read as well as wear these scholarly broadsheets, I would have discovered that while they did little to enlighten readers on world events, they unfailingly listed every eye-watering and salacious detail of all recent cases of rape, sexual assault and indecent exposure.

8

THE VESTIGES OF WAR

Mum had to cope with the needs of her family; she had little time left for playing with us. She used to insist that my brothers took me with them and this did not go down well. They would be setting off on some manly adventure when she would shout:

'And you take that little 'un!'

A chorus of resentful groans would ensue:

'What? Oh, no! Not 'er, we don't want 'er, she can't keep up!'

On a few magical occasions though, Mum came with Jean and me for a walk down the back fields that lay between Campdene and the hamlet of Hatford. We would clamber down the bank into a field that had been shaped and undulated by the ridge and furrow system. Here the land, studded every autumn with an eruption of gigantic horse-mushrooms, lay in long, regular whalebacks like the waves of the sea rolling away into the distance. We walked beside blackberry hedges to the end of the field where the ground became marshy, where bright yellow kingcups, or marsh marigolds, sparkled beside plump cushions of coarser grass. 'You'll have to pick your way,' Mum would call.

'Stay on the tuffets!' Soon we could see the various irrigation channels created by Brigadier Kellie for his market garden. He had diverted the stream, inserting sluices and creating new waterways. There was a little waterfall over a concrete step providing the refreshing splash of water and always, always, the v-shaped wake of countless water voles, swimming fast and furious with their noses up and their brown furry backs sculpted into points by the water. We disliked them, thinking they were rats, and the boys threw stones meaning to hurt them.

From the waterfall, two courses of action were possible. You could turn back through the kingcups and go home the way you came, or follow the stream until it met the Hatford footpath, where black-and-white railings marked the tiny bridge. The path had a sandy surface, and ran away across two fields to Hatford. The first field was an ancient meadow where steers were put to graze, where in the spring cowslips bloomed fiercely in long, creamy drifts. We children picked fat, pink-stemmed bunches of the flowers, unaware of the briefness of their tenure, not knowing that in a few decades they would be gone, the land ploughed, fertilised and condemned to a round of growing endless cereals.

That field was like a jewelled cloth laid over the soil, perfected over centuries, sumptuous and species-rich. The memory stays with me, those vanished wild flowers blowing in their season and the exquisite quaking-grass that we called wiggle-waggles, with herringbone-marked bobbles that rattle in the wind and down the years.

The footpath ran in a straight line over the second field to Hatford, and I was taken there at a very young age to see a house that had been bombed. Young as I was, it made a dreadful impression on me. There was a terrace of cottages with blue slate roofs and through one a jagged hole had been smashed where shattered slates hung like teeth. The stricken house was an appalling scene of brutal destruction among soft, bee-buzzing gardens. Some people said it had been a 'stray' bomb dumped randomly after a London raid, others said someone must have lit a cigarette at an unguarded moment so that the dark, watchful presence in the sky was able to see and take aim. At any rate, on the night of 19 September 1940, three children died in that house, two of them evacuees sent away from their homes to a place of supposed safety. Mum said she could see the flames from across the fields. With a rare gruesomeness, she said, 'I could smell the burning. I could smell the smell of death.'

The war had ended by the time I was born, but evidence of it was still everywhere to be seen. On Cottage Road, there had been an RAF hospital, and behind tall, chain-link fencing the flat-roofed buildings remained, along with a reservoir for fire-fighting and a grass-covered air-raid shelter. To the west of Stanford in the Vale lay Shellingford Airfield, where during the winter of 1941, No. 3 Elementary Flying Training School began operations, using fifty-six de Havilland Tiger Moths housed beneath metal arcs known as blister hangars. From 1943, Horsa glider pilots trained at Shellingford in preparation for the D-Day Landings in 1944 and a large shifting population of troops moved through the village as the war progressed.

Their impact upon the insular community must

have been tremendous. Black Americans arrived, stunning people who had never seen a black face in their lives, and white Americans, the RAF and soldiers of all kinds and nationalities. The tracks of their tanks mutilated the village green. In the build-up to D-Day, sweet country lanes were lined with piled boxes of ammunition ready to be picked up and swept down to swell the great armoury amassing in the south.

Large areas of military accommodation were created for the troops. A cookhouse and cinema stood on the land behind Bear House and a strange kind of mortuary too, with ceramic body-shaped indentations let into the floor for the burned or the dead; we only speculated, we did not know. Those who could have told us were gone, scattered like corn by the winds of war. I have no mental image of those transient soldiers but my older brothers do; they remember the laughing men who smuggled them into the cinema through the open windows and concealed them under benches so they could watch the film; the kind, homesick young men who tried to soften the harshness of the boys' lives and supplement their meagre food rations by giving them chocolate, chewing gum, handfuls of currants.

What I saw was the gradual absorption of these premises back into the landscape, these structures built with such urgency slowly falling into decay. Brambles began to climb the walls of the silent cinema. Ivy softened the rusting legs of the water tower, windows were broken by mischievous stones and chickens scratched at straw strewn in former barrack rooms. Algae clouded the steep-sided fire-fighting reservoirs; rain washed the concealing turf away from air-raid shelters, leaving unexplained lengths of massive concrete pipe marooned in fields. The tautness of chain-link fencing around the airfield gave a little, nettles grew up and flakes of paint began to peel from the angry Keep Out signs. A gentle, imperceptible shift occurred as innumerable army huts found new purpose as stables, cowsheds, stores. Squatters moved in, babies were born; empty buildings threw off their silence and became makeshift homes.

Though large tracts of the former military areas still lay sombre and redundant, the village itself was busily shaking off the austere fetters of war and moving into more prosperous times. It was well equipped to tend to its own requirements. Along the curvaceous High Street were a pair of Esso garages, the two sweet shops and three grocers, one of which was gloriously named Rant & Tombs. There was a café, the two busy builders' yards, the butcher, a Post Office, blacksmith, cycle shop, electricians and a seed merchant, where I collected the 7lb bags of corn and layers mash for Mum's chickens. There was a draper, six public houses, a large school, two chapels and our main St Denys Church possessed of a disintegrating casket said to have once contained the holy finger of St Denys himself.

Disabled people fared as best they could by offering goods and services. Opposite the bus shelter lived Mr Swann who seemed in poor health, but who nevertheless made leather purses and other stitched items, which he then offered for sale in his cottage window. All shoe repairs were undertaken by deaf-and-dumb Wally the snobby, or cobbler, who wore an oversized tweed cap and lived with his mother in a tiny cottage up behind The Red Lion pub. The whole place was

45

busy, purposeful and self-sufficient. Numerous farmyards led off the High Street and in a leisurely fashion herds of cattle plodded through at milking-time, leaving scattered cowpats behind them as they went. Hardware and wet fish, which were not supplied by village shops, turned up in ponderous vans calling weekly from Faringdon, as did Mr Ball, irreverently known as 'ole Bally', who plodded round the villages with his horse and cart, selling paraffin and buying scrap metal. Our village was full of constructive activity. It was moving ahead; all traces of wartime were being thrown aside. The war was past and gone; it was history.

9

A NEW BIKE

The acquisition of your first-ever bike is a momentous occasion. I must have been about seven when I had mine and I remember it distinctly. I absolutely detested it.

Like many things that came into our house, it was handed down. Mrs Rooney from Hatford passed it on to us as she kindly passed on many useful things, but this time I wished Mrs Rooney from Hatford had kept it. It made me stand out in a way I did not like. My new bike was different and conspicuous. For a start, it was bright red, when everyone else I knew had a black bike, or dark green or navy blue. This was hand-painted fire-engine red. Furthermore, it was already too small when I was given it. To ride a bike that is too big gives you a daring, ambitious, devil-may-care look, somebody who is moving on up. To ride one too small gives a squatting, preposterous appearance, of knees akimbo on a baby's thing, only one stage up from a toy. However, far, far worse than the garish colour and inadequate size was this: it had no bell. Where there should have been the standard bun-shaped bell with a large thumb-friendly paddle, this had *a horn*. A red-painted trumpet with a black rubber bulb was screwed to the handlebars. To warn anyone of your approach there was no question of briskly ringing a crisp-sounding bell. Instead, you had to pinch the bulb of the horn. Pinched sharply enough, it would make an excruciating, lewd farting noise. I would rather have died under a bus than pinch that horn. My much-anticipated new bike was a disappointment on all fronts. There was no way I could tell Mum because she was ecstatic. 'That'll do you a treat my gal,' she said, 'it's just the job!' I knew my ingratitude was disloyal and contemptible, but I felt it all the same. I wanted a grown-up-looking bike. One with a *bell*.

Dad helped me to learn to ride it. This involved him in a great deal of fast running while bent double, until I mastered the elusive business of 'getting your balance'. I can still hear his pounding footsteps, laboured breathing and short, staccato instructions. He sprinted, holding on to the back of my saddle while I nervously pedalled. Up and down Cottage Road we went until Dad had to stop for a breather and a fag. Out came his worn tin of Old Holborn tobacco and orange packet of Rizla papers. You had to run the tip of your tongue down the gummed strip to make it all hold together. Eventually 'the balance' came to me and I could propel myself forward without falling to the side. I can still remember the rising joy when I realised I was doing it on my own; I was upright, I was forcing those pedals down and Yes! I was surging on! I left Dad standing; I was off.

Seeing that I had more or less cracked the business of learning to ride a bike, my brothers moved in if not for the kill then at least for a damn good laugh. They gathered round and explained that for the sake of my own safety I had to be able to warn people of my approach, and should therefore learn to sound the horn while riding. All I needed was some practice. It would be an act of great skill, they mused, if I was able to ride my new bike down the slope in front of Mr Whiles the magistrate's house next door to Campdene, and *simultaneously* parp the horn. It would probably be too great an act of co-ordination; no, it was too difficult, it couldn't be done.

Gullible to the last, I agreed to give it a try. My four brothers and their friends lined up eagerly by our garden wall. Halfway down the slope, I reached across to parp the horn, wobbled and shot off. My brothers disappeared behind the wall, creased with silent hysterical laughter. Eyes brimming with tears, fighting to keep a straight face they arose to spur me on. 'You nearly had it, our Pam! You'll do it this time, have another go! You just need a bit more speed!'

Again, I pushed my red bike to the top of Whiles's slope. Starting from further back this time, I came down it at breakneck speed, tried to reach the horn and in so doing turned the front wheel at right angles to the direction of travel. There was a moment of mad one-legged running as I fell off sideways and the bike cartwheeled away. As a man, the brothers doubled up and dropped

48

behind the wall, biting the backs of their fists. 'You get straight back on Pammie! Otherwise you'll lose yer nerve!' And I did get back on, seduced by their supportive tone. I must have been catapulted off my bike ten times before it dawned on me that this was in fact a spectator sport; they weren't trying to help me at all. I finally limped indoors and Mum, who had seen all this going on through the window, said to me, 'Well, you must be a mug.'

In time I became adept on my bike, extravagantly and flamboyantly so. Pedalling exuberantly through the village one day with both hands on my hips, I shot past an unseen presence, the lurking village policeman known to all as Copper Mayall. His voice boomed forth and frightened the life out of me:

'Don't you NEVER let me see you do that again Pammie!'

Horrified and chastened, I grabbed the handlegrips. I have never let go of them since.

P.C. Mayall played a strange dual role in the village. My father was deeply wary of him, unsurprisingly, as Dad spent a good proportion of his time helping himself to other people's pheasants, but the village policeman was often called upon to act as friendly advisor. People knocked on his door when baffled and in need of clarification of official letters for instance, or the tricky small print on forms. I liked his presence. He made me feel safe and protected.

10

VISITING OUR RELATIONS

Most outings from Campdene consisted of riding our bikes to neighbouring villages to visit relations, although there were several exceptions. Occasionally Mum and Dad took Jean and me on the back of their bikes to a pub called The Fox at Denchworth. This was a hazardous means of transport because there was no actual seat for the pillion passenger at all, only a flat platform about the length of a shoe box above the back wheel of the bike. This was padded up to form a seat using somebody's rolled-up coat, which you then sat on with legs held well out to avoid both the oily black chain and the spokes of the wheel. I remember the silky feel of the roadside grasses parting over the front of my feet as Mum pedalled stoically on towards the pub.

The Fox had a garden with chairs and tables, and here for a treat Jean and I would be given a bottle of Queen's Toast, a fizzy drink in a garish shade of orange. I could never understand why it was called toast. Another treat was a bag of Smith's crisps with a fat blue paper twist of salt to sprinkle over the contents.

We liked The Fox because it had a resident pony. The wretched animal was kept in a windowless shed in the garden, and peering through a crack in the planked wall enabled you to make out its shape. It had no daylight at all. At the time I was undisturbed by this and thought that must be how you kept ponies.

The majority of other outings involved seeing our relations. I adored visits to my paternal grandmother Ada and my grampy Bill in their thatched cottage on Uffington Common. Adjoining the house was a dark shed with a stand pipe, tap and drain where I loved to play. I was perplexed that Mum always got cross about this and insisted that I come out, only later discovering that it was the drain down which the men habitually piddled.

Grampy Ayres was born into a family of thirteen children living in a cottage at Moor Mill near Uffington. Over time, the millrace would become obstructed by silt, enfeebling the mechanism and slowing the milling of grain. To overcome this, the millrace received an annual clean in which my grandfather participated, and which regularly stranded a vast harvest of thick eels. These were then kept alive in tin baths until required for eating.

At the age of twenty-one Bill Ayres was hedging in one of the small fields around Uffington, cutting back bushes with a slasher, when a blackthorn flew up and penetrated his eye. It became infected and could not be saved; he was fitted with an artificial glass eye. My brother Tony, as a small boy, was staying with Granny and Gramp and could see into their bedroom from the alcove where he slept. Having no clue about the glass eye, he was astounded to see Gramp take a surgical tool like a buttonhook, remove his eye and place it into a glass of water.

Gramp worked on a farm owned by a Miss Laker who later emigrated from Uffington to Tasmania to join her brother, a doctor. Half a century later when I was touring Australia I found her, and we sat drinking tea in her home in Launceston. Miss Laker told me poignantly that she had taken Bill to hospital to choose his glass eye; he had asked her to come and match the colour.

My own memory of him is a little regretful; I wanted to get to know him but feel I never really did. He spoke little and gave me an impression of weariness and remoteness, constantly using his handkerchief to mop his eyes. One was enlarged and bulbous, and both looked inflamed and sore. For reading, he wore glasses that were cloudy on one side and had a thick lens on the other, and for as long as I knew him he had a large white moustache with waxed tips.

From the back of their cottage, they could see the Uffington White Horse carved into the chalk face of the hillside. As an old man, Gramp developed a cataract on his only eye, and was terrified that the operation to rectify it would ruin what sight he had. After the operation, my brother Tony asked him anxiously how he was. Gramp replied, 'I can see the White Horse again Tony, and it's bloody wonderful.'

As a young woman, my grandmother Ada was in service at Ashdown House, perched on the Berkshire Downs near Lambourn. A lovelorn Lord Craven built this beautiful building of Dutch-style dolls-house appearance in the seventeenth century for Elizabeth, sister of King Charles I, in order that she might avoid the plague in London. Tragically, she died without ever seeing it.

In the footsteps of the great, and on a somewhat lowlier level, my granny worked here at menial tasks, rising at 4am to clean fireplaces and blacken grates. She contracted breast cancer and underwent a double mastectomy, although this fact was never, ever, stated in such bald terms. Instead, in a hushed voice Mum confided in Jean and me that when she was younger, Gran had been found to have 'a growth'. She must have suffered greatly at a time when less was known about the condition, and treatment was primitive. Yet she was lovely, slim and elegant, with smiling eyes and high rosy cheeks. Her long hair was swept up and round the top of her head in typical Edwardian fashion and she favoured elaborate blouses with ruffled, pin-tucked fronts, possibly to disguise the utter flatness of her chest.

I loved going to see her. She used to make macaroni puddings from sweetened pasta and milk from the farm. You could suck the macaroni into your mouth with spectacular speed and satisfying whistling noises until Mum prevailed. Gran had a large run with black chickens that she called 'the fowl' in a way that gave the word two syllables. 'Come on Pammie,' she would say, 'we'll go and feed the fow-ell.' Elsewhere the family kept Berkshire pigs with their black bodies, white facial blaze and turned-up snouts.

Up their garden, they had a pleasant pale wooden lavatory; ivy had inveigled its way through the slats. In contrast to our lavatory, theirs was very smart. Few families had toilet paper. Everyone used newspaper; it was only the presentation that differed. Gran cut her newspapers up into squares and neatly threaded a string through one corner. These were then hung up discreetly and conveniently on a little interior nail. At Campdene, ours was pretty much as it came off the presses. Whole newspapers were strewn across the wide seat and concrete floor: it was just a question of ripping off the quantity required to both clean the bottom and simultaneously blacken it with newsprint.

Gran's sister Clara had lived in a cottage next door to Gran and Gramp on the Common, and was much admired for her spectacular auburn hair. The houses had no electricity then and were lit only by oil lamps. One day there was a horrific accident; the lamp which Clara was tending flared up. She rushed it outside through the low doorway; the flames blew back towards her igniting the thatch and the beautiful abundance of her hair. Clara perished in the inferno that followed; the cottage burnt to the ground and was never rebuilt.

On a trip to Uffington, it was customary to call in and visit other relatives. One was Mum's brother Uncle Les, who lived at Baulking in the small stone house where their mother Florence brought up her family of five. Mum always called it 'over home'. To reach it you pedalled past the parish church of St Nicholas, down the narrow footpath running the length of the long village green, having first paused to view the coot-dotted pond, and then steered left across the grass to reach the semi-detached cottage.

Here, my Uncle Les lived his disappointed and increasingly out-of-focus life. I learned later that as a young man he had watched his siblings disperse, George to Woolstone, Sam to nearby Challow and Mum to Stanford. Only Oliver remained to come home; Oliver, who had tired of the monotony of farm life and enlisted, whose photograph was displayed proudly in the home, handsome in his Guards uniform and smart moustache, the fun-loving brother who adored dancing, played the harmonica and took my infant brothers on his shoulders to pinch apples from irate local landowners. Throughout the war, Les had waited eagerly for Oliver's return to break the silence of the house, to brighten it and fill it with good cheer. Instead a telegram came. He had been blown up in a tank. The Germans, with their 88mm anti-aircraft guns lowered, had fired first upon the front tank, then upon the last in order to trap the convoy. In leisurely fashion, they picked off the rest. Whatever remains of my uncle lies at Heverlee Cemetery in Belgium and in 2008, I went there and placed on his grave a handful of blossom pulled from the hedgerow at Baulking, where in his youth he exulted among the green fields.

The news, when it came, was a mortal blow to Les, and a dreadful change began to creep over him as he realised he was likely to be alone in the house for the rest of his life. Gradually his standards slipped and he ceased to tend either the home or himself. Both became grubby and imbued with the musty smell of neglect. He worked for a local farmer and was known mockingly in the hamlet as 'Sugar'. Uncle Les walked back and forth to the farm, ate his solitary meals in the foul house and talked endlessly to himself while the fruitless years rolled away, unlived.

Once, Mum, Jean and I had been over on our bikes to visit him and for a treat on the way back to Campdene we stopped at The Anchor Inn at Stanford for lemonade and crisps. Mum was talking to a friend and said we had been over to see Les. 'Oh!' I exclaimed in distaste, wrinkling my nose. 'He's a dirty old thing!' Mum continued her conversation and I forgot about my comment. The minute we left the pub and were on our own, she turned on me with fury. I was angrily slapped and told that I had said a terrible, unfeeling thing, that I had no clue what Les had been through, I was a little clever-dick who should think before she spoke and there were things in families you kept to yourself, and didn't shout about in pubs. I was horrified. I'd had no inkling of how protective she felt towards him. I rode my bike home in disgrace, censured, shocked to the core.

Uffington at that time was filled with lives wrecked directly or indirectly by the two world wars, and this must have been only a tiny example of what was happening in towns and villages all across the country. Down a bent lane in a gloomy cottage filled with photographs lived Gran's elderly sister Beet, whom we also used to visit. Her young husband of only a few weeks was killed in the First World War. Without him, she could not progress, and she lived out the rest of her disappointed life with only his memory for company.

The plot of land next door to Gran, where her sister Clara's cottage once stood, had been left as a piece of waste ground. Upon it in a hand-painted green caravan lived their brother Alfred. A sniper during the First World War, he had been gravely injured by a Turkish homemade bomb in Mesopotamia, present-day Iraq. A metal plate had been inserted into his skull and Alfred was left abysmally affected by the myriad conditions which, lumped together, were known as 'shell-shock'. He would groan 'Oh, my head, my head' repeatedly, and slap at his legs, or the air, all the time whistling in a weird, uncontrolled manner. In the harsh way of those times, this made him a figure of fun and in the village he was disparagingly known as 'Sheddy'.

As a very small girl, I remember being taken

with a gang of others to bait him, for a laugh. His small, bottle-green caravan stood in front of a tall, sheltering hedge. All along one side of the caravan lay a sloping, malodorous and vermin-infested heap of tin cans that had contained Kit-e-kat for his numerous stray cats. The caravan door was open and I could make out a shadowy figure wearing a greatcoat. The idea was that you made him come out by jibes and catcalls and then doubled up with laughter as he whistled and slapped at the air. With shame, I remember how he snarled at us to clear off.

At home, I have a photograph of him in his uniform. His face is full of mischief; his eyes twinkle and, beneath his arm, he is carrying a little 'swagger' stick in a jaunty way. He looks full of life, bright, cocky and ready for a lark.

It was the misfortune of Alfred and of all his generation that he was born into a time of bloody carnage. It was a time of profligacy with the lives of young men, and of callousness towards the maimed. With his stray cats, he lived out his life in the bottle-green caravan. People reached in and stole money through his windows. He was taunted and ridiculed by the senseless and the ignorant, including, shamefully, me.

Countless young men of that era were immersed in scenes of unimaginable horror. They had no choice. Mum's brother Leonard was always known as Sammy. During the Second World War he was a guardsman based at Wellington Barracks in London where he was batman, or valet, to a Guards officer, whom he liked very well. On Sunday, 18 June 1944, the service had just begun in the packed Guards chapel. A buzzing was heard, which grew into a roar, drowning out the hymn.

The fearsome sound suddenly cut out and a V1 flying bomb fell upon the concrete roof of the chapel, exploding on impact. The terrifying weight of masonry dropped on the congregation, killing 121 and injuring many more. It took two days to dig out the dead and among them was Sam's officer. In the aftermath, Sam was asked to stay on to help look after the officer's bereaved wife and young family. I heard this from others; I never once heard him talk about it himself.

11

CHALLOW STATION

Sam worked as a porter at the railway station in the hamlet of Challow, on the A417 between Faringdon and Wantage. He was tall with intensely brown eyes and a tremendous nose, and he lived with his wife Dorothy, my father's sister, and their two young sons Oliver and Raymond, at the end of a row of six red-brick homes called Station Houses.

Their outdoor lavatory was the smartest I had ever seen. At the window in front of the frosted glass were hung plastic curtains of a colourful fish design. On the sill stood an Izal toilet roll, the only one seen among the entire spectrum of our relations. They had an equally rare spectacle in the kitchen; it was a plumbed-in bath. Of homemade construction, it had a hinged wooden lid that dropped down to form a table when the bath was not in use and, whenever we went to visit, we used to implore Auntie Dorothy to raise the lid so we could marvel at the pristine white porcelain below.

How rude our own soap-plugged tin bath seemed by comparison.

I liked Auntie Dorothy; she was pretty and feminine and Sam thought the world of her. Every Friday she came on the bus to visit Mum at Campdene. She had crisp new dresses, her hair was salon-tended and attractive, and together with the two boys, they seemed a loving, affectionate family. She was cared for and cherished as our mother was not; it must have been hard for Mum to see the way her sister-in-law was treated and not make comparisons.

Auntie Dorothy occasionally came out with things that I found acutely embarrassing. Sex was never mentioned in our home. One day the radio was on and the subject under discussion was the playing of romantic melodies during sexual intercourse. 'Well Pammie,' Auntie Dorothy quipped to me, 'me and Sam'll have to do it to the music!' My jaw dropped and I nearly died of shame. Fancy *admitting* that you *did it*!

On another occasion when our family was together, I stood up from the sofa to walk out of the room. Dorothy watched me go. 'Pammie got her skirt stuck in her bum,' she observed loudly, as all eyes swivelled to look. I was enraged that she had directed everybody's attention to the undignified sight.

Auntie Dorothy owned interesting things. In a cupboard above their fireplace, she had plaits in a box. They were her own plaits, thick braids of perfect blonde hair lying wrapped in tissue paper in a shoebox. I remember a feeling of distaste as I looked at them, a worrying sense of amputation, of something morbid that should still have been attached to somebody. It seemed to have been quite common, this cutting off and keeping of particularly good hair. Perhaps it was a coming-of-age ritual, a sign of growing up. Girls either kept it all their lives like Auntie Dorothy, or used it as an insurance against hard times when they could sell it to wig-makers.

All visits to Challow were enhanced by the presence of the family's pets. Dorothy owned a series of corgis called Jenny, each one crabby and of prodigious fatness. The Jenny of the day used to be served a fried egg for her supper, which scandalised my mum, struggling to feed eight people every day. 'A fried egg! A fried egg for a DOG indeed!' she would exclaim with disbelief. The Jennies were all one-woman dogs who adored my auntie. They wanted nothing to do with me and snapped nastily. I was disappointed; I loved dogs and craved one of my own.

More accommodating was their tortoise, which lived in the heavily shaded back garden surrounded by concrete walls. I could fuss him to my heart's content though it was an unrewarding pastime, he being steadfastly unmoved. His house was a small wooden box and the garden was scattered with lettuce and tomato for him to eat. He would lunge at the food, opening his triangular chops to reveal a fleshy red interior in sharp contrast to his ancient-looking skin. He paced the concrete of his Challow home for many years.

Tortoises at that time were ten a penny; the pet shop in Faringdon churned with them; it was a wicked trade. You could see them in the windows, in shallow trays filled with wood shavings, endlessly milling and grappling over each other in a tawny, wretched mass. As pets, they were uncomplaining; for the most part they led brief, unhappy lives

60

owned by people who had no clue what their real requirements were. I was one of them. Mine had a hole bored in the edge of his shell by which he was tied to a length of string. All day he struggled fruitlessly against his restraint, his big hands scraping little hollows in the dust. In the end, he escaped. I hope he found the freedom and amenable environment denied to him by me, but I doubt it.

Uncle Sam and Auntie Dorothy had a pig. The old practice of cottagers keeping a pig had largely died out by this time; theirs was the only one I knew. He was kept in a pigsty made of railway sleepers at the bottom of their garden and I used to go and marvel at him, his bristly pinkness, enquiring white-lashed eyes and distinctive piggy smell.

Once we had arrived at Challow and parked our bikes against the outbuildings, Mum and Dorothy would sit and enjoy a cup of tea and specially made fruitcake. Visiting children, once the initial happy greetings were over, did not then take long to get bored. One day when I was very small, that is exactly what happened and I dawdled off to look for something more interesting. There was a communal path that ran along the back of the row of cottages; it was easy to peer over the gates into people's yards. In one a pram was parked and I stopped to look, walking in and round to the front so that I could peer underneath the hood and see the baby. I looked and was aghast. The pram was entirely filled by a huge male child restrained by straps; he looked at me with a steady gaze. His head was a strange shape. I gaped at him in horror; he began to make whimpering noises and thrash back and forth wildly in the screeching pram. The

61

scene was awful and I ran away in terror, breathlessly back to my mum and auntie at the end house. I told them what I had seen and their reaction reflected the attitude of the time. They blamed the mother, shaking their heads in a she's-a-fool-to-herself sort of way. 'He wants putting away,' they said in a disapproving, under-the-breath manner, 'but she won't part with him.'

I don't know what was wrong with the little boy. Perhaps he had hydrocephalus, treatable today but then a condition ending only in death or institutionalisation for mental retardation. Now I find it unspeakably sad to think of that mother who couldn't bear to lose him, who, despite being pressured from all sides to lock him away, placed her boy outside in the garden to enjoy the sunshine.

Often, when we had biked the two miles to Challow, Mum would walk across to the railway station to see her brother Sam in his place of work. There we would sit on one of the platform benches, in what seems in my memory to be constant shimmering summer heat. Once again, as the adults talked, I felt excluded and bored beside the searing railway lines in the stillness of a country railway station. It was a relief when a straggle of passengers gathered, indicating that Challow was about to be shaken up by the arrival of a steam train. Expectancy could be felt. Activity would be seen in the signal box, bells rang and signals flopped into the down position. At first sight, the locomotive looked like a small, dark coin far down at the end of the tracks. As a child I was afraid as it approached, unnerved by the eyeless black face looming up through clouds of smoke and steam. The noise was massive like a wall; the harsh clank of metal, mournful shrieking whistle and furious exhalations of steam as if from a living thing that breathed. Then it would be upon us and, as the huge locomotive slowly inched past, the hellish conditions within could be glimpsed. Blackened men, stripped to the waist, shovelled coal with rhythmic strokes into a fiery furnace, and the flickering flames reflected on their sweat-drenched bodies as if they were themselves on fire. It looked diabolical to me and I cringed back in fear, yet as the train halted the cheerful figure of my Uncle Sam in his immaculate black uniform and peaked cap would appear strolling amiably beside it, his feet obscured by steam, opening leather-strapped doors and shouting, 'Challow! Challow Station!'

The station building was small and sweet with a kind of wooden frill running below the eaves. It was painted in the brown-and-cream livery of the Great Western Railway and various large signs were affixed to its walls proclaiming the presence of Stationmaster, Left Luggage and Waiting Room. Beyond, enticingly, was the wooden railway bridge with steps up, over and down to the far platform. It was a feat of heroism to stand on the bridge as a through train passed underneath. To remain frozen and doomed as the force and power of a 'Castle' steam engine cannoned towards you, white smoke and steam pulsating furiously up from the funnel. That rising unstoppable roar, the breathless shock as it flashed under, the whack and shudder of the bridge, clacketty-clack of points and engulfing smoke, which shot up instantly on both sides of the bridge with an evocative, now gone-for-ever smell. Then, the subsiding fear and flood of relief as the mighty train forged on to

Paddington or Swansea, its tarred carriage roofs snaking away and diminishing to nothing except for threads and fibres of vanishing steam. After the tumult came a laying on of silence like a quilt; the peaceful return to tranquillity, birdsong and buzzing of insects over the silent rails as if nothing had ever happened.

Challow was a busy place then and important to us. It had action, emotion and excitement. Red-faced people ran for the train, excited families went on shopping trips to Swindon, uniformed national servicemen came eagerly home on leave, hurrying back to their families in modest but yearned-for village homes. It was a place of joyous reunions and heavy-hearted farewells, of a never-ending passage of goods over the platforms, coal, mail, feedstuffs, bicycles, boxes of day-old chicks and racing pigeons glimpsed in wicker baskets.

12

A RIDE UP WHITE HORSE HILL

A much-looked-forward-to treat, which I never looked forward to much, was a bike ride up White Horse Hill. It was such a strenuously herculean effort, such backbreaking and sweaty hard work that always seemed to be undertaken by Mum and Dad in conditions of blistering heat. The first part of the ride was fairly level and nice enough, up to the T-junction in Baulking and left past the red-brick former schoolhouse. Mum's first job was in this house, working as a homesick fourteen-year-old nanny for a couple who didn't get on. Mum was not allowed to go home to see her mother half-a-mile away across the village green, and coming from a peaceful, loving home herself, found the sound of arguments night after night unbearable, alone in her bed in the house by the railway.

Below the house, further along the railway line, my grandfather Corporal George Royal Loder was killed by a railway train on the night of 6 January 1916. He had been drinking with a few pals in the pub at Uffington Junction, and it was their custom, albeit an illegal one, to take a short cut and walk home to Baulking along the railway line. Mum said perhaps he'd had too much to drink and stumbled as the train passed so perilously close. In other quarters people thought that rather than return to the unimaginable horror of the trenches, he had committed suicide, which in those days was heavily stigmatised. I do not know the truth but whatever it may have been, someone approached Florence's little stone house late that night and broke the news to her that her husband lay dead on the railway line and thenceforth, at the age of thirty-four, she was a widow with five children to fend for. My mother, the youngest, was just six months of age. Florence was brave and feisty; she took in filthy farm workers' washing from local landowning families to survive. A brother who had emigrated to Australia sent money when he could and she succeeded in keeping her family together despite the odds. In photos, they were tall, good-looking and well nourished. In 1941, by which time Mum had a young family of her own, Florence died of tuberculosis at Christmas. She was fifty-nine years old and had lived a life of gruelling hardship. Mum was tormented by anguished memories of her mother's difficult life and painful death.

Leaving the railway bridge behind, the road sloped pleasantly down what Dad called the turnpike and soon crossed the fast-disappearing remnants of the Wilts and Berks canal. We used to stop and look at it from the road, and I was thrilled and enraptured to imagine a time when there was a waterway with boats and strangers actually sailing through these placid green fields. I implored Dad to tell me a story of what it was like, how it had been. He only ever shook his head and declared that it was before his time. He had heard, he told me, that the bargees stole children; they snatched them from the banks. I looked at the old canal with awe, at the expanse of parchment-dry, pale rustling reeds carving a lighter path between scrubby thickets of hawthorn. I could hear the haunting cries of the stolen children as they were borne far away from their homes.

On towards Uffington we pedalled and by now White Horse Hill looked a lot closer. One of the reasons I never liked the epic ride much was that we were always so hard up; we could seldom stop for an ice-cream or lemonade. In my memory, the outing was always associated with sweat, agonising pain in the legs and a raging thirst.

This became all but unbearable after you reached the crossroads at the foot of the hill and started the final ascent. A redeeming factor was Dragon Hill, which loomed up on the right-hand side. I liked it very much. Flat-topped and easy to climb, it was most certainly the genuine place where St George slew the dragon, for you could see all the white dribbles running down the sides where the blood, being so thickly black and toxic, prevented the grass from ever growing again.

The final climb in blazing heat was indescribably

awful; a ghastly blend of red-faced exertion, unfit gasping and detestation of the whole stupid idea. Beside the road in its final traverse, in a landscape formed during the Ice Age, the land falls dramatically away down into a spectacular flat-bottomed valley known as The Manger. Kindly breezes blow up suddenly and soothingly to cool small, angry faces. At this point, the struggle to ride our bikes up the ferocious incline was abandoned; we all got off and pushed. Finally, the chalky, rubble-strewn road levelled out, and in varying degrees of exhaustion we reached the top.

Even this triumph preceded a disappointment. 'Let's go and have a look at the old castle!' Dad would shout, striding off towards another long, uphill slope. A castle to me was something with battlements, knights, flying pennants, a drawbridge and mighty clunking portcullis at the very least. Uffington Castle was an earthwork; just ancient mounds of soil arranged in a vast circle, nothing more. Skylarks sang there at all times, the velvet grass was embroidered with countless fragile harebells in a perfect shade of blue, the air was sweet and a panorama of sunlit fields lay spread out to the very horizon, but I could not appreciate these things then. At this Iron Age hillfort there was no ice-cream and no moat; therefore it was a waste of space.

The White Horse lies to the north-east of the single rampart and ditch that makes up Uffington Castle. Three thousand years ago, the shape of this extraordinary beaked horse was dug out and the resulting ditches filled with chalk boulders. Why this thing, which can only be seen fully from the air, was built is not known. It is intriguing to wonder who was it for, who was meant to see it and why people toiled in that inhospitable place to create a work they could never see in its complete and finished form.

It was lovely to run down the soft sloping grass to the White Horse. Its eye was formed from a perfect white circle of chalk and here every person would stand to make a wish; it was a vital part of any visit. As with all wishes, you could never disclose what you had asked for or your effort would be fruitless, but it now seems safe to reveal that I always asked for Mum and Dad to get on better, that our home might no longer be blighted by grim silences lasting for weeks on end.

13

ALONG THE RIDGEWAY

Dad was born in Uffington; he knew the area and all its secret places in fine detail. I remember when he first told me about Wayland's Smithy; I was enchanted. He told me seriously, as if it was fact, that if you rode your horse a mile or so along the ancient Ridgeway towards Ashbury, you would come to a place where you could have the horse marvellously shod for sixpence and you would never see who did it. The place was called Wayland's Smith Cave. All you had to do was to tie your horse up quietly and respectfully, leave a silver sixpence on the capstone, then go right away to a point where you couldn't see any activity. It was a mistake to leave more than sixpence, because Wayland would be offended, as if considered grasping. Nor should there be any mischievous peeping back or it would not work. On your return, if all the proper etiquette had been observed, you would find your horse immaculately shod and the coin on the capstone would have mysteriously vanished.

Wayland is a Saxon god of metalworking, and the Neolithic burial chamber known as Wayland's Smithy was begun in 3700BC. Archaeologists discovered twenty-two bodies, some broken 'as if the roof came in on them' in 1919 and 1962. It is a leafy place, atmospheric and eerie. I had no doubt then, and have none now that the legend is true. One day I'll leave my horse to be shod and I know that Wayland will take good care of him.

As far as exploration of the area was concerned, we now cast off our parental bonds. Instead, as a loud nucleus of gangling children, its numbers alternately swelled or reduced by passing brothers, sisters, cousins and cronies, we swarmed over the landscape on an unprepossessing collection of bikes.

A visit to The Dingles was popular and, apart from the rubbery flexibility required to clamber through fierce barbed-wire fences, not much trouble to access. This wooded valley at the foot of White Horse Hill was private; trespassers were forbidden and we went most Sundays. It was a charmed place of pristine chalk springs flowing into lakes thick with watercress. The pools were criss-crossed by fallen trees, their trunks softened by shaggy, lime-green moss. In these shady depths, you could lie on your front along the carpeted trunks and peer down into the pure crystal water. It was so beautiful, the peppery cress so dark and plentiful, a secret place of silence, springs and musically flowing water, which had fallen as rain on the hills above.

A less picturesque destination, but one visited regularly by us for the sake of variety and cheapness, was the Blowing Stone near Kingston Lisle. This waist-high boulder of sarsen is thought to have been carried in the glacial embrace of the Ice Age to its first resting place high on the nearby hills. Some time before 1761, it was brought down to the cottage garden of the local blacksmith, remaining there as the property became first an inn, and then a dwelling house.

Wreathed in legend but of unprepossessing appearance, its craggy exterior is blemished by a few rocky holes. The stone is grey but around the holes, pinkness has appeared as if generations of straining lips have left their mark. For this stone can be made to speak. The following method is the one usually employed. The prospective blower approaches the stone with menace, grasps it by both ears, plants his legs widely apart and bends forward from the waist. Bravely ignoring the snails that can often be seen within, he opens his mouth to gigantic proportions and applies his lips to the largest cavity in an effort to seal it. Inhaling massively and with the lungs of an elephant, he then blows with all his might into the blowing stone. All too often, nothing happens and he arises purple-faced and defeated, but for the gifted few, there is a spectacular result. After long seconds of straining, the appearance of numerous prominent veins about the face and the most strenuous endeavour, a deafening drone rises up that can only be likened to a tremendous, gruesome fart. It wails and mourns stupendously across the wooded hills and resonates in the valley. Resident snails are paralysed; the triumphant blower is lauded to the skies and helped away, crippled, from the scene.

You were expected to make a contribution to the stone's upkeep, though it is hard to imagine what it could have required. A chained moneybox was placed prominently to the fore and certainly, in the early days of our visits, access to the stone was severely controlled. A kind of trapdoor with padlock had been affixed to the blowing hole to discourage revellers from blowing it in the middle of the night. In order to have it unlocked, you had to apply to the lady living in the adjacent cottage. She would emerge clutching a checked tea towel and unfasten the blowing stone's blowing hole. You then went through the ritual of trying to blow it under her somewhat unwelcoming and impatient gaze. If there were several of you, in a nod to hygiene, she would take the checked tea towel and mop up the copious saliva of the previous assailant before the next person had a go. After we had all failed, the trapdoor would clang shut and the moneybox would be rather aggressively shaken. It was not our favourite destination. We liked the legend though, and were absolutely certain that this was the stone King Alfred had used to summon his troops. To what and from where, we couldn't say, but it was true all right, you could be sure of that.

Our outings were to free places, to the homes of relations or to natural spots where water, woods, or rock had combined in a landscape, which, with a little ingenuity, could be made ripe for excitement. Tree houses were popular; one was built and lushly carpeted beside the brook near Hatford. This provided languorous relaxation until an envious rival gang set fire to the host tree with the occupants still in it.

71

My brothers and the older boys did sensational things; near Hatford, they created a dugout, a subterranean cave with a chimney that could be seen thrillingly smoking in among the meadow grasses. They hung thick cables of rope over streams so by sprinting up and grasping the rope in a monkey-like fashion, you would be swept over the water and far out to the other side. They made unlikely rafts to sail the River Ock, and took death-defying risks to obtain eggs that were taken home to be cooked and eaten; pigeons' eggs from the trees and moorhens' eggs from the riverbank.

It was lovely to be out with my brothers, though for them the presence of a small, easily tired girl interfered with their heroic pursuits. They did spectacular, daring things and when I was with them, I felt supremely safe and protected. This could have been optimistic on my part considering that I was present one day when they bombed the Ock. A net was erected across the river at one point, and further upstream a Camp coffee bottle containing a lethal cocktail of ingredients including weedkiller was lobbed into the peaceful, flowing waters. There was a brief, somewhat disappointing explosion and a large, paisley-shaped globule rose indignantly out of the stream. No shoal of fat trout appeared obligingly stunned on the surface, no shocked eels or pike knocked senseless. Downstream the net failed to bulge with an illicit catch, and the disenchanted bombers drifted away to some new pursuit.

Another day along the Ock my brother Allan threw me in. I was wandering along behind him and his friends when he picked me up with great bravado and said, 'C'mere Pam, I'm going to throw you in!' I knew he didn't mean it and clung on to him as he did three mighty swinging movements. 'One! Two! Three!'

On the shout of three, he lost his footing and we both fell into the river. I was completely unafraid and noted the deep greenness and warmth of the water as it closed over my head. There was panic on the bank as the other boys, all of whom had sisters of their own and suspected that parents preferred them undrowned, rushed to haul us out. As I was spectacularly soaked through, Allan decided I ought to be taken home. Mum had gone to Wantage on the bus so Allan had to confess to Dad who, being uncertain of the right response, gave him a good hiding. This grieved me deeply as I knew he had not meant to harm me and, indeed, had solicitously brought me home. Dad normally had little to do with our day-to-day care, and was unsure of the right treatment of a half-drowned infant. After some consideration, he stood me in the washing-up bowl, sluiced the river water off me and in the middle of the afternoon put me to bed with a jam tart. Mum then came home from Wantage, got me up again and told me off for being so damned stupid in getting near the river in the first place. It was an exciting day.

14

TREATS

Throughout my childhood, there was great freedom to range over the area. The only boundaries were invisible ones imposed by a landowner's unfriendliness, fields where it was best not to venture for fear a bellowing employee might appear brandishing a stick. The riches of the geography were there to be enjoyed; the only crucial tool was a bike. Without one, you were legless. I can think of few activities that cost money. Pubs served no food except crisps, or peanuts at a push. There were no restaurants that I knew of, but in any case, we would have run a mile from their prices and poshness.

I was taken to a pantomime once when I was very young, to see a production of *Jack and the Beanstalk* at the New Theatre in Oxford. I was anxious because I was not with my own family; the invitation must have been kindly proffered from elsewhere. Oxford was a foreign country to me, far distant from all I knew, and I felt homesick and afraid. I did not much like the panto. I was baffled by the whole thing but stoical enough until the dame, impatient at being unable to find Jack, announced to the audience, 'When he gets back here I'm going to skin him alive!'

At that point, any scant pleasure I was getting out of the show deserted me; I was gripped by horror. She was going to skin him while he was still alive, put him on her big dreadful table and pull his skin off over his head, revealing his livid red muscles in the way I had seen Dad skin rabbits. I was going to be made to watch; I would have to listen to poor Jack shriek as she did the unspeakable deed. The show could not end soon enough for me.

That night in my bed beneath the window at Campdene, I woke up screaming and terrified. Mum came bustling in; she was tired and said impatiently, 'Well, you're not going to any more pantomimes if it's going to finish up like this!' I was never so glad to hear it; the show had horrified me with one throwaway line.

Each year there was an exciting Christmas party in Stanford. This was due to the efforts of Becky Keene, a little round lady who wore her grey hair in a bun. She kept a small sweet shop in Stanford and also catered for parties of touring cyclists. It was not uncommon at the weekends for me to be wandering round the village waving a stick and to be suddenly taken aback by a high, singing sound, which I couldn't place. Spinning round, I would see a colourful group of cyclists streaming towards me along the village street. They would whisk past on smart, thin-tyred racing bikes and for a moment I would be surrounded by a sea of drop handlebars, water bottles and sinuous brake cables. They sped past, assembled, dismounted and parked their bikes on the gravel outside Becky Keene's hall. I do not know why she had a hall, but it was capacious and attached to the side of the sweetshop. Into the building the cyclists would troop to enjoy what, I discovered later, was a monumental and legendary tea.

In this same hall each year when we were infants, Becky would lay on her Christmas party. Jean and I would leave Campdene absurdly early to hurry down the village and join the queue. All the village children were there, so it was a massive undertaking for Becky. The trestle tables in the hall were heaped with sandwiches and cakes. Jean and I had a great favourite: the bum cake. This was a cake comprised of two round pink meringues sandwiched together with cream, and undeniably bum-shaped. You were lucky if you got one, as the bum cakes were much in demand, creamy, brittle and super-sweet. Becky's party was a feast, a noisy unmannered scramble for luxurious foods by kids who seldom had the chance. It was looked forward to eagerly.

Far more lavish and varied was Dad's party. The Southern Electricity Board arranged a Christmas party for their employees' children and this took place in the splendid Roysse Room in Abingdon's Guildhall. It was a beautiful room with an exquisite plaster ceiling and panelled walls. We poured excitedly into it for wildly anticipated treats: first the feast and then there was a *film*! A loud and swiftly ticking projector would be set up and we would have the unprecedented joy of watching a Laurel and Hardy film. We hardly ever saw one so it was unspeakably exciting; we shouted and rolled with laughter. One year they showed a film that made you feel that you were in a sleigh! You were looking out at the horse's back, at his flowing mane and bobbing head. He wore a sleigh bell headdress that jiggled as he trotted and on each side a spectacular landscape passed, of snow-laden pines, lakes and distant mountains. It was enchanting; I never wanted the ride to end.

Most eagerly anticipated of all, after the feast and the film, Father Christmas would come! He would sit at the end of the Roysse Room and, incredibly, call out the name of every child present! How could he possibly have known who would be at the party? Awestruck, we would go up and receive a wrapped gift from the hand of Father Christmas himself. It was a perfect party that created the most wonderful childhood memories. I don't know how much money it cost the Electricity Board, or indeed whether the dads paid into a fund, but it could not have been better spent.

I can only remember having one birthday party

at No. 2 Campdene and I got into trouble for saying the wrong thing. At the time, we had a dark brown leatherette sofa in our front room. Someone had unwisely attempted to adapt it into a chaise-longue; this involved the insertion of a metal shank with a large round knob on the end, which stuck out under one arm. A person approaching the sofa and wishing to stretch out full length would grasp the metal shank and wrench it upwards. Deep within the horsehair, some defeated mechanism would disengage and the battered arm would lay down flat. It was a criminally ugly piece of furniture. Prior to my birthday party Mum laid a tartan blanket over it, tucking it in carefully to hide the ugly knob and cracked worn-out leatherette. It looked so much nicer that I couldn't contain myself, and rushed out to tell the assembled guests who were waiting outside to storm in and annihilate the food: 'Mum's tucked a new blanket over our old sofa!' In the house Mum heard, and cringed, as her little ploy was laid bare. I was told off. I don't think I had any birthday parties after that.

15

TREATS COSTING MONEY

A couple of events that took place in the village needed to be paid for, and one was Jumbo Collins's Fair. I understand now that this was just a little tinpot travelling fair, but to Jean and me at that time it was a sensation. It trundled into a field bordered by the Ock and set up operations, bringing coconut shies, a test-your-strength bell, dodgem cars and the matchless delight of swinging boats, where you heaved on a thick, knotted rope and the boat soared high in the air above its gaudily painted frame. The unprecedented bird's-eye view and the thrill as the boat paused in mid-air then swooped ecstatically down were more deliriously exciting than anything I had ever done before.

Once I went to the fair with Mum and Dad, and he tried to ring the test-your-strength bell. He was tremendously strong and six feet tall; I had no doubt that he would do it straight away and I waited proudly, but though he swung the hammer again and again, the bell didn't ring. Dad said there was a bloke standing behind it who moved something to stop it from working. He hurled wooden balls repeatedly at the coconut shy but every time they seemed to glance off the great hairy nut and thud uselessly into the canvas behind. Dad said they were stuck into their cupped posts with glue and probably they were; few people ever seemed to win one. Dad said it was all fixed, all a set-up and I expect it was. Nevertheless, I cannot remember ever being happier than I was that night, coming home with Jean, between Mum and Dad, still breathless from the swinging boats, my face smeared with candyfloss, and carrying, clutched in a plastic bag, a goldfish.

A great annual event that also required the outlay of cash was Lockinge Point-to-Point, a day of amateur horseracing high on the downs above Wantage. It attracted a massive crowd, most of which was conveyed up to the event by a crawling shuttle service of buses from Wantage. It was a beautiful course, laid out on the sunlit hillside, fringed by woods and interspersed with straight dark jumps. The first time I went was with Dad when we were given a lift by 'ole Mainy', more politely known as Les Maine, the publican of The Red Lion, a popular Stanford pub. It was the first time I had ever been in a car. It was an Austin with the seats softly upholstered in shiny sage-green leather sewn in strips. How entrancing it was to glide along, warm and comfortable, not having to pedal, just looking out of the window at passing scenes.

As a young child, I wandered round the packed racecourse on my own in a way that might raise an eyebrow today. I didn't know what to make of it. The pictures had a hard edge; different scenes appeared and were then obscured by crowds. I glimpsed the bookies on their raised stands chalking on blackboards, the eerie hand-language of the tic-tac men communicating with persons unseen over my head, a marquee bearing the baffling name of Tote, where queues of people standing in a litter of discarded tickets shuffled up to hatches and passed in their money.

Wandering over to the enclosure I looked at the diminutive silk-clad jockeys mounted in such a funny way, their little legs bent sharply back and up into the shortest of stirrups. A profusion of persons whom Dad casually identified as Nobs strolled among the horses, dressed in the country uniform of covert coats and dark brown trilby hats, greeting each other in educated tones so different from the soft brogue my ears were used to hearing.

Although I was a country girl it did not dawn on me until I was nine or ten years old that the farm animals I saw in the fields were destined to be slaughtered for meat. This sounds unlikely but is perfectly true. The signs were all around me but I would not or could not see it. Our family knew I was besotted with animals, so perhaps no one wished to be the person to spell it out to me. Therefore, I loved animals in a childlike way for their own charming individuality, their soft noses, kind eyes and friendly presence.

At Lockinge, for the first time I observed people with a different view. Their way of regarding horses was different; it was admiring but had no trace of sentimental affection. This was to do with money, a kind of calculating appraisal; the cooler glance of a gambler working out the odds. An environment where animals were seen as money-makers was new to me. I could feel the tension, the rising excitement as the start of the race approached, but even at that young age, I felt a sense of dread because I knew that in the final analysis the horses were considered expendable. They could get it wrong; at the end of the race, they could lie dead under a green sheet.

When a race started, I went to stand beside a jump. As the field drew near, the sound was like the rhythmic beating of some great earthen drum; a rising clamour; an urgent pulsating blend of snorting exhaled breath, saddlery, hooves and quick muttered words of encouragement.

At last the great surging mass of horses thundered into view, intent and determined; a sudden moving frieze of undulating heads, manes, sheepskin nosebands and dark bodies streaked with foam. I saw the brightness of small goggled jockeys standing in their stirrups, buttocks angled up into the air, whipping the horses with sharp, spiteful strokes. At the jump a few horses miscalculated and faltered; some fell with appalling pained grunts but the rest careered on, front runners, also-rans and the riderless with reins loose and trailing. Occasionally a horse did not get up; it thrashed on the ground. Then a canvas screen was swiftly erected about it, a vet came in a Land Rover and the crowd drifted uneasily away.

There was always a jellied-eel stand at the point-to-point course and Dad made a beeline for it straight away, as it was his favourite. I watched the scene as the men queued up before the stall and bought little white ceramic dishes of grey fish in urine-coloured jelly. They scooped up and gnawed the chunks of eel, then spat out the central spine section on to the grass. The whole area was littered with white cartilaginous material. My stomach churned; it looked revolting. Not much better was the whelk stand; there the ceramic dishes contained great curled muscular whelks, three or four to a serving. They were grey and of immensely gristly appearance; everywhere chewing men chewed doggedly on.

On my first visit to Lockinge, Dad gave me two shillings in a single coin known as a florin. It was a substantial amount of money, far more than I had ever had at one time before and I was thrilled. As I walked round the racecourse, I met a man wearing a cardboard tray loaded with chocolate bars round his neck. Clutching my coin, I approached him and asked, 'How much is a bar of chocolate?'

'How much yer got?' he demanded roughly.

'Two shillings,' I replied, looking at the florin Dad had given me.

'Thass how much it is,' he snapped, taking the money and shoving a bar of red-wrapped Peter's chocolate in my hand. I was stunned. I didn't even like Peter's chocolate; it was nothing like as nice as

81

the Cadbury's or Fry's that I usually bought with my pocket money. I wandered on, disgruntled and resentful. I wasn't very old but I knew that I had been diddled. I decided that Lockinge point-to-point wasn't for me; either it was too hard or I was too soft.

16

SCHOOLDAYS

Children's clothes were seldom retained once they were outgrown, but were swiftly handed on to other families. 'Pass it on!' was the constant cry of our mother as the clothes circulated. 'This'll do somebody else a good turn!' The feeling was of co-operation and support, since nobody had anything much in the way of possessions. It was nice.

In this way, a Fair Isle cardigan came into our house, and Mum dressed me in this for my first day at school. Knitted intricately in thin two-ply wool, it was a work of art in red, white and green with extravagantly puffed short sleeves and red buttons. I hated it, with its stupid perked-up shoulders. A fawn Fair Isle knitted beret had arrived with the cardigan and Mum was keen that I should sport the whole ensemble. I felt conspicuous, and a twerp.

Although she was overloaded with chores, Mum somehow found the time every morning to plait my hair. I can see now that this showed a great degree of maternal care and affection but I cannot say I felt much gratitude at the time. It was always done with great briskness, the hair drawn back so tightly from the temples that for the first few hours of the day I showed off a credible face-lift. I had masses of hair, a great thicket, and the ordeal of twisting and pulling seemed to last forever, particularly if it was bulked up by a recent perm. Finally, it was over. Two yellow slides like sunflowers were inserted either side of the central parting, bows of ribbon were tied at the end of each chunky plait, the Fair Isle beret was slapped on top of the mask-like face and I was ready for my first day at school.

Stanford in the Vale Church of England Primary School stood chunky and school-shaped, on the corner opposite The Red Lion, the pub belonging to ole Mainy at the far end of the village. It was a long walk from Campdene for a five-year-old girl. Beside the school was the house of the headmistress Mrs Perkins, predictably known as Polly, a tall, dignified woman in large, grey, flat sandals. A luxuriant laburnum stood in her garden, the graceful boughs rising up and extending far out over the pavement. Each summer a marvellous cascade of golden racemes was produced, and in time these shed a thick carpet of poisonous seeds that were crunched underfoot by the crummy footwear and nailed boots of the arriving scholars.

Entering the school for the first time as a new member of the infants' class, I was alarmed to see sinister, black, cage-like frames. These proved to be racks of coat hooks in the cloakroom. Beyond were four classrooms, each with their resident teacher. Pupils started with Miss Edmonds in the infants class and moved up through the hands of Miss Bedford, Mr Biggs and Mrs Perkins before being passed at the age of eleven into the hands of either The Elms Grammar School or the Secondary Modern School in Faringdon. Success or failure in the eleven-plus examination decided the destination.

On my first day, Miss Edmonds stood me in front of an easel and let me loose with a paintbrush and a selection of gaudy poster paints. I loved her from that day on. She gave us containers of wallpaper paste coloured with powdered paint, and a comb. The idea was that you brushed the thick paste all over your sheet of paper then used the comb to create marvellous swirling patterns. It was hypnotic. I had a wonderful mother who took great care of us under less-than-perfect circumstances but she never had the time, energy or know-how to set up simple creative projects such as these. I was very happy in Miss Edmonds's class. She could make you understand things. I remember learning addition from one to ten with matchsticks. She laid out the sticks so you could see there were ten. Then she moved one apart and explained that $9+1$ still made ten. Then she moved another and I could see that $8+2$ made ten as well. So did $7+3$ and $6+4$. This is a tiny thing I know, but I remember the triumph, the sense of achievement; I could see how to do it! I could add up!

Once I could write numbers and the alphabet, I was able to join in with the popular pastime of car-numbering, where Jean, Margaret and I sat on the grass verge with pencils and little notebooks from the Post Office. When a car went by, you wrote down the number. With so very few cars, it was exciting to see if the next one bore a number that nobody had in their book! Lined up like small birds on the grass verge, we strained our ears for the distant drone of an engine.

I kept my car-numbering notebook and other belongings in a bag I thought was a satchel, which I carried to school each day. It was leather with a shoulder strap all right, but I now think it was some sort of cartridge case dusted off from the depths of Dad's shed. I loved it anyway, but one day the strap came away from the body. I was heartbroken and showed Miss Edmonds in the playground. She took me into the classroom and mended it with a brass cotter pin. Also, in her drawer, she had a roll of the previously unseen Sellotape, which could mend papers in such a way that they could *still be read*! As far as I was concerned, she was a miracle worker. I heard in later years that she was a close friend of my Uncle Oliver. One day at school during the war, Tony told her a telegram had come to Southdown saying he had been killed, and Miss Edmonds cried and ran over the road to Mum.

Miss Bedford was a different kettle of fish. She had a fearsome reputation and most of the children were scared stiff of her. I certainly was, and when I left Miss Edmonds to go into her class I went with an unhealthy sense of foreboding. Like Miss Edmonds, she wore the attractive, full-skirted dresses of the day but otherwise she was desperately different, firm, grey-haired and unsmiling. In fairness, I cannot think of anything she did to warrant such extraordinary fear, but an aura surrounded her and I prayed that I would do nothing to attract the cold, unforgiving stare.

I had an arithmetic exercise book with an orange paper cover. One day as I lifted the lid of my desk, I accidentally lifted the orange cover as well and it ripped. Suddenly there was a great tear halfway across the front of the book. Panic gripped me, and a sense of cold seeping dread as I realised that there was no question of confessing what I had done; I was too terrified of her reaction. I could see only that somehow I would have to avoid any situation that involved handing the book over to my teacher. Thus began an extraordinary period of feigned illness lasting for months, spiralling up out of the seemingly insignificant matter of the torn book. I started to lie. I claimed that I had stomach pains though I was perfectly well. The doctor was called and diagnosed 'grumbling' appendix. I claimed I had a bad arm, a bad leg or I felt sick; I was at home for weeks. In the end, I think Mum began to smell a rat and unbeknown to me went down to speak to Miss Bedford, a thing that was unheard of at that time when the demarcation line between parent and teacher was drawn straight and strong. Perhaps Miss Bedford then searched my desk and found the damaged book, I don't know. At any rate one day in the silence of the classroom, she said the electrifying words: 'Pamela, bring me your arithmetic book.' I felt as if I had been stabbed through the heart. This had been such an enormous crisis to me for so long. Cornered, I burst into terrified tears. 'I've torn my book!' I spluttered.

There was a pause. 'I see. Bring it here.'

On limbs turned to water, I crept forth and cringingly placed it before her. She looked down at it. She looked up at me as I quaked. I imagine that into the abyss, some colossal penny silently dropped. Taking a roll of Sellotape from her drawer, she calmly stuck the torn cover back together. The relief I felt as I watched this simple remedial act was immense, out of all proportion. Miss Bedford said something quietly to me about her not being an ogre, that I could have just come and told her what had happened, so perhaps she had realised what had been going on. For myself, I felt the weight of months of fear lift up and disperse. I returned to my desk light and breathing free, no longer having to invent a daily illness.

It was in Miss Bedford's class that we began the long process of learning to understand and operate the Imperial system of weights and measures, and the monetary system of the time, which was pounds, shillings and pence. It was astonishingly complex and took years to learn; I do not know how any foreign visitor ever coped with it. There was no symmetry; unlike the metric system, which is calculated in tens, the method in use then could involve twelve, as in pence to the pound, twenty, as in shillings to the pound, sixteen, as in ounces to a different kind of pound, 112 as in pounds to the hundredweight, and so on. Oddities littered the landscape: guineas, half-crowns, ten-bob notes, threepenny bits and florins. There were acres, gills, chains, fathoms and stones. It was fiendishly difficult yet all of us, by steady, grinding repetition and endless patient explanation over a period of years, eventually mastered it. The time would come when a pair of shoes at 39/11d was no mystery to us. When we would know that half-a-crown less two bob left you with a tanner, or that four threepenny bits added up to a shilling. In Miss Bedford's class, we started out on the long journey to enlightenment.

17

SCHOLARLY DELIGHTS

A run of low buildings took up one side of our school playground; it contained a coke store, lavatory cubicles and a smoothish wall, which, with its underlying channel, formed a urinal. In this area, there were various things of interest. In the coke shed, slung upon slopes of the peculiar grey featherlight coke, were gas masks discarded at the end of the war. They were of inhuman appearance and horribly sinister, with huge round eyepieces covered by yellowing glass and a dreadful perforated mouthpiece like a macabre trunk. A tangle of straps surrounded the masks and they gave off a rank smell of perished rubber as they rotted on the coke. The idea of having one strapped to your face was suffocating, unspeakable.

Further along the low building was a row of cubicles enclosing bucket lavatories. The wooden seats were crusted and filthy. I had a bladder infection for much of those early years at school, and assumed it was normal to constantly, uncomfortably need to pee.

Beside the fragrant toilets was the urinal wall. Although there were four boys in our family, behaviour at home concerning bodily functions was modest and discreet. Therefore, it came as a shock to me to see raucous gangs of boys bawling with laughter, leaning over backwards, endeavouring to pee over the top of the wall on to unsuspecting fellow pupils standing thoughtfully on the other side.

Mrs Jones was the school caretaker, a vast, slow-moving woman tightly wrapped in an overall. Her grey hair was worn in a bun; she spoke very little. From time to time, she would appear in the lavatories, fling a pail of disinfectant at the urinal wall and stump off. Pupils were sick in the playground on a fairly regular basis; Mrs Jones would be summoned. After a long interval, she would emerge expressionless with a bucket of water and a broom, deluge the unsavoury pool with water and sweep it all with painful long-windedness into the central drain. Eventually with all gruesome evidence washed away, Mrs Jones would heft up the bucket and trudge ponderously back into the building. Perhaps she was weary; perhaps she wasn't very well. Either way, she gave off an air of not liking children very much.

Mrs Perkins ringing a hand bell summoned us into class at the start of each day. We formed lines and filed into the biggest classroom, that of our only male teacher Mr Biggs, and there we stood for prayers. With Miss Bedford on the piano, a hymn or two would be sung and we would listen to a morally uplifting talk, often given by the vicar of St Denys, Mr Street. As an orator, he left much to be desired, frequently choosing as his theme 'Spreading and Growing'. He would describe throwing a pebble into a pond, an occupation I would have much preferred, and then aided by extravagant circular movements of his arms he would describe the subsequent ripples Spreading and Growing. As the dénouement, this was likened to the worldwide spread of Christianity. We had heard it all before, we knew the end. Then Mrs Perkins would offer a blessing, a nice one that went

'May the Lord lift up his countenance to shine upon you, now and for evermore' and off we would go to lessons.

I see those early schooldays in a series of little scenes like watching a film. It is winter. I can hear the sound of the nailed boots of the boys as they shot across long slides created on the icy surface of the playground. One after another, they would pelt up to the start, turn sideways and slide at great speed across the ice amid the harsh gritty roar of hobnails. Their play was rough. Rocks encased in snow hurled with gargantuan force at the opponent's skull stood in for snowball fights; as a non-participant it was best to cower back out of the way.

There were crazes: some game or activity would come into fashion then suddenly be old hat. Marbles were such a game. I had a soft bag of them and knew each one individually. My finest marble was big and ice-clear with a tremendous red flare like blown silk through the centre. One day I played with an older girl called Penny and she won it from me. I can still remember the gut-wrenching grief as she dropped it casually into her pocket and ran off. It was mine! My favourite! Why had I risked it? I've had a lifelong dislike of gambling; perhaps losing my marble sowed the seeds.

Just over the stone wall of the playground was a dark pond surrounded by willows; we were forbidden to go there. In the summertime, long fronds of willow hung over the wall. The slender leaves bore hard red tumours, which when split open with a fingernail contained tiny white larvae. At other times, the trees cast a white cotton-like froth that lay in drifts on the playground. One breathless day a swarm of honeybees alighted in the willows and hung quivering from a green branch, a great pendulous brown cone glistening with tens of thousands of wings, seeming to breathe and undulate like one single other-worldly creature. We were terrified. Pandemonium raged. Everyone imagined themselves writhing on the ground, black with stinging bees. A beekeeper summoned by Mrs Perkins appeared later in the day and could be seen moving stealthily towards the swarm. Clad in white and blackly veiled, he puffed smoke through a spouted contraption as he came on. Producing a straw skep, he manoeuvred it beneath the bees, severed their bowed branch and lowered the swarm gently in. Covering them solicitously, he moved silently away leaving only a wisp of smoke, a circling bee or two and, for Stanford school, the memory of a deeply thrilling event.

Many children kept silkworms as an interesting novelty and unresponsive pet. I think we brought the small white caterpillars home from school in the first place, but thereafter Jean and I kept ours in perforated shoeboxes under our bed. Fed on enough mulberry leaves they would grow large, develop a black face and sprout horns before enveloping themselves in a self-spun golden cocoon of silk. Obtaining the mulberry leaves was hazardous and effortful as the nearest tree was at Hatford, a bike ride away along the sandy footpath. The tree stood in a field immediately in front of Hatford House so any endeavour to remain hidden from the occupant was useless. A swoop technique was employed whereby a crowd of us would arrive, fling down our bikes, run commando-fashion across the grass while bent double, then swarm up the tree snatching off as many leaves as possible before the irate owner emerged brandishing a shotgun. One of the older girls pointed to a pond at the bottom of the sloping field and assured me that if I were caught I would be thrown in. The pond, she added confidently, was *bottomless.* Bottomless! The word terrified me. I saw it writ across the sky in great Gothic letters. It was an awful price to pay for a silkworm's breakfast.

Once there was a school project to send some of our wild flowers to Poor City Children. In a way that would cause consternation today, we gathered armfuls of them, which were carefully laid in a flat box by Miss Edmonds. On top was a beautiful drift of snakeshead fritillaries with their mauve chequered petals. I suppose they were sent by train from Challow Station to the Poor City Children, and I hope they liked them. For myself, I now have apple trees encircled by those same chequered fritillaries and my love of them stretches back in an ever-lengthening strand, to the ones in the flat box in Miss Edmonds's class.

Our school had no playing field, but permission had been given by the Reverend Street for us to use the vicarage lawn. Once a week, weather permitting, we would stream out over the closely mown grass. I was good at high jump and had developed an individual full-on style. Not for me the delicate approach from the side, the elevation first of the right leg followed by the left. No, I thundered towards it full tilt from the front and leapt with both feet raised together. I must have looked like a Shire horse. After each jump, I have a clear memory of Mrs Perkins turning away discreetly to the side. I could still see that she was shaking with laughter. Once a year we had a Sports Day on the vicarage lawn and Mum always came. It was the one occasion each year when teachers and parents stood together, although they seemed remote from each other, like two unconnected factions.

If the weather or the season precluded visits to the vicarage lawn, then exercise was taken in the Village Institute next to the school. Built in 1921 this was a large creosoted wooden building with a corrugated tin roof. During the war, troops had been billeted in it but when I became aware of it the Institute was used for dances, billiards, entertainments, the WI and as an adjunct to the school. It was on that wooden stage, now demolished, that I first tasted the joy and terror of acting.

At an early age, cast in the lead role of King Marmaduke's imperious queen, I graced the stage while draped in noble robes made of old curtains. The name of the play is now lost to me in the welter of years, but the script specified that the queen stared haughtily at her subjects *through a lorgnette.* These hand-held spectacles on a dainty gold shaft were a rare phenomenon indeed in the straw-sprinkled streets of Stanford in the Vale. Nobody had ever seen any. Undeterred, the task of providing a pair was given to the balsa-wood craftsmen of the school woodwork class and in due course the instrument turned up. Featherlight and painted a violent yellow to simulate gold, it was four times the required size and deeply owl-like. I remember looking at it dubiously and thinking the balsa-wood boys hadn't quite cracked it. Nevertheless, when, at the age of seven, I stepped out on to the Village Institute stage followed by the curtains, stared over my lorgnette and summoned my king in a fine, cut-glass accent: 'Marmaduke? MARMADUKE!' the ripple of laughter that shot round the parent-filled auditorium was deeply thrilling. My brain went on full alert. So *this* was acting. I couldn't wait to treat the audience to more.

PE in the Institute consisted of Team Games and Dancing. I have forgotten the nature of the team games, where you donned a diagonal coloured sash and sprinted about on the dusty floor, but the dancing was memorable indeed. Large, embarrassed country children squired each other round the floorboards in oafish versions of the Gay Gordons or the Valita. Then from the ancient gramophone, a crackling invitation would issue, 'Take your partners for the Boston Square Dance!' We formed a square and couples would gallop diagonally across, often with a bone-crunching collision in the middle to liven things up. We lacked grace. My favourite was the Progressive Barn Dance where the inner ring of dancers constantly moved on and your partner changed. One with a snotty nose could be passed swiftly on to somebody else.

In our classrooms we learned by rote. Each day we chanted our times tables until we reached the pinnacle of the twelve times, and every morning we took a spelling test of twenty words. For me this worked a treat, the information was inculcated into the brain by constant, droning repetition and there it stayed. We were taught to sew and to embroider and within those four modest classrooms I received what I now think was an impressive educational grounding; a good foundation on which to build.

94

English was easily my favourite subject. I was good at spelling and had consistently good marks for written work. My stories and compositions started to be pinned up on the classroom wall. I found writing enjoyable, an escape, and I liked the praise.

A terrifying cloud appeared on my horizon when I was bullied. For some reason a much older boy called Phillip started to pick on me. I was scared stiff, and someone must have told Mum because she tackled him. I didn't know she'd cornered him, or what compliments she used to describe his character, but afterwards, ripe for revenge, he came to find me and jabbed me repeatedly in the chest. 'I-haven't-got-to-poke-fun-at-you,' he sneered, punctuating each word with a hard prod of his bony finger. Mother had prevailed though, and the bullying came to an end. I can't think why I attracted his attention; he was so much older than me.

There were only a very few unsavoury presences in the village; whenever a crowd of girls played on the green in front of Campdene, one big boy always lay in the longer grass and invited the girls over beside him; he had something to show them, he said. He never offered to show it to me.

Another, older man was more menacing. Soft-spoken and cultured, he charmed the mothers into letting him take their little daughters out and about. He took the mothers in; they thought he was delightful and so *kind* to the children. They would have been less charmed to see him when he had the little girls to himself. None of those so trustingly handed over to him were harmed, but I remember him with profound disquiet. He was silkily manipulative and we were most certainly

95

at risk.

18

THE CREEP

At home in the meantime, high fashion struck our family a swingeing blow when my third brother Jeff decided to espouse the Teddy Boy look, newly arrived from the States. The main components of the look were the three-quarter length 'drape' jacket, drainpipe trousers and suede shoes on a white crêpe sole of startling thickness. Crucial for authenticity was the right hairstyle, massively quiffed and combed into the back to form a DA, or duck's arse. One evening in the kitchen, Jeff materialised in this gear while practising the steps of the latest dance craze, the Creep, which was simple to learn as far as I could see as it only involved creeping menacingly up and down past the sink. His drape jacket was blue velvet, and an excess of hair oil from the duck's arse dripped steadily on to his collar. When Father saw this spectacle, it was like a red rag to a bull. He was beside himself, enraged, but Jeff, undaunted and defiant, exited the house and went on his way in the full regalia, still dancing the Creep.

19

WE MIGHT WIN A FORTUNE!

Every family I knew did the football pools, each week entering a competition that required you to predict the outcome of innumerable football matches played each Saturday all over the UK. Vernons and Littlewoods were the two major companies involved. They offered enormous cash prizes, the topmost being £75,000, which at that time was a fortune beyond imagining. The companies employed agents to collect the money; they would call at the house on a weekly basis so that a person's 'little flutter on the pools' was made ever so easy.

References to winning the pools were a part of everyday conversation: 'Look at that smart car! We'll get one like that when we wins the pools!' or, dolefully, 'I don't know where the money's going to come from. We shall just have to hope we wins the pools.'

It was everybody's dreamed-of escape route from the iron restraints of being hard up; a golden staircase that would drop from the heavens direct to your back door and allow you to ascend while making V-signs at the boss and draping the wife in mink. All you needed was eight draws on the coupon.

When the football results were broadcast on the radio at about five o'clock on Saturday evenings, a feverish scratching could be heard all over the land as people wrote crosses and noughts against their chosen teams on the blue grid of the coupon. In our house during this time, concentration was so intense that everyone was forbidden to speak. Any slight sound brought forth a long drawn-out snarl of 'ALL RIGHT!' from Dad, hunched over the kitchen table, hoping against hope for the avalanche of cash that would never come.

Some time later there was unprecedented excitement when Tony had a win. At about £200, it wasn't the longed-for fortune but it helped him to buy a new Ford Popular in Ambassador Blue.

20

A HARD HAT GONE SOFT

I liked animals. I had four pet rabbits up in the chicken run, knew all the laying hens by name and was on good terms both with Mum's budgerigar and the dog from next door, but I was about to discover a new and larger love.

Our butcher was called Phil Wentworth. He was curly-haired, prosperous and drove a dark blue Jowett Javelin. His two daughters had a pony each and when I was nine, I discovered that his eldest daughter Jill offered riding lessons for three shillings an hour. I saved up my pocket money and nervously went to see her. She was lovely; seventeen years old with dark curly hair and a bright 'I'm-on-your-side' manner. A lesson was arranged for ten o'clock the next Sunday morning and it proved to be the first of many. We fell into a lovely and, certainly for me, much-looked-forward-to routine, of walking to the field to catch the ponies, leading them back, grooming them, putting on their saddles and riding off. Their names were Tarka and Poppet. They were Exmoor ponies, strawberry roans with mealy muzzles. I loved them and I idolised Jill. It really was a lesson; she taught me about the subject of riding in a serious and cerebral fashion. I had to learn the Points of the Horse starting with the withers and other words I liked the sound of but had never encountered before: stifle, gaskin, pastern and the dainty word fetlocks. I had to memorise the various parts making up a horse's tack and here were more intriguing words: pommel, cantle, throat latch and the melodious martingale, which sounded like the name of a bird. We cleaned the saddles and bridles with Propert's saddle soap on rainy days when we couldn't ride and, when we could, we went to a fragrant conifer wood called Hatford Warren where the ponies' hooves were barely audible on the sandy soil. It was like a cathedral, a place where it was preferable to be silent. Winds murmured far up in the canopy of tall trees, but at ground level, all was quiet and still. Mossy pines had fallen across the pathways; you could press your pony to canter up and jump over them. The riding was calm and leisurely, but it could be fast and thrilling too, tearing down stubble fields with the pony's mane thrashing and your heart nearly bursting with joy. One Sunday after my lesson, I was walking away down the driveway of the house and Jill was crossing the lawn to go in and have her lunch. She was vivacious, tall and slim in her black jeans, and she called to me in her fun-filled, encouraging voice. 'You're improving!' is what she said.

A few days later, I heard that Jill had been thrown from the back of her boyfriend's motorbike. Her spine was irrevocably injured; she spent many long months in Stoke Mandeville hospital and for the rest of her life was unable to walk unaided. When I first heard this news, I was distraught and cried in the chicken house for a long time.

Stanford welcomed Jill home, now as a disabled person, and she became a much-loved sight around the village, either in her wheelchair or in a little blue electric car. She acquired a puppy, which grew into a large black-and-brown dog called Simon; he trotted alongside her and seemed to have taken it upon himself to look after her. In time she married a friend of my brothers, a quiet, thoughtful, village boy named George, and they had two sons.

It was my affection for Jill Wentworth and her ponies that coloured my writing at that time. Like countless small girls of nine or ten, I had become pony-mad. I thought of nothing else. My brothers charitably observed, 'She even walks like a bloody horse.' The excitement of riding fired me up; it was so hard to wait until the next time so I assuaged my impatience by writing about it. Asked at school to write an essay or something imaginative about a photo we'd been shown, even if it was of Mount Everest, I found some way of involving horses. 'Amazing horse climbs Mount Everest.' My compositions were about big horses, small horses, brave, loyal horses that saved people's lives and wild, undisciplined brumby horses streaming across remote tracts of Australia. I mustered my growing vocabulary to describe them and I am sure that as my new teacher Mr Biggs read my florid works, he felt himself obliterated by trail dust.

There was a less attractive side to my love of horse riding. It appealed to my snobby instincts as well. I had found a pair of jodhpurs at a rummage sale, and someone had given me a navy riding hat gone soft with age. Dressed up in this finery, riding through the village, I felt a step closer to Mrs Bean, the aristocratic woman who seemed to me to epitomise smart living. Mum, knowing I was so keen, kindly helped me to find the money to pay for my riding lessons, but ironically once I'd had them, I started to look down my nose at Campdene. One day I made the mistake of asking Mum if I could have a pony, if we could rent a field. I shall never forget her reaction. 'WHAT?' she gasped, incredulous and scornful. It was not one of my better ideas. My parents were working long, thankless hours just to feed and look after us all; the idea of any money going to buy me a bloody horse was bloody rich. Shamed, I crept away in my jumble-sale jodhpurs.

It was not only money; it was to do with class. An expression that I heard a lot and disliked was 'out of place'. Dad used to say you couldn't do this or that because you would look out of place, and be a laughing stock. I learned that there were mystifying unwritten boundaries that governed what was acceptable and proper. If it could have been explained to me, it never was. I saw life in a series of fragments. I could see, for instance, that my family and the Campdene children went to our sort of school, the village primary and then the secondary modern in Faringdon, yet other village children did not do that. They went to the grammar school, The Elms at Faringdon, and this set them apart. The girls who went there had to wear grey felt hats and gymslips; we wore what we liked. They waited for transport on their side of the green, and we waited for our outdated bus on ours.

Some children, the offspring of the top tier of Stanford society, disappeared from the village altogether. Sent away from their homes, they would reappear hugely grown at summer and Christmas. Later I learned they had gone to places like Shrewsbury, Wellington or Harrow, but I did not know where those places were, or why you might be sent there to be educated. I knew one such boy called Robert; he was about the same age as me and I liked him. He was the son of Brigadier Kellie, the market gardener whose land adjoined the Campdene gardens. One warm summer's day Robert and I were playing on a sand-heap near the greenhouses. His father appeared and ordered his son indoors. He pointed his stick at me and said 'Go away' in such a cold voice that I felt like vermin. Clearly, I was 'out of place' and had made a mistake in playing with Robert but I couldn't see why; I couldn't understand the rules. There were invisible barriers, who you could mix with, who you could talk to. Decades later, I interviewed my former head teacher Mrs Perkins for BBC Radio 4; she said of the village, 'It was feudal; it was *so* feudal.'

Therefore, to my ten-year-old self, riding about the village on a pony while wearing a hard hat gone soft gave me a distinct feeling of having moved out of my allotted place and slightly upwards. I felt as though I had thwarted the system a bit; I had inched nearer Mrs Bean.

21

BICYCLE BUSINESS

The purposeful population of Stanford usually pedalled round the village on bikes, and the pace varied from sedate to must-want-his-head-tested according to the infirmity or pent-up vigour of the cyclist. Bikes were the usual form of transport for the hard up and nearly everybody had one. Only the grand few owned a car. Between us, our family had eight bikes and this could cause disaster when Father came home from his nightly visit to the pub.

There was no street lighting at Campdene; at night, all was in darkness. You knew it was time to take cover when from outside in the pitch-blackness you heard Father's progress up the garden path halted by a stumble, a grunt, a metallic clatter and furious roaring curse. This meant firstly that somebody had forgotten to put their bike away and had left it lying across the path, and secondly that in the inky darkness, father had fallen over it. You then braced yourself for the crashing impact as he seized the errant bike and hurled it far out on to the garden—this was the price you paid for your negligence.

He would then enter the family home, eyes blazing with the white light of fury, and demand to know which daft bastard had left their bike on the path where anybody could go a gutser over it. These preliminaries often signalled the start of a monumental, frightening row. One night I ran away, the door was open and I slipped out to escape the horrible bellowing voices. I went down the village to the ponies' field and talked to Poppet and Tarka. They smelled nice, accepted the cuddles and listened with great equine wisdom. After a time, to my astonishment Mum and Dad loomed up out of the darkness seeming anxious; they had come to look for me. It was a weird feeling; I'd had no inkling that I was important enough to search for.

Bikes were crucial. Without them people could not get to their place of work. There were desirable bikes and old-fashioned, laughed-at bikes. Drop handlebars had just come in and were all the rage among young men; women raised an eyebrow at the crouching, buttocks-raised stance. Cable brakes were also becoming more common, snaking racily over the handlebars, and all the latest trends were studied enthusiastically. People cycled in all weathers and some would tuck a rolled-up cape behind the saddle to be shaken out as a flimsy defence from the rain. The bike was a major purchase for everybody's budget and had to be properly maintained. From time to time, a bike belonging to one of my brothers would get a puncture and he would sit on the back step of No. 2 Campdene to mend it.

First, the bike would be upturned amid the contents of a puncture outfit and a large, spread-out assortment of tiny, intricate tools. Tyre levers or battered spoons were used to prise the tyre off the wheel. Mum's washing-up bowl was filled with water and the inner tube submerged, rotated and drowned until it revealed the puncture's whereabouts by a string of tiny bubbles. A small square rasp was then used to graze the surrounding rubber, a tube of rank-smelling glue known as The Solution applied and the repair sealed with a rubber patch of suitable size. A little pack of powder puffed round the edges to prevent unwanted adhesion finished the job. During this operation, the craftsman's paraphernalia would spread out over such a large area that it was very difficult to get into or out of the back door without inadvertently crunching some minute tool into the concrete and being savagely shoved off and cursed.

Rarely was a bike taken elsewhere to be repaired; normally you did it yourself. Only if the problem was beyond the skill of you or your neighbours was it deemed necessary to visit the cycle repair shop, and this was a carefully considered step of last resort because it involved parting with money. The shop, situated next to Mrs Miles's sweet shop, was housed in a building of rough creosoted planks like a large wooden shed. Inside it was exceedingly dark and gloomy with a strong invigorating smell of chain oil and fresh, new rubber tyres. A bell rang as you entered, and after an age the proprietor slowly emerged, a Mr Day. I hate to be unkind to Mr Day but it must be said that he was of unprepossessing appearance with melancholy, frog-like features. He would place his hands wordlessly upon the broad counter and wait. Above his head hung a tapestry of cobwebs and in the wide shop window, upon a thick snowfall of dust, lay a solitary bicycle pump to entice passers-by. New bikes were available to order from Mr Day, and when my eldest brother Tony started work as an apprentice electrician in Faringdon he earned £1 5s a week or £1.25. He gave £1 a week to Mum for his keep, and kept the modest balance. By so doing, he saved up £15 and bought a racing bike from Mr Day. It was at the pinnacle of modernity with drop handlebars and cable brakes. People came round and admired it; the undisputed Rolls-Royce of Campdene.

22

AN EIGHT-INCH SCREEN

By the mid-Fifties, at least two of my brothers had started work and were contributing to their keep. Mum had to claim the major part of their wages, and this taking of what she saw as the lion's share seemed to perturb her in later years. None of us needed convincing but she would say earnestly 'I had to have it. I had to have it or we couldn't have managed'. Mum was prudent and ran our home brilliantly with little money; her six children were tall, warmly clothed and well nourished.

As each son joined the workforce, she must have felt some slight easing of the financial tension, and relief that the family income was now arriving from more than one source. If a husband was the sole wage earner and became ill, the family's horizon grew dark. A breadwinner 'on the sick' was exceedingly bad news.

At home, excitingly, one or two things began to arrive, which could be classified as luxuries rather than necessities. We bought a flight of three plaster mallard ducks that winged their way across the front room wall. Several Campdene families had them; they were new and trendy and I loved them. My brother Tony, the apprentice electrician, keen to introduce a touch of much-needed modernity to No. 2 Campdene, brought home the latest word in light fittings and affixed it to the ceiling. In appearance, it was not unlike a flying saucer. It had a pale blue convex centre encircled by a white fluorescent tube and this chilly combination of colours laid a ghastly pallor upon us all.

A breathtaking bold sign of our slightly less perilous financial setup was the arrival of a television. One day, coming home from school, Mum suggested we go and look in the front room. Jean and I burst in excitedly and gasped: on the cherrywood drum table loomed the huge bulk of our own television. It was gigantic. Manufactured by Pye, it was shaped like a waisted cube with a skirt of horizontal ribs and tiny greenish screen eight inches wide. Gilbert Harding, a famously irascible TV personality of the day, was in mid-flow. 'You'll see a lot of him,' Mum said confidently, 'debatin' about stuff.'

Jean and I loved a police series called *Fabian of the Yard*, which was based on the memoirs of Robert Fabian, a real-life Scotland Yard detective. Inspector Fabian stalked criminals on the London streets, and would emerge from a mighty Humber Hawk to solve hideous crimes while sucking a pipe.

From 1953 to 1961, Johnny Morris appeared as *The Hot Chestnut Man* and engaged children in a delightful way with his stories. Johnny was my absolute top favourite with his confiding manner, sack of chestnuts and large perforated brazier.

By stark contrast, some time after 1953, BBC television brought something darker into our house. They began to show a science fiction series named *Quatermass*, which I found bleakly terrifying. I had never seen any kind of manufactured horror before, nothing specifically designed to frighten, and I found it deeply disturbing. Understandably, my brothers were agog to watch. There was an appalling moment when in some crashed and buried spaceship an ungodly presence was detected. A mortified scientist staggered out and whispered the blood-curdling words: 'It . . . it *walked through the wall!*' I freaked. I went berserk with fear. On a regular basis thereafter my brothers loomed up out of dark places at me and with rounded eyes and a deathly expression, informed me that it had walked through the wall. On the nights when the programme was shown, I was faced with a dilemma. I could watch it and be mortified, or remove myself to another part of the unheated house and there, frozen and alone with my imaginings, quake anyway.

23

THE CALL-UP

As my four brothers grew up, the shadow of conscription loomed, whereby all young men aged eighteen and over had to perform two years of military service. They enlisted in the army, navy or air force, and in our family Tony, being the eldest, was the first to go. It must have been terribly difficult for Mum to see him walk away. Those village boys, callow for the most part, were drawn out from their homes in a constant stream. The destinations to which they could be sent were many and far-flung. They left their families, most never having been away from home before, and the mothers watched them go with uncertainty.

For me as a young girl, conscription, National

Service or 'the call-up' meant the sudden unwelcome disappearance of a familiar brother from the home and his reappearance some weeks later with an astonishing brand-new look. The old figure would have vanished; in his place clumped a shaven-headed, booted soldier clad in rough khaki battledress and shouldering a kitbag. When Tony came home for the first time, fresh from basic training and 'square bashing', his talk was of places as foreign to us as the moon: Blandford Camp, Barton Stacey and Andover. His speech was newly peppered with unfamiliar titbits: something was smashing, a real *brahmer*, or it was no good any more so it was *played out*. I hoovered these novelties up eagerly so I could drop them into conversations at school and be sure of sounding urbane and worldly-wise.

I missed my brothers as each one was called up, but was consoled by the glorious foreign gifts they unfailingly brought home. I shallowly felt that I could stand the separation, and that on the whole conscription was a good thing, so long as the brothers returned laden with presents, preferably for me. Tony went into the Royal Electrical and Mechanical Engineers, better known as the REME, as a driver, and was posted to Germany. He brought home a beautiful clock for Mum. It knocked spots off the sturdy utilitarian job normally planted on our mantelpiece. This was heavily decorated and raised up on pillars so its workings were visible. I watched it for hours, this little enclosed world where tiny golden wheels and springs revolved and interacted beneath their glass dome. Also from Germany, Tony brought me a silky headscarf bearing a scene of the Brandenburg Gate, and a model of the Town Musicians of

109

Bremen, a donkey, dog, cat and rooster who stood on each other's backs and scared away robbers! Though I was always an earnest nail-biter, he also gave me a lavish green manicure set, with little tools laid out on cream velvet.

Next, my brother Jeff joined the Royal Navy and served on the aircraft carrier HMS *Eagle*. He came home in a fabulous sailor suit, with a lanyard knotted round his neck and his bell-bottoms pressed into complicated horizontal pleats. He described the sea as he himself had seen it, filled to the horizon with leaping dolphins. From out of his kitbag, he drew jaw-dropping treasures: exquisite shell lamps, exotic pink satin pyjamas and kimonos embroidered with dragons, silk rugs, wooden camels and gaudy gewgaws delightful to my sister and me.

When it was Roger's turn to enlist, Mum and I stood at the window to watch him as he walked away across the village green. She had given him a hug and said 'So long, old boy', which was her way. Her maternal love was particularly fierce towards Roger; as a child, he had not thrived and he was less sturdily robust than his brothers. Dad had been declared missing in wartime Germany when Mum was expecting him. It was shattering news and she was racked with worry, not knowing if her husband was dead or alive. She felt that Roger had suffered as well, that she had not given this baby the good start he deserved.

On that day, as he made his way across the green and down the street, I watched him go and was unmoved. I was always waving my brothers off. However, when I turned back and looked at Mum, I was shocked to the core to see that she was crying. Tears streamed down her face as his slight figure became more distant. It was unbearable. I thought she was tough and wiry, that my mum meant business and you didn't get in her way. Yet here she was unguarded; crying openly as her boy reached the corner of the village street and, without looking back, disappeared from view.

That was in 1957, when Roger joined up and went into the Ox & Bucks Light Infantry, later to become a battalion of the Royal Green Jackets. He was posted to Cyprus and I wrote long letters to him in Limassol. When he wrote back, his letters were sprinkled with the names of distant, intriguing places: Nicosia, Larnaca and the juicily named Famagusta. He brought me home a beautiful writing case of soft brown leather, finely made and smoothly zipped, a thing especially for writers! I couldn't believe I had been entrusted with it. I have always treasured it.

They were generous, my brothers. They never came home without gifts for us, although they couldn't have had much spare cash. We were close; there was a strong bond between all members of the family. Everyone adored Mum; she was the heart of our home. In addition to the exotic clock, Tony brought her a beautiful scarlet-lined jewellery box from Germany. When the lid was lifted a ballerina danced and a little music box played 'The Blue Danube'. It enchanted Mum. We weren't allowed to touch it but had to wait until she proudly played it for us. Mum loved the song 'Isle of Capri', which Gracie Fields used to sing; and so from Cyprus Roger brought her a gondola made of mother-of-pearl. It revolved as a little music box picked out the tune; the young man steering his boat as his sweetheart reclined upon the cushions.

Our home, when I look back, seemed to embrace two extremes. On the one hand, our furnishings were exceedingly cheap and plain, yet interspersed among them, as a legacy of conscription, was a scattering of bright goods from the far corners of the earth.

The armed forces touched the lives of all families then. The welfare of called-up sons, relatives and friends was the first topic of conversation among the villagers as they greeted each other. How long until their boy went? Where had he been posted? How much time did he have to serve before demob? Everybody had this one thing in common.

Regardless of where my brothers were stationed around the globe, they would receive the local paper from Mum once a week. Off went the *Wiltshire Gazette and Herald*, rolled up and trapped in a tube made from an airmail envelope, addressed in her instantly recognisable handwriting to the relevant British Forces Post Office number. Three of my brothers did National Service before conscription ended in 1960. They travelled widely and made friendships that endured over many decades.

At Campdene, my life at the age of ten was enriched by the comings and goings of my brothers, I was happy at Stanford school, I could keep up with the work and I went riding whenever I could. However, by stark contrast with these homely aspects of my life, I remember being acutely conscious of the monstrous shadow of nuclear war. I don't know why this was, because the invasion of the Bay of Pigs had not yet occurred, nor had Khrushchev and Kennedy faced each other during the perilous Cuban missile crisis, but I was aware of it nonetheless. I knew that in the event of a nuclear strike there would be a two-minute warning. At school, I spent a lot of time seriously wondering if it was possible to run the length of the village in that short time to be with Mum when the end came, so that she would not face the terror of annihilation on her own.

24

A COACH TRIP TO WEYMOUTH

From time to time, during the long, languorous days of our school summer holidays, Jean and I would be galvanised by tremendous news. To our incredulous and ecstatic disbelief, Mum would announce that we were going on an outing to the seaside. Someone in the village would have 'got up a busload' for a day trip, usually to Weymouth in Dorset. The excursion never varied but always followed the same pattern. Agonisingly early in the morning, families who had managed to afford the fare would queue in various spots around the village. Faces drugged with sleep, they would be surrounded by a vast number of bags containing everything deemed necessary for a successful day. This would include coats, cardigans, plastic macks, umbrellas, sunglasses, sunhats, rainhats, newspapers and magazines. Swimmers would require caps, costumes and towels, and all the families would have prepared colossal quantities of food and drink so that they wouldn't have to buy anything. The provisions would be modest but substantial; hearty sandwiches filled with corned

113

beef, fishpaste, reeking hard-boiled egg, a wet mush of cheese and tomato or Spam, the sugar-pink 'luncheon meat', which had to be forced out of a tin and which may at one time have seen a pig. To all this was added slices of great doughy cake, Swiss rolls, currant buns, Arthur Shepherd's lardy cake and huge dented vacuum flasks of tea. We were all set.

At last, the laboured drone of the approaching bus could be heard over the early-morning silence still blanketing the fields. Excitement surged up through our tiredness as the huge vehicle roared into view and pulled up alongside, wreathed in noxious fumes and throbbingly hot. Deafened, choked and brandishing our bags like battering rams, we barged on board to grab the best seats and be ready for an adventure!

By the time we reached the coach park in Salisbury, anticipation had turned to anguish as bladders were strained beyond endurance. The sight of the cathedral, miraculous and mist-shrouded as it might be, counted for nothing when compared to the sight of a toilet and the prospect of a long-awaited, luxuriant piddle. Like pilgrims to a shrine, we hobbled cross-legged over the tarmac to seek relief.

On emerging radiant, the next task was to procure some souvenir with Salisbury Cathedral on it, and present it to Mum. We bought her ashtrays although she never smoked, plaster cathedrals with thermometers affixed, pokerwork toilet-roll holders and small embellished spoons. We gave her teapot stands although there was no surface in our home likely to have been harmed by a teapot being placed straight on it. We particularly liked gifts bearing little sentimental verses. This was one, printed on a gilded plate:

Who is the one to whom we turn
When all the world is grey?
Who is the one for whom we yearn
When we are far away?
Mother.

A present from Salisbury.

We loved to give her things; it was part of the outing's joy. Once, when I was taken to see the famous Roger Bannister run his four-minute mile at Long Hanborough sports field I could find no gift stalls at all, so I took Mum home a bag of sugar.

Back on the bus, she accepted all our offerings, protesting that we shouldn't have spent our money on her, but exclaiming upon their beauty or usefulness and tucking them safely down among the packs of sandwiches. With all the adventurers safely back on board, the bus toiled on again for Weymouth. Impatiently, hours before there was any hope of seeing it, we peered between the hills for a glimpse of the sea.

At long last, after a journey of interminable crawling length, the coach would wheeze out on to the promenade, proceed along to the Jubilee clock on Weymouth beach, and stop. The driver would switch off the engine and, as it shuddered and died, sit back in his seat, stretch and relax.

There, finally, it was. All the breathtaking splendour of the seaside spread out before us: the sparkling ocean, warm lapping waves and an endless expanse of shell-dotted sand littered with seaweed. There lay the tattered eel-brown ribbons for predicting the weather, and beyond it blistered bladderwrack ripe for popping. Here were bare-bottomed kids with buckets and spades, sandcastles, deckchairs, parasols, baggage, windbreaks and striped stalls, the whole glorious line-up fluttering in the breeze. And lifting our eyes up to the horizon, we saw ships, naval vessels, boats, lilos, all manner of craft unknown to us in our village homes. The smell of the sea and everything it stood for thrillingly filled our nostrils as we poured ecstatically down the stairs of the bus, down the rasping beach steps and out on to the clean yellow sand, now loose and fine, now wet and ribbed, weaving madly through families each encircling their precious belongings, searching for the right spot where we too could set up a base, drag out our swimming costumes and run, run for that first mad, freezing, joyful splash into the sea!

Getting settled on the beach was a bit like the wagons of the old West forming a ring to protect themselves from the Sioux. Deckchairs were hired and placed so they enclosed the piled heap of baggage dumped in the middle. Mum didn't swim, so once ensconced in her deckchair she would always offer to take care of the bags, and spend most of her day watching over them, periodically ransacking our own collection for food for her two ravenous daughters. Those roughly sawn sandwiches were nectar to us, cold and blue after too long in the sea as we were. Mum provided a changing service for us as well, holding up a towel to guard our scrawny modesty as we scrambled in and out of the gritty embrace of a wet, sandy costume. All she ever asked for was a cup of tea. 'Run and get us a cuppa tea you two,' she would say to Jean and me, and we'd queue up at a stall. If

116

it wasn't hot she would look at it with contempt. Weak or strong, cups of tea were prized according to their degree of blazing heat.

The worst thing that could happen was that you lost sight of Mum in the hordes. She would drum it into us: 'I'm here look, just to the left of the clock, you just look for the clock,' but of course we didn't take in what she said in our headlong sprint for the sea. It was easy, as you jumped and played, to stray a considerable distance along the shore. Having decided at last to come out of the water, there was nothing more awful than to stand in the surf scanning the multicoloured mass of humanity, the countless faces of strangers, and be unable to pick her out. The feeling of panic, loss and terror was unspeakable, overwhelming. She must have kept a close maternal eye on us, however, because I never stood desolate for very long. She would materialise from the crowd to claim me and take me back to our own encampment, safe among the busload of familiar Stanford faces.

Sometimes Dad came on the Weymouth trip with us and that made going into the sea much more exciting. Unlike Mum he could swim; he would hold my hand and take me much further out than I would have dared to go alone. He never sat about on the beach with us though, but always went off for a wander. He liked to have a bet on the horses, and to search the back streets for the most outrageous of Donald McGill's saucy postcards to send to his mates. Finally, he always went to look at the harbour with its weight of memories.

Dad was in the Weymouth area during the war when the beaches were readied against invasion and armed with barbed wire. He helped to build fake guns along undefended stretches of coast, pitiful cubes of corrugated iron with protruding lengths of drainpipe to resemble gun barrels so that from the air the beaches looked armed and dangerous. He saw the influx of American troops prior to the D-Day landings, those endless columns of youthful soldiers who were packed into landing craft in that same harbour and sent prematurely to their deaths on merciless beaches far from home.

He was there on 28 April 1944 when, further along the coast, a soft, kindly landscape turned bitter, when 749 soldiers and sailors died in one night in the catastrophe of Operation Tiger on Slapton Sands in Devon. The dead drifted on the tide. Dad was one of those who saw the bloated bodies wash ashore, saw hands lift and carry them silently from the water. All witnesses were sworn to silence lest the planned landing on Utah Beach was compromised. 'They was all in American uniforms,' Dad told my brother Tony in later years, 'we couldn't ever talk about it.'

At six o'clock in the evening, our day at the seaside ended. The coach reappeared beside the clock and weary families made their way towards it, lugging baggage made knobbly by innumerable shells, ropes of seaweed and heavy waterlogged towels. Small sandy hands clutched colourful windmills. The space taken up by food on the outward journey was filled now with further gaudy souvenirs and large quantities of seaside rock with 'Weymouth' written through it, in strange stretched letters. It was a triumph of nastiness, from the lurid pinkness of the outside shell to the violent artificial mintyness within. Once sucked it became rough and spiky in a way that lacerated the mouth.

Robbed of its cellophane wrapper and conjoined with the fresh air, it soon oozed a sticky sludge. Pink runnels of it appeared on arms, and blobs found their way into the crease of an elbow or the back of a knee. Loathsome as it was, a stick was unfailingly taken home for every family member who had been unable to come on the trip.

There now commenced the long, grinding journey home, which was livened up by a pub stop at the halfway point. The joy tended to be more in the anticipation, but it was nevertheless a thrill to pull into the forecourt of a pub you didn't know at all. One had a playground with a friendly donkey over the fence. Another had slides you could play on while parents were inside the bar. Children were not allowed to enter and we waited hopefully outside for lemonade and a packet of crisps to be handed out, if our sparse remaining funds could stand it.

During the final leg the revellers burst into song. All the ghastly old numbers were roared out on beer-loaded breath. 'Show Me the Way to go Home' was one, 'Roll out the Barrel' another, 'It's a Long Way to Tipperary' and countless others. At some point a cloth cap would be produced, and someone would proffer it down each side of the central gangway collecting contributions for the driver. When the heavy, clinking cap was handed over to him, the passengers fondly looked on, noted his correct grateful response, then threw back their heads and gave him an alcohol-fuelled chorus of 'For He's a Jolly Good Fellow'. Soon, as darkness began to gather, the sound of the engine and gears took on a soporific quality. Thoughts fogged by the powerful beer, the heads of the weary travellers began to droop in snowdrop fashion as one by one they fell asleep. Arriving in Stanford at last was a rude shock and, as sleepily as when they got on the bus that morning, the families stumbled out into the darkness. Amid neighbourly cries of 'Good night all!', they made their way home to bed. At No. 2 Campdene, there was no bath or shower so Jean and I got into our shared single bed still crusty with sand. The bed had a pronounced sag in the middle and, over a period of days, the quantity of sand built up to satisfying beach-like proportions. We did not have many days at the seaside, but the few that Mum and Dad managed to afford stand out like joyful beacons. They were well worth the money.

25

WE SWIM WITH BEETLES

At home, we usually swam in the River Ock as it travelled across the bottom of Wentworth's field. It was crossed by a wooden bridge, and in the rushes beneath it one year when the Ock was quick and swollen by floods, the lost toddler son of a village mother was found drowned. Mum told us about this in a voice hushed by the enormity of the tragedy, but I didn't take it in then; I could not imagine the tearing anguish of the heartbroken mother until I had little sons of my own.

Crossing over the bridge and turning left brought you to a rounded bowl in the river that we called Big Ben. Here on summer evenings where the water ran cool and brown we learned to swim with bundles of knife-sharp rushes bundled up under our ribcages for buoyancy. I remember those first three or four strokes with which I crossed miraculously to the other side. It was unbelievable! I had done it! I could swim! I rushed home and told Mum.

Sometimes we went to the Thames at Tadpole Bridge or Radcot where there was no softness to the river. Here, by contrast, it was deep, fast and businesslike; a great volume of water surged under the bridge and onwards. Yet it could be tamed: age had lengthened our skinny arms and legs and our swimming had become sufficiently strong that the current no longer frightened us; it became instead a pleasant challenge. We learned to go with it, to be carried along and just to strike out for the bank further downstream. Having once been in the river a person's skin bore a tell-tale smell, brackish but not unpleasant; you could sniff yourself and think of the good time you'd had in the water.

It was nothing short of a sensation when we discovered that the nearby town of Wantage had a swimming bath, and a gang of children, including Jean and me, rapidly embarked on a new routine. Saturday mornings would now find us in our erected-for-the-Coronation bus shelter, rolled-up swimming kit under our arms, waiting to catch the bus to Wantage. It was doubly thrilling; a bus ride followed by a swim in an unfamiliar and purpose-built place. Unlike the river the municipal pool was not free; a modest sum was payable for admission. Sixty years after its official opening in June 1899 as a memorial of Queen Victoria's Diamond Jubilee, it looked past its prime and bore an air of neglect. Along the side, set back a little from the pool, were changing cubicles with partial, saloon-type doors or the brittle remains of a plastic curtain. On the surface of the water lay great undulating drifts of black beetles that parted as you swam. I do not know if they bred in the pool, or if like lemmings they leapt into the soupy waters as part of some calamity of nature, but at any rate if you swam at Wantage, you swam with beetles.

26

TESTING TIMES

At Stanford in the Vale Primary School, I had progressed through the four levels, starting with Miss Edmonds's infants class, continuing through the hands of the fearsome Miss Bedford, the affable Mr Biggs and finally arriving in the senior class presided over by Mrs Perkins. I liked being there. I could do the daily spelling and mental arithmetic tests; I loved English, could knock out a good essay and I could draw. She also taught us more advanced needlework techniques, appliqué and couching. By that time I had acquired a luckless pet starling named Starkey, which through ignorance I fed on a diet of bread and milk. Mrs Perkins let me bring him to school with me until one day in the needlework class, Starkey's guts revolted against his unnatural diet and he excreted spectacularly all over the work surface. As a result, he was ousted by Mrs Perkins and excluded from the school.

At home, we had very few books. One was entitled *Character from the Face* and was filled with close-up photographs of facial features and the corresponding character traits to be expected of the bearer. There were pages of noses for instance, ranging from cute button to alarmingly hooked, alongside voluptuous or meanly thin-lipped mouths, and sections of great fleshy ears. It was a very peculiar book, as was another that kicked about the house for years. This was a bird book where all the birds had been given supposedly comical personalities. The 'sparrer' was a Cockney pearly king for instance and spoke in painful, apostrophe-laden dialect. They were horrible, pointless books to me. We had a few Roy Rogers books printed on thick, card-like paper where the colour-blocking was askew and the rich brown of Roy's horse was some distance from the horse itself. One story revolved around a *mesa* and a *pueblo*; nobody at Campdene knew what they were. Jean and I had a few Christmas-gift *Rupert* annuals but these I ungratefully disliked. The interminably laboured verse of the stories irritated me, and I couldn't make myself care about the characters. By contrast, I adored the *Brer Rabbit* stories by Joel Chandler Harris and Mum bought me those whenever she could. For the most part the books in our house were a ragbag assortment. Nobody had chosen them; they drifted in and lay about unloved.

At school one morning, an announcement was made to the effect that we now had a school library. Inspection was invited and I went along to see. The library was housed on one bookshelf presided over by Miss Edmonds who greeted me in a friendly fashion and asked about my interests. She chose two books for me, both of which I would love and remember for life. One was *Black Beauty* by Anna Sewell and the other *Just William* by Richmal Crompton. These were real, crafted stories and hugely potent. One made me cry, one made me laugh and both whetted my appetite for more. Miss Edmonds handing me those two books was a simple act of immeasurable significance.

Now for us the eleven-plus examination loomed, when a great portcullis fell down between those who had passed and those who had not. It was the norm to fail. Most of us did not expect to pass and claimed not to want to anyway; there was a strong sense that being selected for The Elms Grammar School was vaguely traitorous. No one doubted that you would have to wear a uniform, talk posh and become a snob. This nonsense was absorbed by some kind of awful osmosis. Nobody spelt it out; it was not uttered by any teacher or parent but we all sensed it just the same. It was to do with the unwritten rule of knowing your place. I remember actually being afraid that I might pass, that I would be set apart and separated from my friends. They were everything I knew. The baffling business of 'getting on' or 'getting a good job' didn't come into it. Confusingly, at the same time I was fairly competitive and wanted to do well.

On the day of the exam the vicar, Mr Street, joined the teacher who was adjudicating. It is a fact that they talked and laughed together throughout the examination and I remember being incensed at the distraction. Inflamed by the injustice, I even considered asking them to be quiet, but they were important authority figures and I did not have the courage. I failed the exam, and probably I would have failed anyway, but fifty years on it still rankles ever so slightly that I was unable to sit the exam in silence.

I could tell Mum was disappointed that I failed. I had always done well at school and she was proud

124

of me. 'Oh yes,' she would confide to Auntie Dorothy, 'our Pam got a good headpiece on her.' My good headpiece and I had fallen short of the standard required for The Elms, however, and so in due course I left the kindly old village school and moved on to the secondary modern school at Faringdon.

27

HEALTH AND WELLBEING

I was not aware of much illness in Stanford. One poor lady suffered from a massive goitre, which she made a pitiable and largely unsuccessful attempt to hide with a little chiffon scarf. A lot of children had minor things like chilblains, the inflamed swellings known as 'gatherings' and whitlows. Measles swept through from time to time but mothers did not dread it or connect it with any serious complications liable to follow. It was an inconvenience, a rite of growing up. Similarly, children caught mumps but there were no fears for the fertility of the boys; parents were simply unaware of the danger. Fertility was a thing taken for granted and never discussed.

One village girl was a polio victim; she wore an iron calliper and ugly built-up shoe like a man's black lace-up. Callously, I ignored her because she was different and though she was nice to me, I never bothered much with her. Years afterwards, I heard that people suspected she contracted polio from playing in the River Ock.

I became aware that all was not well with

Maurice Hull, a good friend of my brother Tony. I liked Maurice. His father and mother ran the little pub called The Cottage of Content just up the road from Campdene, and I was often dispatched there to buy Dad's tobacco, an ounce of Old Holborn. It was an interesting place. Mrs Hull had an Indian mynah bird, which could be heard squawking just out of sight in their living room adjacent to the tiny bar. With a certain lack of subtlety, a gentlemen's urinal had been built outside the front door of the pub. From the other side of the road we watched men emerge from the bar and make their urgent way into the roofless cubicle. The sound of copious flowing liquid could then be heard from within. From our side of the road we cackled with coarse laughter. It was thin entertainment, but better than nothing.

Mr and Mrs Hull had purchased one of the first televisions in the village, long before one arrived in our house. On 2 June 1953, Jean and I, aged six and eight, were invited into their home to watch the coronation of Queen Elizabeth II. We were agog, sitting cross-legged on the floor watching the splendour of the event unfold on the tiny black-and-white screen. Clearly, the coronation was an occasion of unparalleled importance because there was a special ceremony at school when each one of us was presented with a commemorative blue glass beaker, smartly boxed and bearing the royal coat of arms.

Maurice Hull from The Cottage of Content was a kind, pleasant young man. His hobby was breeding budgerigars and sometimes he let me go round to the back of the pub to see them. Here behind the stacked beer crates, their cages were arranged in rows. They were lovely to look at, bright hopping little birds in turquoise, yellow and green.

But Maurice became ill. Suddenly any mention of his name was charged with shock and sadness. When I asked Mum what had happened, she took a deep breath and told me that Maurice had been found to have a shadow on the lung. Mr and Mrs Hull's only son had contracted the dreaded TB. Tony and Maurice had gone together to the new mobile X-ray unit, but only Maurice received a letter calling him back. He was hospitalised in Abingdon and, soon afterwards, Tony with a group of friends cycled the fourteen miles to visit him. When he saw his friends from Stanford, Maurice told them despairingly he had to stay in for six months and as they left to go home, he broke down and cried. In Stanford, the little pub must have become silent and fearful. But the treatment for TB was changing at last. From a situation where bed-rest for up to two years was the only hope, now antibiotics both stopped a patient from being contagious and killed the TB. In time Maurice was welcomed back safely to the village.

Though I was a robust child with few illnesses, I did contract yellow jaundice and was delighted to find that the whites of my eyes had become spectacularly yellow. Because of this, I was promoted during the daytime to Mum and Dad's big bed in the front bedroom, where there was a lovely view down over the green and village beyond. My brothers queued up to be revolted. 'Ugh!' shouted my brother Allan. 'You looks like a ghost!'

My illness was serious enough to warrant a visit from the vicar's wife, Mrs Street. One dark stormy night she appeared on our doorstep wearing owl-like spectacles and a little brown hat, proffering a basket of nice things because she had heard I was *poorly*, a word we had never encountered. It was kind of her; there was lemonade and fruit, but while nothing was actually said I had the impression that her visit was not appreciated by my parents, that she was felt to be snooping, and that they were perfectly capable of looking after me on their own, thank you very much.

For minor ailments, a trusted remedy still very much in use was the poultice, formed from a range of fragrant ingredients, which could include bread, mustard or cooked onions. Many people suffered from boils. Dad was plagued by a crop on the back of his neck and I too sprouted an impressive boil on my knee. It was taut, red and shiny. Boils were discussed in terms of ripeness, in the same way a person might comment on a rosy apple, and the favoured treatment for inducing ripeness was the bread poultice. The preparation process looked horrible. First, a quantity of bread was soaked in boiling milk then squeezed and kneaded between scalded fingers to form a hot slab. While smoking hot it was slapped on the boil to 'draw it out'. Numerous blazing poultices were applied to my knee with no apparent effect and Mum said I would have to be taken to the Cottage Hospital in Faringdon to have it lanced. The word hung in the air in great jagged letters. *Lanced!* I had a good grasp of English and my hair stood on end. I was no fool. I had seen pictures of the Bengal Lancers in books by Rudyard Kipling, and I imagined someone thrusting such a deadly javelin into the heart of the protuberance. Luckily, whilst trotting alongside Mum soon afterwards, she accidentally struck it with her handbag and the thing burst.

Though the spectacle was gruesome, I was ecstatic. I had cheated the lance.

The use of poultices was part of the general attitude that you should 'doctor yourself up' at home. Mum was never without a reeking bottle of TCP, used as a gargle for the treatment of sore throats and colds. 'You gotta try and help yourself,' she would urge us, 'get on and have a gargle with that, as strong as you can stick it! It's *marvellous* stuff!' Certainly, it burned like fire. Our eyes streamed with tears, but we gargled on.

Equally pungent was Sloan's Liniment, which came in a ribbed brown bottle bearing a picture of Sloan himself. This liquid was poured into the hand, then massaged into muscular aches and pains as the choking odour spread all through the house. Dad thought very highly of it. Highly regarded, too, were Beecham's pills in their tiny round box. Small, shiny and putty-coloured, they were taken for constipation, and the world-famous slogan on the package proclaimed they were 'worth a guinea a box'. Alternative remedies could be tried. Liquid paraffin was a popular option for constipation, particularly as, with breathtaking versatility, it could also be used as a dressing for the hair.

Accidents befell people. Allan when much younger had been climbing a tree beside the school pond, and put his foot into a wasps' nest. Once again, a sick child was promoted to Mum and Dad's bed and the rest of us queued up to gawp at him as he lay swollen and throbbing, misshapen like the Elephant Man and groaning with pain.

Roger came off his bike in an accident on Faringdon Hill. Dad came into the kitchen and his exact words to Mum were, 'Don't get panicky like, but our Roger's come off his bike . . .' Her reaction was instant and frightening; she spun round, terrified, snapping out questions to him, gauging the situation. Later that evening Roger came home from the Cottage Hospital. He had fallen from his bike at speed, careering along the road with his face in the dirt and stones. All evening he sat grim and silent by the kitchen table, his skin raw. Clear fluids trickled from the great weeping graze; he mopped at it with his handkerchief.

28

FARINGDON SECONDARY MODERN SCHOOL

It was 1958 and I had now started at Faringdon Secondary Modern School. As an adult, decades later, I became friends with some of the staff who taught me, and was surprised when they told me the school had been considered rough. 'Oh my God,' said one, shaking his head and grimacing, 'oh my God, that was a rough school.' I remember being astounded. I had never once thought of it in that way.

The great thing about being the youngest child of six was that you seldom had to brave things alone. Whatever it may have been, the older members of the family had usually been there first and got to grips with it. So it was with the move to Faringdon School. Allan and Jean were already there, I could see them around the place, confident and reassuring. They were far above me in the hierarchy of the establishment and kept to their

My great-grandmother Sarah Anne Ridley, with her pet jackdaw taken in Richmond, Surrey in 1847.

My great-uncle Alfred Ernest Ridley, known as Sheddy.

Dad as a young boy, about 1920.

Mum (left) and her friend Maud, members of St Nicholas Church choir at Baulking, 1920s.

My grandmother Florence Rose Loder with her son, my uncle George, at Baulking.

(Below) My grandparents Ada and Bill Ayres, at Uffington on their golden wedding anniversary.

(Above) My grandmother Ada Ayres with her son Grenadier Guard Stanley, my father. On The Common, Uffington, about 1935.

The Uffington White Horse, which you could see from the back of my Ayres grandparents' cottage.

Me aged about five on the garden path at Campdene. Our chicken run and greengage trees in the background.

'Jeannie first, Margaret second, Pammie last!'

Mum, Jean and I at Campdene, 1950s. Jean is wearing my Fair Isle knitted beret!

Dressed ready for school
with brother Tony at
Campdene.

School photo, Stanford,
about 1953.

Allan and Roger, with Jeff at the window,
No. 2 Campdene.

With Mum and Jean at Vandiemans. I am wearing my full circle skirt!

Jean and me with Tony's Watsonian motorcycle combination.

At Jeff's wedding to Edie in Uffington, about 1959. Taken shortly before the car accident.

Me beside a large trout hanging on the washing line.
I am the one with the perm.

The hard
hat gone
soft.

Joey the budgerigar. I crafted the skirt myself.

Mum and Dad arriving for Roger's wedding in Wolvercote, early 1960s.

Dad and Tony by the River Thames at Tadpole Bridge.

Hairdos of the Day.

The Cottage Loaf.

The Dusty Springfield.

The Windswept (while serenading the dustbin).

The Well-lacquered. Aged sixteen, bridesmaid at Roger's wedding.

own groups of friends but I knew they would come to my aid in a crisis.

We travelled the four miles to school each day on a coach from Eagle Coaches in Faringdon. Painted cream and brown, it looked old-fashioned even then. As far as I was concerned, the bus ride was a thrilling bonus that topped and tailed the school day. On arrival in Faringdon, we were dropped off beside The Swan public house and trailed down a long pathway to the school. The original building with its cream-and-green paintwork could not cope with the baby boomers, the huge numbers of children born shortly after the war, so other space had been hurriedly found. To receive our education we traipsed round a series of unlikely sites and my enduring memory is of walking in the wet. The sodden crocodile marched in an eternal figure-of-eight to reach classrooms, which, if they were not in the main school, would be found in nearby temporary terrapin-type buildings, a former prisoner of war camp known as 'the huts', or in sections of a disused marine camp miles away over the railway line and past the screaming sawmill at Butts Close. Sport was played on a recreation ground at the end of another traipse through a red-brick housing estate called Marlborough Gardens. Regardless of the weather, we plodded grimly on. It was a lesson well learned; how to walk uncomplainingly for long distances with wet legs and feet. Finally, we squelched into the far-flung classroom to receive the lesson and, underneath our desks, the cheap wet leather of our shoes warmed up. Chilblains flourished in the hothouse conditions, and athlete's foot cracked the spaces between toes.

On one side of the main playground was a tall

building where boys learned practical skills in woodwork and metalwork. They made pokers with twisted shanks; Mum received four. Fireside companion sets were produced along with breadboards and bedside cabinets. In a cavernous ex-barrack room at Butts Close we girls were promoted from hand sewing to sewing machines, and the two halves of my brain revolved in opposite directions as I tried to work a treadle. It was desperate; I could not do it.

New vistas opened up when we were taught to cook. It was lovely; there were clean tables, sinks and shining cookers in an airy classroom filled with the drifting scent of pastry. We made raspberry buns where you poked a hole in the top and spooned in the jam, parkin, rock cakes and Swiss rolls. We were taught to make bread and I discovered the curious resilience of yeast; the crumbly grey other-worldliness of it, foaming up when fed and giving off so seductive and enticing a fragrance when bread was taken freshly baked from the oven.

Mum, who had to shovel out vast meals every day for the family, was a bit scornful about the cookery classes. 'I like that!' she would say as I measured out her currants and flour to take to school. 'You cooks it and then you sits down and eats it!' It was true; many products of the lessons never managed to make it home.

My new form teacher at Faringdon School was a Miss Harding; she taught English. My memory of her is coloured pink and white. Her unusually florid complexion contrasted with the white cotton wool-like fluff of her short hair; she was middle-aged and substantially overweight. Miss Harding had a mannerism that I found deeply disconcerting; when she spoke to you, she closed her eyes, forcing you to address her closed pink eyelids. Winter and summer, she wore long pink interlock knickers elasticated at the knee. This was serious underwear. It was her habit to perch on the corner of her table at the front of the room, and coquettishly to raise one leg and reveal the enormous bloomers. I do not know why she did this. If it was her dark intention to foster and inflame the developing lust of her schoolboy pupils, then she failed to achieve it. Instead, in red-faced, shaking ranks along the back of the classroom they fought to contain their hysterical laughter.

I was the sixth Ayres child to attend the school. On the first day in the form room when Miss Harding asked all our names, I nervously offered 'Pamela Ayres'. She stopped dramatically, closed her eyes, raised her leg and exclaimed, 'Oh no! Not *another* one!'

There was an art classroom, which was new and exciting to me. It was untidy and cold but the teacher Mr Pottinger was friendly and easy-going. I drew a lot of horses and my drawings attracted attention and were displayed on the walls of the room. Sadly for me Mr Pottinger left and was followed by a young female teacher who seemed distant and disdainful. She brusquely told me that I could not draw horses and should stop trying. This hurt my feelings and I started feeling indifferent towards the lessons. Her ideas were tedious to me; we were not allowed to invent, instead she made us copy things. One, which could well have reflected her hopes for our future, was Anubis, the Egyptian jackal god of embalming.

At the new school, I began to feel a depressing

133

sense of being left behind. I missed the close supervision of Stanford School where everyone was kept up to the mark. Here the maths teacher was a Mr Badger, naturally nicknamed Brock. He had the look of the mad professor, with wispy clumps of hair above each ear, a bald pate and tiny round glasses. He taught us algebra, geometry and logarithms but I lost track in algebra and stopped being able to solve the equations, or calculate what X and the variously shaped brackets meant. Mr Badger had a reputation for strictness, for standing no nonsense and I didn't like to confess that I hadn't understood or would have liked him to repeat what he'd already said. Previously I had liked arithmetic but now the pleasure and confidence slipped away.

I had hoped that I would shine in English, and that it would be my strong card as it had been at Stanford School, but depressingly Miss Harding didn't seem to attach much significance to anything I wrote. At the end of the first year I was shocked to discover that although I had started in the A stream, I had now been demoted, not even to the B class, but to the C stream. I was embarrassed at my fall from grace. I had sensed my own early promise but now, at this new school, I no longer seemed able to excel.

I was terrified of my new form teacher. He taught PE and was fit-looking in his glossy navy blue tracksuit, dark-haired and handsome in a grim, malevolent way. He was rumoured to be ex-army. His form room was the previously delightful domestic science classroom, now incongruously filled with desks shoehorned between the cookers and sinks. He taught English after a fashion and was violent. I sat next to my friend Lucy Clements, also from Stanford, and it soon dawned on us that in being relegated to this new class we had drawn an exceedingly short straw. This so-called teacher was explosive and unpredictable. With little provocation, he would erupt, crimson-faced and swift, crossing the room in huge menacing strides to seize a child by the collar, the jacket, the hair. Possessed of great strength and fitness, he would drag the pupil backwards on helpless scuffling feet to the cloakroom outside. He kept a terrible sort of order by fear and physical violence. At twelve years of age Lucy and I were scared every day; I learned nothing in that class except how to keep your head down, how to disappear.

At Faringdon, there were formal music lessons where a teacher named Mrs Thomas endeavoured to teach us notation and melodious song. We had already learned a wide if somewhat startling range of songs at Stanford School where I think they may have been grooming us to join the military. The great naval sea shanty 'Hearts of Oak' was one; 'Kijje Was a Warrior Bold Who Fought so Bravely for the Tsar' and 'The Minstrel Boy to the War has Gone' were others. We struggled through the impenetrable Latin-laden dirge *'Non Nobis Domine'* and eight-year-old children sang 'The Ash Grove', cheerfully bashing out the doleful lyrics: 'With sorrow, deep sorrow, my bosom is laden, all day I go mourning in search of my love.'

Music as taught by Mrs Thomas was a different proposition altogether. She dealt in minims and crotchets. A stave and clef appeared on the blackboard and a large question mark appeared over the top of my head. I couldn't grasp it. I did, years later, but then I peered but nothing came

135

through the fog. Mrs Thomas had a short fuse. One day she asked me what notes went into a certain bar. I had not a clue. 'Two minims and a semi-quaver?' I ventured. She made me stand up. 'How on EARTH could you POSSIBLY have arrived at THAT?' she bawled, red in the face and blazing with anger. I felt my interest in music clutch its throat and die of shame.

I was hopeless at sport. I didn't like anything about it. I hated the dark cloakroom and the endless search for your plimsolls that somebody else had nicked. I usually emerged from the changing room in two left plimsolls of differing sizes belonging to someone else. I saw no point in standing about in the cold in less clothing than you would usually wear. As I was tragically unfit, any running about left me breathless and convulsed by searing pain in the lungs. Nobody chose me for their team in netball, as I was apt to throw the ball towards the wrong end. On the court I could not remember the circles and lines you were supposed to stay inside or not cross. I liked rounders because I could understand the rules, but one day having struck the ball a mighty crack I flung the bat behind me with such vigour that the girl standing behind me was knocked unconscious. My only redeeming feature was that I had great long legs, so rather like a sluggish horse I could run or jump obstacles if sufficiently prodded.

It was 1960 and I was not doing well at school. I shone at nothing. In art I decided to craft a monumental head and, having failed to stick the wet, heavy plaster of Paris on to the flimsy wire frame, I lost interest and instead used it to fill up Janette Weaver's fur-lined gloves. Not unreasonably, Janette Weaver was indignant and I was sent to the headmaster for a wigging. He suggested I try the other creative arts since possibly, as far as sculpture was concerned, I lacked the necessary aptitude.

At about this time the school made a half-hearted attempt to introduce the teaching of French. I was in the class used as a kind of guinea pig and the teacher was a man named Mr Hill whose fleshy downturned mouth and squat appearance earned him the nickname of Froggy, by which he was known to all. I went eagerly into the French lesson but soon it became obvious that Froggy might lack the patience required. The class members, drawn from the country town of Faringdon and surrounding villages, found difficulty at first in grasping the strange concept of feminine and masculine in the French language, and instead of saying *le* correctly as 'luh' they mispronounced it and said 'lea' by mistake, because that was how it looked on the page. After a few nervous pupils had erred in this way, Froggy had had enough. He knitted the fingers of both hands together above his desk, looked at us with dislike over his spectacles and said matter-of-factly: 'I will *hit* the next person to say "lea".' I remember feeling differently once he said that, because I had found it interesting and enjoyable to learn the names of things in French, but now we were back on the same old footing; learn or be subjected to violence.

The French class was short-lived but before it was abandoned, the school did organise a trip to France. There was no question of me going; our family could not afford it. When the travellers returned, boards were put up in the school hall bearing rows of jolly photographs: windswept happy groups on the Channel ferry, clusters outside spectacular chateaux. I remember looking at the photos sourly and feeling jealous.

I did go on a school trip to the Ideal Home Exhibition in London, the first time I had ever been to our capital city. The journey took many hours. The Exhibition itself didn't do much for me; it celebrated everything I was too young or immature to appreciate: cookers, refrigerators, advanced whisks. One innovation was coming into vogue: the wall-to-wall carpet. This appealed to me as an unattainable but blissfully luxurious alternative to the freezing lino and depressing bits of mat that greeted my own large feet every morning as I got out of bed. Also, as I wandered the aisles a salesperson gave me a free sample of hand lotion: it was thick, cheap and sugary-pink but I was ecstatic; I hadn't had to pay for it.

The only other school trip was to Buscot Water Works, a mile or so out of Faringdon. We went on a bitterly cold day when the north wind cut us to the bone. We climbed down from the bus, clutching our coats around us and were shown a series of rectangular concrete tanks, a dozen or more, let into the ground like small swimming baths. We were invited to make our way along them during which time it was pointed out to us by the waterworks guru that the further we went, the more we would see quantities of fluff accumulating in the water. With great drama, he declared that it was not really fluff at all! It was alum! Alum had the characteristic of clustering round impurities in the water, enlarging the unwanted particles and making it possible for them to be extracted in the filtration process! This information was delivered with the same aplomb as might accompany a rabbit being produced from a top hat. As yet I have not found a use for this knowledge. The perished onlookers nodded acceptance, their teeth chattering, as we waited, frozen, for our ordeal to be over. I cannot remember any school trips other than these during the four years I was at the school.

Other impressions from that time stay with me, one of an unfortunate girl who suffered from epilepsy, of the embarrassment and shock I felt when she had a fit in the playground, the sight of her twitching and writhing; the dark pool of urine that spread out beneath her on the dusty ground. Unkindly, I hardly bothered with her after that.

I have a memory of another girl with short, chopped hair. She was plain, isolated, haunted. Her father interfered with her, they said, but not in such genteel terms. I looked at her with incredulity, almost with fear. I had never heard of such a thing. I didn't bother with her either, not after hearing that. How casually mean I was as a child. I didn't go out of my way to comfort anybody.

We believed such stupid things, for instance, that if you lined your shoes with blotting paper, all your blood would be sucked into your feet and you would faint. I tried it once but lost my nerve and ripped it out of my shoes before I fainted away. Girls were starting to menstruate and old wives' tales abounded. I heard that you should never shampoo your hair during your period, or even worse have a perm. It would be courting disaster! DISASTER!

I asked in what form but nobody knew.

29

A NARROW ESCAPE

There was an exciting development at home when I was twelve years old and it nearly cost me my life. Jeff, the sailor from HMS *Eagle*, met a beautiful, dark-haired Uffington girl called Edie and they decided to get married. Jean and I were to be bridesmaids at the wedding in Uffington church. I was speechless when I saw my lovely dress; it was lemon-coloured with a scalloped neckline. I had never had anything so sensationally feminine and romantic. Jean's was the same design but pink, and a third bridesmaid, Audrey, wore blue. With his bride beside him, Jeff knelt at the altar rail during the ceremony, revealing in the time-honoured tradition the price sticker still on the sole of his shoes. His brothers stifled gales of irreverent laughter in the pews.

At the reception in the village hall there was the treat of a sit-down tea, and the cutting of the cake. Soon, Jeff's new wife slipped away, to reappear shortly afterwards in her going-away suit as was the custom. The newlyweds were leaving from Challow Station about three miles away. Two young men, guests at the wedding, ushered the three bridesmaids into the back of a car to go to the station and wave the couple off on their honeymoon. The driver was drunk and had no driving licence.

On the way back to the reception, we were speeding through countryside known as Baulking Fields. The small car was packed with a crush of five people and assorted wedding presents; I was holding the glass jug of a water set. We approached a sharp bend at breakneck speed and the car crashed through the fence, rolling far out into an adjoining field. The sensation inside was of a mass of people pitching and twisting. When the car came to a halt, I was looking at a swathe of fresh blood across the grey upholstery of the ceiling. The car was on its side, doors down. There was a stench of petrol. The glass jug I had been holding was gone; now I was gripping the jagged, snapped-off handle.

Painfully, people unwound themselves and after a time the men managed to open the uppermost door and scramble out. In our full regalia, we stood dazed in the field, a multicoloured straggle beside the upturned car. My lemon bridesmaid's dress was stained with blood; I was bleeding from my hands. Someone, I don't know who, stopped and drove us back to the reception where we caused consternation and were given densely sweet tea as a remedy for shock. I was taken to Faringdon Hospital to have my hand stitched.

In the car, we had been trapped and fully conscious; we could not have got out had it caught fire.

The experience had an effect on me which lasted for years. I developed a fear of travelling, of getting into the school bus or any other vehicle, and a dread of being driven at speed. Although I had previously looked forward to any journey, now I spent a freakish amount of time worrying that the driver would go too fast, that it would end in disaster. Eventually, after a period of years, the feelings wore off, but it was a blight for a long time.

30

MANOR FARM

At home in the village, there was a new and wondrous development. Somehow, I had heard that the daughters of Commander Herbert Acworth of Manor Farm, Stanford in the Vale, had gone away to university. They owned a horse called Paddy, now hopefully in need of exercise. I tied on my best pink-spotted chiffon headscarf and knocked nervously on the mighty front door, having no clue that it might have been more appropriate to go round the back. It opened after much clattering of bolts to reveal Mrs Isobel Acworth, white haired, cultured and immaculate in a powder-blue cashmere jumper. She studied me dubiously as I stated my case, saying that I would really love to ride their horse if it was possible. Mrs Acworth invited me to allow her to consider it.

No doubt she asked about me in the village, perhaps from the Wentworth family where I had learned to ride, but shortly afterwards I was invited back to the farm and told that the answer was yes, on condition that I paid 2/6d towards each shoeing. I was overjoyed, ecstatic. I loved horses and had no hope of ever owning one. This was unbelievable, because not only did it give me a big, beautiful grey horse to ride and look after, but also it meant that I could come and go freely to Manor Farm, an exquisitely beautiful property with a perfectly proportioned, ancient red-brick house and adjoining farmyard. Set round a central tree stood a marvellous group of barns, stables and darkly fragrant feed stores with bins of cow-cake. There was a dairy where the brothers Mike and George Hedges operated an Alfa Laval milking parlour; you could see the warm milk surging along transparent pipes. In the long, low cowshed there were sounds of the utmost niceness: the Red Poll cattle munching their cubes of cake, a gentle suction of milking machines and an occasional holler of protest as a cantankerous old girl called Fairy kicked out at George. There was a high-railed bullpen containing a sad, satanic Friesian bull, a tack room with racks for Paddy's saddle and bridle and for the stiff, dusty harness of working horses now replaced in the fields by a grey Ferguson tractor. Oh, but it was a perfect farm; all was harmonious, set among green fields. I was enchanted. It represented the perfect home to me for the rest of my life.

I fell into a happy routine. On Saturday mornings, I would bike down the main road to Manor Farm and bring Paddy in from his field. I would give him something nice to eat, tie him up outside the barn and groom him with a dandy brush. He liked rolling and was always caked in mud. George and Mike Hedges would appear in the door of the dairy and good-naturedly ask if I ever thought I was fighting a losing battle. I never did. Then I would put on his saddle and bridle and clop off down the poplar-lined drive for our ride.

We explored Hatford Warren with its silent sandy paths; on Paddy, I was tall enough to break off rhododendrons to take home for Mum. Amid the quiet beauty, only the gruesome gamekeeper's gibbets with their rotting, pinioned creatures sounded a clashing and discordant note. We tried not to look but it was hard. There were a lot of

143

them.

Paddy and I splashed through the shallow ford at May Board and followed the quiet green Ock beyond Hunters Corner to where willow trees were grouped, tall and graceful, and the undersides of great trees were cropped ruler-straight by browsing cattle. In the autumn we went mushrooming along Horsecroft in the direction of Charney Bassett, or roamed among the ghosts on the old airfield. We explored the whole area in the nicest of ways. My hands rested on his unruly mane, the sound of his hooves was soft underfoot and, ahead of me, pricked up and alert, were his nice grey ears.

Sometimes I rode him to Campdene feeling very proud and full of myself and, indeed, indistinguishable from Mrs Bean. Mum, upon whom the charm of horses was lost, would come out in her apron and cheerfully shout 'Giddy up!', which grated on me as failing to strike the right admiring note. Pomposity punctured, I would ride for Manor Farm. There I would turn him out, give him an apple and watch as he rolled ecstatically on the ground. I put his saddle and bridle away, got on my bike and rode back home.

My life at that time was enriched by being able to ride Paddy. I could go to the farm whenever I liked; it was a haven to me. The kindness of the Acworth family brought a joyful and unexpected change to my life and my weekends were transformed by having access to the beautiful farm.

Commander Acworth bred Wessex Saddleback pigs, which were free to root about in the fields. One day as I arrived at the farm I found the drive cluttered with obstructions: barricades of disinfectant-soaked straw, a trough for washing boots and a grim notice hand-painted in dribbling red letters reading 'Foot and Mouth'. I didn't know what it all meant and went to find George. He said Foot and Mouth disease was in the area and if any of our animals caught it then the whole lot would be slaughtered and burned. It was shocking, unbearable, but though other farms faced despair and were forced to incinerate their animals in loathsome pits during those 1960s outbreaks, the disease skirted us and Manor Farm was spared.

My life during those years of my early teens contained two great contrasts. On the one hand were the dismal days at school where I didn't seem to be able to get going, where I was competitive but couldn't make a start, where I grew discouraged and took to mucking about. On the other hand there were the peaceful idyllic days spent on a farm with which I had fallen in love. By letting me ride their horse, the Acworth family gave me a glimpse of a different kind of life. They couldn't have imagined the impact it would have on me. It boils down to having something that acts as a driving force; something to long for. I didn't think about it in those terms of course. I was never chummy with the family; they were kindly but remote, and their way of life was far removed from anything I knew. They had a luxurious grey car, a Rover. Their speech was crisp, correct and free of any countrified accent. Their four children were schooled in some way I didn't understand, which involved them being sent away from home for months at a time. That seemed intolerable to me, going gratefully home to Mum as I did at the end of each school day. Clearly, by our standards, they were a wealthy family, but I did not envy them their money so much as the understanding they had of what to use it for, the grace and comfort, the quality and age of their possessions. They had an Aga that was warm and cosy all day. On rainy days, I sat beside it in the boot room and cleaned the tack. Inside their house, they had book-lined rooms and the doorknobs were made of old, faceted crystal, cold and angular in the hand. Beautiful rich carpets lay on polished wooden floors and, while nothing stood out on its own, all elements combined into a feeling of quality, substance, warmth and welcome. I dreamed of one day having such a home for myself in so beautiful a setting. I imagined owning my own farm as I sat on stacks of hay bales in the big barn, felt the softness of the grasses and inhaled the sweet perfume of summer, safe and preserved for wintertime.

*   *   *

By contrast with Manor Farm, at about this time I saw something horrible when friends of the family took me to visit Marlborough Mop Fair. I assumed the event was a funfair that happened to have a weird name. In fact it was an October hiring fair dating back 800 years, one of hundreds of similar fairs held all over the country at Michaelmas. These acted as a kind of labour exchange, where agricultural and domestic workers could go to seek work. Craftsmen and those with a trade would traditionally show some token to indicate their skills: a shepherd would carry his crook for example or wear a lock of wool pinned to a shoulder. A woman with no particular trade would carry a mop. Employers would move among those looking for work, and once a position had been agreed the prospective employee would receive a little money, which was then traditionally spent on the amusements of the fair.

Upon arrival at Marlborough Mop, the family I was with joined the queue for the freak show. I had never seen one before. A spieling showman was outside, raised up on steps, shouting in a harsh voice to entice people in. Once we had paid and passed through the lurid entrance, we found ourselves in a shabby marquee filled with the overpowering stench of the farmyard. A long enclosure divided into stalls ran down the centre; the paying public shuffled along each marshy side and gawped at what was on offer. There were many animals, all deformed. I saw a pathetic live calf with stunted extra legs sticking out from its shoulders, and an oversized bottle containing a two-headed baby monkey spread-eagled in brown pickling fluid. The whole spectacle was revolting; I was infinitely depressed to think that people would pay to see it.

31

ON THE MOVE

Meanwhile, back at home in No. 2 Campdene, change was afoot. Though she had lived there with her family for over ten years, Mum had never liked the house. It was overcrowded and there were the aggravations of the shared path and the unhygienic presence of the old-fashioned bucket lavatory immediately next to the kitchen where she prepared food. At the forbidding council offices in Faringdon, she had long since placed the family name on the waiting list for a bigger house. At last, the name of Ayres had clawed its way to the top and amid great excitement we were off!

I had seen the new house being built in about 1950. It was one of my earliest memories when, as a child of three or four, I explored the thrilling building site with my brothers and sister. There were massive heaps of sand and one had been made altogether more heart-stopping by the addition of a scaffolding plank across the top to create a gigantic see-saw. The scaffolding plank travelled a colossal distance up and down and, being springy, tended to ping people off at the top.

When the builders finally withdrew, a new row of houses faced the world, some red brick and others pale and rendered. Included were traditional-looking terraced homes and examples of the ubiquitous twin-gabled semi-detached design with narrow horizontal upstairs windows, which were built all over the country in the immediate post-war period. Finally finished, the only thing the new row of dwelling houses required was a name, and one was duly chosen. Vandiemans Road. Mystifyingly, incomprehensibly, these homes in a sweet village in rural Berkshire had bestowed upon them the misspelt handle of a Dutch explorer born in Utrecht in 1593, and were declared open for business.

In 1961, the Ayres family sprinted in. With our bedding loaded into prams and our possessions heaped on any wheeled conveyance we could get, innumerable journeys were made back and forth between the two houses. At the end of the day, Mum said, 'Them kids was *marvellous*, they never stopped.' By then No. 2 Campdene, my first home where I was born in the front bedroom, stood forlorn and empty. I pushed my final pramload of our belongings down the front path and left behind those places that had marked the small parameters of my early life: the chicken run with its greengage trees, the abandoned pump, Dad's shed and the great constantly moving English elm.

*   *   *

No. 16 Vandiemans had a bathroom and a back boiler for heating water behind the fireplace. A mighty, soot-encrusted lever protruded down from the chimney; pushing it backwards with a poker caused the fire to 'draw' whereupon the pleasant pop and crackle would change into a sinister roar. None of us understood the system; the back boiler was seen as a malevolent, bomb-like presence, which if overheated might well blow up and shatter us with boiling water and the remains of the grate.

It was unbelievable to have proper sanitation. In its own little brick-built room stood a high toilet, noble beneath an iron cistern of prodigious capacity. I do not know what massive encumbrance the system was supposed to wash away, but pulling the chain brought about a result not unlike the end of the world; the noise was deafening. First, there came a harsh clank of metal, followed by the roar of a ludicrous amount of water thundering down into the pan. High above, countless more gallons gushed in to replenish the depleted cistern. At last, the ballcock groaned back into readiness and waited for the next assault. It took ages. It was awesome. In time, a seaside souvenir found its way on to the wall. It was a pokerwork toilet-roll holder giving instructions in the event of nuclear blast.

The bathroom was astounding. We tiptoed breathlessly in and marvelled; we had never had one before. There was a small white bath with pot-bellied taps, a washbasin and a *further* toilet! Now the profusion of chamber pots could be pensioned off at last and an enamel bucket no longer stood ready in a shaft of moonlight on the landing. Everybody wanted a bath. Armfuls of logs were heaped on the fire and fanned into blistering heat, but the valiant back boiler was hopelessly inadequate. Once one person had filled the modest bath, there was a wait of hours before the next one was anything more than tepid.

Seated in the unfamiliar bath one day, I invented the tidal wave game. This consisted of bending the knees and drawing yourself as close as possible to the tap end. Then, after a silent countdown, you propelled yourself violently backwards, causing the water behind to rise up and cascade thrillingly forward over both shoulders. It was a sensational game. When an ominous wet stain appeared and spread over the ceiling of the kitchen below Mum was taken aback. What could have caused it? It wasn't there last week! I stared up at the stain blamelessly and agreed that it was a mystery. The tidal wave game though enjoyable was therefore short-lived.

Tony was interested in photography and, by draping the window with a thick blanket to exclude light, he adapted the bathroom as a darkroom. It was fascinating. Bathed in the bloody light of a single red bulb, I watched as Tony placed the photographic paper in this tray and that, rocking the fluid back and forth across the blank page until gradually images appeared and took shape on the white square. There were Mum and Dad on the garden path! There were Jean and I on the front step with, unbeknown to us as we smiled

150

winsomely, our brother Jeff making a V-sign out of the window behind us. All our early family photographs were the product of Tony's bathroom darkroom.

This house was larger than the last one. It had an integral shed and, next to it, a washhouse with a copper heated by the lighting of a fire. There was a large, long scullery, a living room and a small front room that we kept for best and which was virtually unused. Upstairs were three bedrooms and the bathroom. The high, horizontal slitty windows meant that a person in bed could never see out, but was doomed to gaze only at the four walls of the bedroom. We missed the big square windows of Campdene and their amiable view of the green and village street.

The garden was a disappointment to Dad for the dark, much-worked soil of Campdene had been nourished and cared for over the years. Here it was light and sandy, thin and starved. The house was on a corner, so the garden was wedge-shaped, wide at the front narrowing to a point at the back. A chicken run was deemed the best use of the pointed end and one was erected. Into it was placed a new, creosote-drenched chicken house Dad had built, and a beehive, which both reflected his new hobby and unnerved the neighbours. Dad also incorporated into the garden a lawn for Mum to sit out on. Keen to secure the boundaries, he incorporated a large and tasteful iron bedstead into the hedge between us and our neighbours. The family spread itself out comfortably and settled into Vandiemans Road. Mum revelled in the privacy, and the bliss of being able to shut the gate and enclose our own garden. Scarred by battles over the shared path at Campdene and the

151

bad feeling over who had trodden on whose carefully tended flower bed, she said wistfully, 'If I'd only had this when all the kids was small, I wouldn't have known myself.'

32

THIRTEEN DOGS

We acquired a dog. This was extraordinary because for a decade my earnest pleading for one had fallen upon completely deaf ears. The closest I got was dog sitting for a lady called Elaine who lived a few doors down. When she went away on holiday I was given the responsibility of looking after her brown dog unoriginally called Lassie, an animal embodying the best of many breeds. I would let myself into the kitchen, feed her a cheap and cheerful dollop of Chappie and take her out for a walk. It was delightful to me to stroll round the village with a dog trotting brightly alongside, but Mum and Dad were emphatically not interested in me having one of my own. Dad used his normal unfailing technique for ending the conversation by shouting 'FERGET IT!' at you from close quarters.

Therefore, it was a mind-numbing development when Dad himself led home a dog on a length of string. Even the kindest observer could not have called her attractive; she was brindled with strange stripes, large and bony. It appeared that Dad had been working for the Electricity Board on a farm near the village of Appleton when she was a puppy dog. She had taken a fancy to him and followed him around everywhere, bumbling along at his heels. Now he had gone back to the same farm and found the family packing up and moving away. The puppy, now grown up, was going to be put down. Dad couldn't face the thought of it, and to everyone's incredulity and my ecstatic delight he brought her home to Vandiemans Road. I named her Judy, like Mr Howard's nice dog at Campdene, and she was installed in a large kennel, which Dad built and duly creosoted in the back garden. All was fine and dandy until a few weeks later when it became clear that she was pregnant. She developed fulsome teats along the undercarriage and carefully made herself a large nest. I sat in the kennel with her as the puppies were born and handed them up to her at the front end to be licked and fussed over. I was enchanted. Twelve puppies later, I had misgivings and feared that my delight might not be matched by Mum's. This proved to be indeed the case; she was horrified and put forward the unreasonable view that it would be impossible to keep thirteen dogs at No. 16. We had a great tearful row in the garden, Mum with a shopping bag to put the puppies in to be taken down to the vet to be put to sleep and me defending them all. In the end, I had to accept the inevitable and we tried tearfully to figure out which were boys and which were girls. Neither of us had much idea which little bobbles signified male or female but in the end a selection was made and Mum took the tragic shopping bagful to the vet. It was terribly upsetting. I hated Mum and refused to see her point of view.

We kept five or six puppies and found homes for them. The nicest one, Buster, with a white nose, was kept locked up in a shed while the owner

153

worked all day. In the end, the RSPCA came because of his incessant barking. He was taken away filthy and wretchedly encrusted with mange. That was a lesson about indiscriminate breeding that I never forgot.

After Judy had whelped I found it embarrassing to take her for walks, because she developed and kept a great full udder, which ran the length of her underside and walloped from side to side as she walked. Groups of sensitive village youths would double up laughing as we passed; it was hard to look dignified. Countless passers-by urged me to get Judy a bra and I took to exercising her over the fields in the hope that we wouldn't meet a living soul.

33

ON THE PARISH SEAT

At school, things were changing. I had begun to notice boys. A fit-looking, daddy-long-legs of a boy called David Seeley had attracted my attention on Sports Day, as he ran like a great flailing windmill down the athletics track to triumphantly breast the tape. I liked the look of him and I couldn't say why. Youthful feelings of interest began to stir and Helen Shapiro, the fourteen-year-old chart-topping pop singer upon whom all our eyes now turned, brought these sharply into focus. She was the same age as us yet there she was singing 'Why Must I be a Teenager in Love?' on Radio Luxembourg! Furthermore, she was singing about the *very situation* I was grappling with myself, about

154

liking someone who didn't give her a second glance! She understood! We cleaved to her like a goddess; she was singing about us! At a stroke we became part of a new sweeping phenomenon; we laid claim to the brand-new title and proclaimed ourselves . . . Fans!

In Stanford in the Vale, there is a small triangular green set between handsome, double-fronted Bear House, Charlie Robinson the blacksmith and the A417 main road to Wantage. Erected upon the green is an iron parish seat, which we took to colonising on Sunday afternoons in order to hear Pick of the Pops turned up to teeth-gritting volume on a transistor radio. There I lounged with my friends Val, Sue and Margaret, unfazed by the traffic thundering along the main road, listening raptly to the cavalcade of new names that were to become synonymous with the Sixties. The tragic voice of Dusty Springfield washed yearningly over the parish seat, along with Roy Orbison, Del Shannon and the Everly Brothers. Images were conjured up which had nothing to do with everyday Stanford life but instead, drenched as they were in love, loss and high drama, filled us with a shapeless longing. Eager for more, we met up in the evenings and listened to Radio Luxembourg where, in between the crummy adverts for Keynsham's own Horace Batchelor and his football pools-winning plan, we could hear more of the music that thrilled us; music that flung open the door to a new and sensational world. In various cramped council-house kitchens, we danced thin patches on the lino and I choked on my first illicit fags, having been initiated by my sister Jean who had already started to smoke cigarettes.

155

She had surprised me one day as we were proceeding along the churchyard footpath, by whipping out a packet of ten Nelson and a box of matches and offering me a go. We shot over the low wall beside us into a derelict farmyard, and lit up. Crouched conspiratorially together, we puffed at the fags and tried to fathom out what was nice about them. Suddenly we had a shock. A shadow fell over us. Twisting round, we looked up to see, silhouetted against the sun, the large bald head of Mr Chas Frost, husband of Pearl, who lived nearby. He must have seen the smoke and heard the tittering. He peered over the wall at us, and did not smile. I can't remember what we said, what feeble excuse we offered while beating away the smoke, but I don't imagine it was convincing. Mr Chas Frost went on his way and we felt sure that Dad would soon get to hear about it. Though he was an inveterate chain-smoker himself, we knew he would not approve.

Though remote, Stanford was not untouched by the latest trends in fashion. One that swept through the village when I was about fourteen was the Full Circle Skirt. This was a skirt, which, if laid out upon the floor, was shaped like a doughnut complete with hole. Once donned, its immense fullness drooped dejectedly about the ankles until jacked up by its indispensable companion, the Foam Petticoat, available dirt-cheap from Wantage market. This peculiar undergarment was formed out of two materials, the first being white cotton for the waist and hip area, attached halfway down to a deep tier of thin plastic foam coloured a violent pink and trimmed at the lower edge with shoddy lace. The effect of the foam petticoat was to raise up the weighty yardage of the skirt not unlike a crinoline. It was unfortunate, when walking, that friction and the roughness of the foam caused the petticoat to ball up between the legs of the wearer. Anyone underpinned by a foam petticoat could be recognised by their manner of walking: a few paces followed by a frantic grope up the front of the skirt.

Mum gave me my full circle skirt for Christmas and I could not have been more delighted with it. Her timing was perfect; she could see I was growing up fast. For the first time in my life, I went to a dance in the village institute and wore my grown-up skirt. It was a new world; all my brothers were there but in a different context. Now they stood in groups with their friends, eyeing up girls, or dancing with them held close. I had never seen them do this before and it was fascinating. Lonnie Donegan had just come on the popular music scene, singing songs like 'My Old Man's a Dustman' and 'Does Your Chewing Gum Lose its Flavour?' To my surprise at that dance, there was a group on the stage and I knew them all! They were boys from school, all copying Lonnie, playing the washboard and strumming guitars. People loved it! It was intriguing to me that an ordinary person could get up on the stage and, by performing well, be transformed in the public perception, hero-worshipped and sprinkled with stardust. It stood out to me and seemed exciting.

That night my brother Allan, having drunk too much beer, performed a solo Highland fling up and down the length of the Institute to raucous shouts and catcalls. My other brothers helped him outside and tenderly pushed him into the stinging nettles to sober him up.

Now on summer evenings and at weekends, to

Mum's growing unease, I was usually to be found lounging with my friends back on the parish seat. We had become aware of a new and tantalising species, boys on motorbikes. On certain golden evenings, from the far reaches of the A417 towards Wantage came the throaty roar of approaching engines. Suddenly, leaning over almost horizontally as they poured round Charlie Robinson's corner, came a thrilling, revving, deafening, exhaust-wreathed, leather-clad cavalcade of boys on bikes. The aristocrat of bikes was the BSA 650 Gold Star; if a boy straddled one of those, he was desirable even if he looked like a donkey. These boredom-shattering visitors came from Wantage, Lambourn and other villages further afield; we longed for them to stop and talk to us. They brought intoxicating and dangerous glamour, leaning back on to their pillion seats, clad in creaking black leather. Hysterically we giggled and fluttered, each girl an unbearable vortex of self-consciousness and hideous uncertainty. Sometimes the boys would offer us a ride on their bikes but we never went, never even considered it, as our parents would have killed us even if the ride didn't. The boys asked if we went to Wantage Dance on Saturday nights. Up to that point we hadn't, but now we fell over ourselves to get there and get there quick.

First, there came the tricky business of asking Dad. Though Mum was watching with some misgivings my rapid change from being harmlessly horse-mad to much more perilously boy-mad, she always tried to help me achieve my desired result. She didn't mind if I went to the dance, especially as my brothers were likely to be there as well, but Dad had the final say. She urged me to wait until he'd come in from work, had his tea, smoked a fag and mellowed a bit. Desperate for an answer, I unwisely accosted him as soon as he set foot in the door and set out my case for going to Wantage Dance. He listened incredulously. 'You can FERGET IT!' he boomed. Behind him, I could see Mum grimace and shake her head in a *'Why couldn't you wait?'* kind of way. She did persuade him though, but Father relented only after interrogation and the laying down of certain conditions. 'Don't you go getting on the back of any motorbikes!' was one, 'You be back indoors afore eleven!' was another, and finally, the weightiest of them all, this one, this doleful warning that rang in my ears every time I went out: 'Don't you have nothing to do with they stable lads, they ole jockeys from Lambourn—they be *the lowest of the low*!' When I saw them, I realised he was not mistaken. They were all less than five feet tall, but it wasn't their stature he was worried about, only their stallion-like tendencies.

34

THIRD WITCH IN MACBETH

At school, things were looking up. I was outraged that I had, in my view, been unjustifiably demoted to the C class, and I worked hard in my favourite subjects of English and art to show I had more to offer. By my third year I had been promoted back into the A stream and was indescribably relieved to be off the radar of the terrifying form teacher. My new one was Mr Bill Reeves, a rotund, curly-haired, blue-eyed man with chalk-dust on his clothes and a slightly Dickensian appearance. I loved him. He was kind and encouraging, a terrific teacher. He liked my stories and encouraged me to write more. He gave me a new exercise book especially for the purpose and on the cover he had written 'Ayres and Graces' in smart italics. It was the first time I'd heard the phrase but would by no means be the last. I disliked the title but loved the faith he had in me to produce something worthwhile. A school newspaper called *The Conquest* had been started up and I contributed regular stories. At this time I also discovered fantastic poems like Lewis Carroll's 'Jabberwocky' and hilarious songs like Spike Milligan's 'Wormwood Scrubs Tango'. I was also mightily amused by the ludicrous TV advertising jingle for the white hair cream Brylcreem, which went:

Brylcreem, a little dab'll do ya,
Brylcreem, you'll feel so debonair,
Brylcreem, the gals'll all pursue ya!
They love to get their fingers in your hair!

Next, and unusually for our school, there was the production of a play. It was *Macbeth*, in which I was cast as the Third Witch with my teeth blacked out by eyebrow pencil. I loved every minute. It seemed we were finally doing things for which I did have some aptitude, and this made me a lot happier.

I came into the orbit of another great teacher, Mr Holifield, a tall man with pale blond hair and paler eyelashes. He proposed that we put on a revue and the idea really thrilled me. I volunteered to write a funny song, the first time I'd ever thought of it. I chose Diana Dors as my subject; she was a glamorous film actress originally from Swindon, with flowing blonde hair and a shape like an egg timer. Far into the night in Dad's freezing shed, I laboured with a stocking top and raffia to make a ludicrous blonde wig, and I wrote a song I was delighted by. The next morning I went eagerly to school, but when Mr Holifield asked to hear the song, I was overwhelmed with bashfulness. Suddenly it was absurd that I could have ever believed I had what it took to stand there in front of him in my preposterous raffia-fountain wig, singing some pathetic song I had concocted. Despite having worked really hard and having been ecstatically fired up by it, I could not begin to find the confidence to stand up and belt it out. Nerves won the day. Mr Holifield asked if I felt I could sing it into his tape recorder on my own perhaps, but my courage had gone. I remember the disappointment, the hating myself. I knew it was a good song and that its originality would have wowed Mr Holifield, but I was afraid of ridicule: I hadn't had the guts. I looked an idiot and my song shrivelled in a drawer, unsung.

I started to write a few other verses. Some of my girl friends, whose fathers were not prone to bellowing 'FERGET IT!' at them, had acquired proper boyfriends whom they went out with on a regular basis. I knocked out a few funny verses about this or that boyfriend being short or having a big nose or no fashion sense. The reaction was lukewarm. My friends were not much interested; they drifted away before I had reached the end.

*   *   *

It was from friends at Faringdon School that I learned of the existence of Fernham Copse. Variously known as the Primrose Wood, the Bluebell Wood, Barrel or Barrow Bushes, this was an ancient stand of coppiced hazel lying alongside the pale road near White Horse Hill. One warm evening, not knowing what to expect, a few of us from Stanford pedalled over there on our bikes, threw them down on the grass verge and sauntered in through the single gateway to the wood.

With that one pace, we left the hot hard heat of the road behind and entered an entrancing place of cool leafiness, shaded and fragrant, criss-crossed by soft brown paths and banked enchantingly with pink-stemmed primroses. We joined others in gathering up fistfuls to take home to our mothers. Young people ran about the wood, scurrying and picking, but the flowers seemed inexhaustible. Here, during subsequent visits, I would see wild flowers blooming in their season in magical abundance. When bluebells were in flower the scene was exquisite, as if the trees stood in some perfect blue water, intensely fragrant, encircling each coppiced hazel and receding away into the distance. Villagers collected hazelnuts by the boxful, and plates of tiny wild strawberries. It was a heavenly place, the most beautiful little wood I had ever seen.

I could not believe it when I heard the terrible news that Fernham Copse had been grubbed out and destroyed. The thought was unbearable; I couldn't go there. When I did finally pass, any living greenness had gone. All that remained were the root systems of the stricken hazels: huge, silver grey, piled high and randomly beside the newly ploughed land, the beautiful trees that had stood

162

guard over scenes of quiet splendour for generations. It broke my heart. The dead tangled roots clawed up into the sky. I never saw the wood when it was freshly butchered but I heard that in the weeks immediately following, countless squirrels zigzagged on the road beside their ruined habitat.

Many years afterwards, I asked the owners why the wood had been destroyed. They replied that during the Sixties, the government actively encouraged the grubbing out of hedges and copses, both to make more space available for the growing of food, and to remove all encumbrances from the path of the newer, larger machines that were sweeping into agriculture.

Also I was told that the local populace, in addition to enjoying the idyllic gathering of nuts and flowers, had also taken to leaving tokens in the wood in the form of old bedsteads and exhausted sofas. I was glad to have heard both sides of the story.

35

WANTAGE HOP

Now the focus of most of my interest and excitement turned to the dance held every Saturday night in the Victoria Cross Gallery in Wantage. This building was converted from the old Corn Exchange and given to the town in 1900 by the Victorian benefactor Lord Wantage of Lockinge House, who had received the VC for valour during the Crimean War. At the time, I did not know this and, if I had, I wouldn't have cared. All I knew was that every Saturday night there would be a group playing on the stage at one end, and in the body of the hall there would be plenty of good-looking boys and the strong possibility of romance.

At this time, the fantasies of me and my friends were fanned to white heat by floods of American magazines that circulated excitedly among us. I do not know where they originated from; we never bought them in a shop, but reams of them did the rounds and were devoured eagerly. They featured illustrations of teenage couples locked in passionate embrace, usually in a car parked beside a romantic moonlit lake and normally concentrating on the face of the girl who was seen to be wearing a quizzical 'Should I or shouldn't I?' expression. The stories were utterly formulaic and followed a set pattern. Everything happened at High School, a term we liked the sound of but didn't understand. They featured convertibles and drive-ins, to which the same applied. There would be a homely boy in glasses, perhaps named Brad or the more troubling Randy, who admired the girl shyly and hopelessly from afar. Now upon the scene would stroll a sporting hero, fit, scornful and possessed of a cruel curl of the lip. Her knees would turn to jelly. He would snap his fingers and she would go with him in his convertible to the drive-in. After the film he would drive them to the moonlit lake and there gather her up in an embrace of animal passion and strength. He would brook no refusal and she would be carried along on their joint breathless torrent of lust. More or less at the point of penetration, she would realise what folly she was about to commit, climb out from

164

under, retrieve her drawers and flee into the night. By astonishing serendipity, she would then meet Brad or Randy thoughtfully walking his dog or reading a scholarly book beside the water. Without his glasses, he looked not half bad. They had a fairytale wedding, settled down in a little house with a white picket fence, Brad or Randy turned out to be a prodigious sexual athlete and all was well. Fired up by this twaddle we set off to Wantage Hop in the hope of having similar experiences.

The dancing was subject to wildly fluctuating trends but all were easy to learn. We scorned proper dancing and had not a clue how to do it. Instead, we danced The Twist, which involved three types of movement performed simultaneously. The body was twisted from side to side in a corkscrew fashion; the hands performed a motion like drying the back with a towel; and by the gradual bending of both knees the dancer moved from a squatting position to full height and back again. It required a degree of co-ordination that not everybody had. Quite a lot of people, particularly those awash with beer, couldn't manage the squatting part and toppled over backwards on the floor.

My favourite dance was The Shake, which involved the violent shaking of one leg. When it got tired you shook the other one, and meanwhile like a metronome rocked your upper body vigorously from side to side to the music.

As far as hairstyles went, the influence of Dusty Springfield was everywhere. I myself began to sport a beehive hairdo of prodigious height and lacquered rigidity. There was a sought-after product called Bandbox, which we all sprayed on the front of our hair. This cheap, harsh bleach turned the hair straw-coloured, a brassy yellow on the mousy brown. I know now that I must have looked a sight but then I was ecstatic; I felt I was fashionable, smouldering; reborn as a goddess.

Dusty Springfield dictated our entire look. On Saturday afternoons in Wantage Woolworths we bought Miners make-up and, to give us that coaly-eyed Dusty appearance, selected the thick cakes of black mascara which you spat into, agitated, then applied in clods and dollops to your eyelashes using the little turquoise toothbrush provided. I favoured a Miners lipstick in a shade called Yellow Kick, which gave me the appearance of a bloodless cadaver. I applied it layer upon layer and this, combined with great crescents of bright blue eye shadow, must have given me all the subtlety of a pantomime dame. I was undaunted. Though I may have resembled the Wantage Weirdo, in my imagination I was Dusty Springfield yearning, ever yearning.

Clothes were a bit of a problem, as I had no money. Ingenuity and dogged determination provided the answer; I would make my own. Possessed of no patience whatsoever, I would stalk Wantage Market on Saturday morning and from the material stall buy a length of any cheap fabric of garish design. This I would rush home on the bus, divide into two rectangles, stitch the shoulders and side seams leaving a daring split at the sides, cobble up a belt and behold! A new frock for the dance! In a day! With luck, it held together until nightfall. By considered placement of the belt the dress could be Empire line (tied under the bust), Waisted (tied round the waist) or Hipster (tied round the hips). All this, combined with towering new black patent high-heeled winkle-picker shoes embellished with chains gave me a look that I felt could not be improved upon. At fourteen years of age, I tottered into the VC Gallery and unleashed myself on to the Wantage boys.

The unrestrained flamboyant vigour of my dancing soon sent the steel tips flying off the precipitous heels of the winkle-pickers. Reduced to sharp spikes these then stabbed everybody's flooring until I offered them in at the door of deaf-and-dumb Wally the Stanford snobby for repair. Wearing his tweed cap, he looked at my worn-out black plastic shoes and their tarty chain embellishment. He looked up at me. Speechless but eloquent, he handed them back with a look of cold disgust, and closed the door.

Mum watched the change in me with anxiety. When I went to the dance she would say urgently, 'You stay away from any fighting!' not realising that there was *always* a fight. It would break out after closing time, when the disgruntled occupants of innumerable Wantage pubs had been winkled from their crevices. Beery and red-faced, they would congregate by the stage of the VC Gallery for the last hour or so before the band packed up, running their eye over the assembled talent and assessing the odds of a good punch-up. Soon, a ripple, a current of unmistakeable excitement would course through the crowd. A fight! There was a fight! I never sensed fear from anyone, only anticipation of the spectacle. Often a chair would be seen scribing an arc over the heads of the dancers as those nearby scuttled back out of harm's way. I never saw any knives or anything sinister, only fisticuffs and posturing that seemed to be an expected part of the night's

167

entertainment. Immediately the doormen, not yet known as bouncers, would close in and the troublemakers would be escorted outside, sporting a bloody nose or cut lip. It was highly satisfactory; we felt we had got our money's worth.

I never found it shocking or seedy. I was used to the horseplay at home between my brothers; this seemed more of the same. I can see now that people would think it was a poor sort of dance, coarse, rough and rustic, but I had never been to any other sort and thought they were all the same. Wantage Dance was our night out and we loved it with a passion.

Unfortunately, passion itself was not something we could afford to enjoy. The risk of coming a cropper was too great, the results too grim and far-reaching. Girls were chaste through fear of the consequences of pregnancy outside marriage. Though the thought of sex was dark and thrilling, we had none of the courage required to indulge. The impact of becoming pregnant while unmarried is hard to overstate. It was a bombshell, a catastrophe. The girl and her family were shamed. They fell from grace and became the target of whispers, sniggering and ridicule. An unbelievable double standard operated as she became the subject of scorn, particularly from men. She was in trouble, or in the family way. She had been eating new bread; she had a bun in the oven. She was up the duff, up the stick, soiled linen. It was acceptable to say these things because she had forfeited her reputation, her respectability, and so too had her family.

A dismal set of alternatives awaited her. Together with the father she could be bundled into a swift marriage, which had little chance of success.

Alternatively she might seek help from the National Council for the Unmarried Mother and her Child, and be sent to a Home. Such Homes varied but there was no legal requirement for registration and it was common for girls to be denied their rights, to be used as cheap labour, and to lose their babies to coercive adoption. She might manage to retain the baby either by raising it as a bastard at the parental home and facing castigation, or by passing it off as the child of an older married sister.

Either way, it is not an exaggeration to say the girl was ruined. Bastard was a whispered word, but its ugliness and significance roared out. If you had a bastard, no man would want you. Any chances of finding a good husband were slashed. What man would want a girl *if someone else had been there before him?* This was the attitude that prevailed in those days before the contraceptive pill brought revolution. It flourished in Stanford up to the 1960s and beyond, and was slow to wane.

Unattractive as this undoubtedly was, attitudes had at least moved on from the 1930s, when Mum was working in domestic service in Cromwell Road, London. Although circumstances meant she would soon be hastily married herself, she at least had more options than a friend with whom she worked. The young woman became pregnant while unmarried and unable to see any way out at all, committed suicide in the wintry Thames.

36

MY OLD MAN'S A DUSTMAN

By this time, despite the possible pitfalls, I had found myself a nice boyfriend called Pete. This was comforting because I had suffered the discouragement of a false start in the field of romance after Mum asked me to go to Wantage and buy her an ironing board from Woolworths. Previously Mum ironed everything on the kitchen table having padded it up with flannelette sheets; the new ironing board was a step up. On the bus to Wantage, I met Mrs Marshall who made dresses for Jean and me when we were small. On telling her about my errand, she said I was a brick and this was the first time I had ever heard the term. I made the purchase and left Woolworths with the ironing board in my brick-like embrace. It was cumbersome. I was nonchalantly leaning on it at the bus stop in Wantage Market Place waiting for the bus to Stanford, when a young man stopped in his car. I knew him vaguely from the dances; his name was Alf and he offered me a lift home. Burdened as I was, I was grateful and got in. When we reached Stanford, to my surprise and horror, at eleven o'clock in the morning he clutched me to his maroon pullover and gave me a kiss. It was revolting; the last thing I expected and I glanced off his great rabbit-like front teeth, appalled at the gumminess of his saliva and the strange rubbery undulations of his lips. I was aghast and, having lined up the ironing board, shot out of the car. It was like that first fag in the derelict farmyard; I stood on the roadside thinking WHAT in anybody's book could be pleasant about THAT?

*   *   *

I now needed what were coyly described as foundation garments, and I bought a circle-stitched bra from Wantage Woolworths, not having any idea of the right size. They were loosely heaped and you just churned them over until one caught your fancy. Mum also encouraged us to wear a roll-on 'for support' although Jean and I were stick-thin. A roll-on was a white, elasticated tubular garment of impressive strength, which was hauled on before anything else. It extended from the waist down over the bottom and from it dangled four suspenders, which held up stockings and stuck out beneath clothing as four raised bobbles. Roll-ons were also available in racy black for the daring.

The whole business of menstruation was furtive and cloaked in secrecy. Mum told Jean and me that there was never to be any hint of it in front of our brothers; all must be concealed. In the village, there was a curious little drapers shop. From time to time, an indifferent homemade skirt or two would be displayed in the window and, once inside, the premises were similarly gloomy and thinly stocked. It was owned by a seriously spectacular woman called Miss Gunn, who wore a large, floppy, black felt hat over wild escaping hair, half-pinned up and dyed blue-black like a raven. Wearing jodhpurs and brandishing a riding whip she would flounce round the village, or suddenly materialise behind you in a shop, placing her order in high imperial tones. Colourful and eccentric, she was regarded dubiously by the village; rumours abounded about what went on in the upstairs room of the drapers.

Cringingly to Miss Gunn's emporium, we would go to buy sanitary towels. Once within we would guiltily creep up to the counter, mumble the initials STs, and shove the sum of 1/3d towards her in a shamefaced way. Miss Gunn would regard us with distaste and produce an unmarked sky-blue box from some concealed place under the counter while touching it as little as possible. The plain box would be inserted into a plain bag and handed over in silence. It was not a comfortable transaction for either party.

I was never told anything about reproduction or the facts of life either by my mother or by my teachers. What I knew, I picked up from the playground. It was crude and smutty; nobody said anything nice about it.

* * *

I met my first boyfriend Pete at Wantage Dance when I was fourteen. He had dark curly hair and wore a black bomber jacket with thick red stripes down the sleeves. He used to come to Stanford on his motorbike with the other boys, and he and I used to break away and go for little romantic walks along the Hatford footpath, stopping at the black-and-white railings for an amateurish snog. It came as only a mild disappointment to me to find out he was a dustman. Soon even that was dispelled, because when I saw him on his dustcart he cut a fine, flamboyant figure; wearing an American GI's cap he swung easily from a rail at the back and gave me a confident, film-star wave.

For my fifteenth birthday, he gave me a gold locket with a sunray design. It was the nicest piece of jewellery I had ever had; it easily outshone my one marcasite brooch in the shape of a horse's head. I wore it at once. Mum didn't mind me having a boyfriend but knew Dad would hit the roof. She advised me to put my locket away and, as usual, I ignored her. He got wind of it. One evening soon afterwards I was drying my hands on the kitchen towel when Dad loomed up. 'That thing you got round your neck!' he barked. 'You give that back! Where'd it come from? Who give it you?'

'Me boyfriend,' I said defiantly.

'BOYFRIEND? What BOYFRIEND? Who is he? What's he do?' shouted Dad.

'He's a dustman,' I told him.

It was one of the few times he was lost for words. Sadly, a period of bad feeling between Dad and me was approaching, which would improve immeasurably once I left home. On the surface, it was about boys and the freedom to go out and about, but underlying it was the beginning of a miraculous throwing-off of the feeling of powerlessness. At last, there was the undreamed-of possibility of standing your ground, of not being shouted down, the dawning understanding that eventually youth was strengthened and age was stripped away. I was becoming a strong girl. I had seen Dad laying down the law to Jean and I knew it had been much more difficult for her as the groundbreaker to acquire any small independence. Jean made small inroads in the iron rule and I barged through. I wasn't going to be bullied and kept under.

*   *   *

Dazzled by new romantic vistas springing up on every side, I stopped going to Manor Farm and largely forgot about Paddy the horse. One day I sauntered down there on one of my infrequent visits and Mrs Acworth came out to see me. I remember the encounter with shame even now. She said that if I had decided not to ride Paddy any more, if, as was perfectly understandable, I was more interested in other things now, then it would have been nice to have come and told her, especially as I had been so delighted with him at first. She told me Paddy waited for me every Saturday. 'He misses you,' she said.

I felt terrible. He was a loyal old horse and I had turned my back on him, stopped loving him and no longer rode him out and about to interesting places. Now he was slow and boring to me; he waited in vain in his same lonely old field. I have always been sorry for the way I treated him. I support horse charities now to ease my conscience, but I wish I could change what I did.

I was very surprised when Mrs Acworth offered me a job. I was coming up to the school leaving age of fifteen, and she asked if I would like to work at Manor Farm, cleaning and cooking for the family and performing light domestic duties. I liked her very much but was appalled by the prospect. I didn't even consider it. I was acquiring big ideas; I was going to be a somebody. Me, a servant? Yeah, right.

Mrs Acworth went on to suggest that I worked with Mrs Johnson, their current housekeeper, for a day or two to give it a try and see how I liked it, and I agreed out of a misguided sense of

174

politeness. I turned up on the day and crawled round the house dusting skirting boards with Mrs Johnson. There was another girl called Wendy who worked in the kitchen. She was not much older than I was. I stood beside her as she showed me how to wash bone-handled knives without putting the handles into water, and explained how cabbage should be stripped from its coarse veins before cooking. I could have run a mile; fled screaming down the drive. I couldn't bear to think that my future might amount to so little, that I would live out my whole life in that village, dear as it was. I wanted adventure, excitement and travel. I loved the farm but I didn't want to skivvy in it; I wanted one like it.

I was soon to leave school, and a general sense of shoulder-shrugging apathy accompanied the business of getting a job. There was no drive or forward planning, no feeling of laying a foundation for a fulfilling career, only a sense that with a bit of luck something would turn up. I didn't know anybody who had a plan. Most of us drifted into jobs that might do.

As the end of term meandered closer, the Youth Employment Office made a few half-hearted attempts to find me a job. I was sent for an interview to the vast Garrard Engineering Factory, which made turntables and decks in Swindon. It wasn't that I had any interest in turntables and decks, just that the Youth Employment Office sent me there and I obligingly went, wearing an ancient pancake-like hat of my mother's, which I hoped would increase my chances of success. A frosty personnel woman studied the railway timetable from Challow, ascertained that I had no way of getting to the factory on time and apologised that I had been sent on a wild goose chase. Me and the pancake-like hat went home.

The next job interview I attended was at the Atomic Energy Research Establishment at Harwell, for the post of canteen assistant. I wandered in through the impressive gates and presented myself. At the sound of the proposed wage, £4 per week, my eyes lit up. I would be able to afford the new jeans, which were now appearing everywhere! They were only 7/6d a pair off Wantage Market! This was the job for me all right! I was delighted to be offered the post.

Mum looked dubious and troubled. She said it wasn't the job for me at all, that the last thing I wanted to be doing was slaving away in some canteen like a drudge when I had a good headpiece. In many ways, she was a timid person but she didn't hesitate to rise up and defend me. She went to see the Youth Employment Officer. I don't know what she said to him, but it would have strongly featured my good headpiece and her firm opposition to it being squandered on some job scraping plates in a canteen.

I went to see Mrs Acworth and told her I would not be taking the job at Manor Farm, but instead had accepted a canteen assistant job at Harwell. She looked unimpressed as well and told me that I should always try to bring people up to my level rather than sink down to theirs. This caused me to wonder what sort of job I was letting myself in for.

As it happened, I never found out. Through Mum's intervention, I was asked to the Youth Employment Office in Faringdon to sit the Civil Service Exam, which I passed. This enabled me to apply for and obtain a job as a clerical assistant at the Central Ordnance Depot at Didcot, Berks. I

176

was congratulated by all. I had landed something fairly rarefied, an office job, a *classy* job, and furthermore, a *sit-down* job! I felt quietly smug.

It was a lifetime later that I really understood what Mum had done for me and by then it was too late to thank her. She enabled me to show what I could do. By joining the Civil Service, I was automatically included on various further education schemes for young people and these opened up opportunities, different vistas and exciting possibilities.

There was no fanfare when I left school. I walked up the long track to where the bus was parked, got on it and went home. My schooldays, unexceptional as they were, had ended. I was fifteen and it seemed that I had a good job to go to.

PART TWO

37

CLERICAL ASSISTANT

Early every workday morning during the 1960s, three private buses hauled their way round the village of Stanford in the Vale. They were sent by Smiths Industries of Witney, the Atomic Energy Research Establishment at Harwell and the Central Ordnance Depot at Didcot respectively. Stanford was just one of the stops made on a long, grinding route to pick up employees from outlying villages, and take them to work. Jean and I waited each morning for the bus to COD Didcot.

On my first day at work, my initial impression of the place as the bus turned into the main gate was of its vast size. Huge rectangular sheds lined the road for miles; gaunt olive-green warehouses placed one after the other in an endless succession. A network of railway lines served the buildings, running alongside or between them, shining as they snaked across the road. Groups of soldiers wearing fatigues marched along; there were military-looking people, army vehicles and the movement of trains. I had never seen a place like it.

When the bus stopped, I got off and found my way to the Personnel Department where I was processed, and then escorted to the office where I would work in what I assumed would be my exciting new job as clerical assistant. I gaped at the place. It was huge, open and as big as an aircraft hangar. Beneath the jagged, factory-type roof were innumerable desks placed in straight rows.

Countless people worked with their heads studiously bent, and the scene stretched away into the distance. There was a quiet murmur of voices and the occasional ring of a telephone. Here and there, I could see a splash of khaki as someone wearing army uniform stood up and walked about.

Didcot Depot stored some of the monumental range of goods needed by the army, with the exception of munitions, which were housed more securely elsewhere. An army unit situated anywhere in the world that required stores, say for example oil stoves, mosquito nets or countersunk head screws, sent a request to Didcot Depot by submitting a standard voucher. This was a thick, rectangular, multi-layered document with carbon-coated areas liable to blacken the fingers.

At fifteen years of age, I found myself seated at a desk in one of the long rows, flanked on either side by married women much older than me. Teaching me the job was a woman called Joan who lived nearby at Rowstock Crossroads. Her hair was dyed in the fashionable but startling shade known as Black Tulip.

Down one side of this gargantuan office was a run of smaller offices, sealed to minimise the infernal noise of the punched card machines inside. Punched cards were part of a system of data storage and tabulation, which was a step towards automated computing, and the company offering the system eventually merged with others to become IBM. Here, teams of women jabbed rubber-topped buttons on little keyboards. Numbered from 1 to 10, they caused rectangular holes to be cut out of cards the size of a US banknote. Once punched in this way the cards could be read by machine, which massively sped up the processing of data. This system managed and controlled the stores held at Didcot. Four operators occupied each cramped square office, one seated in each corner. At big metal desks amid the intolerable racket, they jabbed their buttons at furious speed. The hungry machines required constant feeding.

The recording of information on to punched cards was only possible if the data was in numeric form, since the system could not process words. This is where I came in. My job was to translate units of issue into numbers, so for instance if kettles were priced at £1 each, the machine could not understand 'each', so I would have to write the figures 00 in a little box stamped on to the front of the voucher. If we were dealing with pillowcases and the price was £1 a pair, I had to write 01 instead. A dozen or a gross had different numbers. That was my job and I did it all day. It did not take long to learn. A short, bald man named Mr Tuck would bring me a stupendous pile of vouchers in the morning and when I had done them, he brought me another twice as big.

After a time, a sense of depression and disappointment crept over me. At the first hint of sunshine, the vast office grew boiling hot underneath its roof lights. Everyone smoked, laying an unhealthy fug over us, which thickened as the day wore on. Boredom set in and I found myself thinking incredulously, 'Can this possibly be it?' All the fuss, all those congratulations on getting into the Civil Service and attaining a sit-down job, is this all there is to it? Entombed in an oven, writing numbers in a box over and over again. It was unbelievable. I was aghast.

My sister Jean was considered to be less

fortunate than me because she worked in the stores, standing on her feet all day in one of the massive green sheds. The buildings were filled with shelving called bins: long lines of green metal racking rising up almost to roof height.

Jean's shed was mostly given over to the storage of nuts, bolts, screws and things of that kind, contained in small greasy boxes made of thick cardboard. Forklift trucks hummed and bustled about under the harsh industrial lighting; I had never seen them before. Driven by soldiers, they glided up and down the aisles marshalling pallet-loads of goods on to the highest shelves. The stores issued by Jean here in the sheds could only be released on receipt of vouchers from the office where I worked. This established a puny but comforting link.

Once or twice, I managed to get a lift down to see Jean in my lunch hour, but it was difficult because the site covered an area of some miles and it was further than I could walk. It was on a visit to the shed where Jean worked that I first saw Pakistani immigrant workers. Grouped anxiously together among the towering racks of shelves, they wore brown warehousemen's coats that seemed to hang on their slight frames. How extraordinarily difficult and lonely it must have been to cope with the strange language, climate and culture. At certain times, they went to pray on prayer mats placed between the industrial shelves. To unworldly people like Jean and me from Stanford in the Vale, this was extraordinary and a marvel, like observing people from a different planet.

Back at my desk, the charms of the job were wearing exceedingly thin. The day ran something like this. First thing in the morning, we alighted from the coach and walked resignedly into the building. A group of young women including me would then drape ourselves over a radiator outside the ladies toilet and put on our make-up. Bridget, one of my friends, used to darken her eyelashes with a fingerload of Vaseline, which I found curious. Though the ladies toilet area was roomy and mirrored, we were reluctant to go inside to beautify ourselves because of a foul device within. This was an incinerator, which despite bearing the appealing name of Bunnie, could not have been more deeply unappealing. Provided for the incineration of sanitary towels it was grimly inefficient. It smouldered and stank; puffs of noxious smoke leaked out of its white enamelled seams.

All too soon, it was time to start work, and I sat lethargically down at my place in the long line of desks. Mr Tuck would pace the length of the office towards me bearing a stack of vouchers and I would start processing them, writing out the numbers: 00 for each, 01 for a pair, blah blah. Hours dragged by until the mid-morning tea break, signalled by the distant sighting of an obese, slow-moving woman pushing a long tea trolley laden with iced buns and an urn. Agonisingly slowly, she moved up the aisles, dispensing as she went. At last, she reached us and there came a break in the unspeakable monotony.

I worked alongside an elderly woman called Mrs Dane who was small and portly with a little fluff of permed hair. However, she displayed previously unsuspected tartar-like qualities one day when it was my turn to fetch the tea. I planted a thick white mug down before her, holding it with my fingers and thumb round the top rim. 'I don't want it like that!' she exclaimed. 'Like what?' I said. 'I don't want your thumb where I'm going to put my mouth and drink! You never know where it's been!'

I looked at my thumb anew, as if it had some unsavoury secret life of its own. After the wigging from Mrs Dane, I was careful to place people's cups of tea before them correctly, by the handle. In my capacity as tea girl, I discovered that people had strong feelings about how their drink should look. I delivered tea to a gentle person called Barbara from Lambeth who spoke with a strong Cockneyish accent and always wanted her mug of tea filled right up to the brim. If it wasn't, if there was a band of white china to be seen above the tea she would say, 'Well! I don't want it if it's got a collar on it!'

Barbara shocked me one day by showing me a photograph of her husband. I gulped. He was bald. BALD! So shallow and appearance-obsessed was my romantic thinking then at the age of fifteen that the thought of a bald husband was worse than the death by a thousand cuts.

A young woman named Sheila worked in our section. Someone whispered to me out of the side of their mouth that she was an unmarried mother, and in accordance with the mores of the time, I was quite shocked. She seemed so open about it, and light-hearted, talking about her little son growing up at home with her mother. She was totally unlike the creeping, eyes-averted, shamefaced girls who had 'got into trouble' at home in the village, whom everyone looked down their noses at or regarded with pity. Sheila was a confident free spirit; she wasn't having any. This did not suit everyone. Older women raised

186

eyebrows to each other in a 'Talk about brazen!' sort of way. Others, particularly younger people, wrote off their views as old-fashioned, as remnants of a once-strong religion now losing its power and grip. They embraced a newer, more easy-going and less castigatory outlook. It wasn't the baby's fault if his mum hadn't got the right piece of paper. That was her business, nothing to do with anybody else. Times were changing and a good job too.

Across from our section was an habitual fainter. This caused consternation at first and then the utmost hilarity. There were many soldiers to be seen around the Depot and several worked permanently in our big office. One day a stunning new officer arrived; it was soon clear that he was well aware of the dramatic effect he had on women. It was unsurprising; he was exceptionally tall, perfectly built, muscular, manly and immaculately uniformed. His hair was dark and wavy; he had a little moustache and a slow, disarming smile. The women, including me, drank in every detail. He was delicious.

After a time, however, certain doubts began to set in among his admirers. He seemed to get up and waft about rather more than was necessary, as if he enjoyed being watched. Also, it was noticed that the chocolate brown eyes that scanned the room did so in a rather cold and predatory fashion. Perhaps he wasn't so delicious after all. Perhaps he was a bit too fond of himself.

Over on his side of the office was a young woman who made no secret of the fact that she was utterly infatuated with him. She was not striking to look at, of rather scrawny build with dyed black hair and heavy make-up inexpertly applied. She took to fainting as he walked past. The first time this happened, a shock wave shot round the office. It was a dramatic sight; he walked past, she dropped like a stone and he scooped her up in his arms. Like a scene from some corny film, she was cradled against his mighty chest, and he turned uncertainly this way and that looking for a place to put her. People rushed to help; he tenderly laid her down and left her to the anxious ministrations of others.

This kept on happening and the initial concern of onlookers began to be replaced by expectant amusement. Now a look of fear and dread appeared on his face if he had to go near her; he realised it had become a spectator sport and was making him look a Charlie. I was close by one day. He walked nervously past her when she sighed and spiralled limply to the floor. Resignedly he picked her up and it seemed to me that her nostrils flared to take in the smell and feel of him, and her lipstick-caked chops fought back a smile of satisfaction to be held in the arms of the beloved in the only way she was going to get there. The business of the persistent fainter gave us all a little, sorely needed, light relief.

Sometimes during my lunch hour, I went for a walk. More often, I sat dully in the stifling office, drained of any energy or enterprise. During one of these occasional walks, my companion pointed out a particular room. The door was ajar and a vast spaghetti of wiring could be seen, thick twisted ropes of it disappearing into banks of electrical equipment running from floor to ceiling on each side and down the centre of the room. The space would have taken a double-decker bus. This, said my colleague in a voice hushed with awe, was *a computer*.

Occasionally the information on my vouchers was incomplete and I would have to search it out elsewhere because I needed to finish up with a correctly detailed description of the ordered item. One day a request came in for a gross of countersunk-head screws. The width was quoted but not the length, and the punched card operators needed both. Armed with the voucher I visited an adjoining office that seemed to be staffed mainly by old soldiers. I shyly approached one of them and uttered the deathless words, 'Excuse me, but could you give me a length?'

The old soldier choked on his tea and his eyes rounded with joy. Turning to his colleague he spluttered, ' 'Ere! Frank! This gal 'ere, she wants me to give 'er a length!' They rocked back and forth with laughter, and tears squeezed out of their rheumy eyes. I stood gormlessly by, clutching my voucher and burning with shame.

*   *   *

One good thing shone through the stultifying boredom of the job, and this was the fact that the Civil Service offered further education to its younger employees. I was keen to be included and arrangements were made for me to attend a day release course at the Oxford College of Further Education, an unprepossessing prefabricated-looking building far up the Cowley Road on the outskirts of the city. It was a laborious journey each Tuesday from Stanford in the Vale, and my recollection is of hours hanging about on cold wet streets waiting for buses. I decided to take some GCE O-level exams, which I would have taken at The Elms Grammar School had I passed the eleven-plus. I took English Language and English Literature, and joined the Drama class. There was an exciting lunchtime club playing the popular music of the day. I was now sixteen and the great luscious soundtrack of that time for me was 'She's Not There' sung by The Zombies.

For English Literature we did Chaucer's *Prologue to The Canterbury Tales*, Conrad's *Typhoon* and *Youth* and other pieces that I've now forgotten. In Drama, we put on *The Devil's Disciple* by George Bernard Shaw and I played the part of the sour and joyless Mrs Dudgeon. This was all much more satisfyingly meaty than my clerical job, which asked nothing of me. I could apply myself to these new projects and feel I was making some sort of progress.

Filling in the identical forms all day became unbearable, and I applied to become a punched card operator. I didn't fancy it that much, and certainly didn't look forward to working in the thunderous noise, but it seemed to me that the operation of the sophisticated-looking machines was cleverer and more challenging than repeatedly filling in soul-destroying forms. You were paid more money as well.

A small, formidable woman named Pearl managed the punched card department. She had a large bust marshalled by corsetry into a high, hard mantelpiece and this gave her the look of a ship's figurehead forging onwards. With nimble fingers, she knitted exquisitely intricate cardigans. I presented myself to Pearl and she regarded me dubiously. Bored as I was, I had gained a reputation for being something of a non-sticker and for showing insufficient respect to the crusty executive officers who sat in front of the various sections, and studied us over their spectacles. Pearl was having no nonsense.

I was shown how to be an effective button-jabber. She demonstrated to me how I should stick out the middle, longest finger on my right hand, support it under the joint with my thumb, and strengthen it from above by laying on the index finger. Training completed, I was all set to start jabbing and time was of the essence. I was given a dummy keypad. With Pearl on the stopwatch and the diabolical racket of the genuine machines roaring in my ears, I was told to depress the keys over and over again in a certain order. The dummy keypad emitted a rubbery squeak. My big fingers were slow and clumsy. Only when you were fast enough could you go on to a real machine. Concentrating fiercely, I jabbed and jabbed. The joints in my fingers crackled, my forearm ached. I couldn't go fast enough. After one final try, Pearl shook her head. Deafened and nursing my claw-like hand, I was ejected from the inner sanctum clutching a form giving the reason for my rejection. On it, writ large in Pearl's firm handwriting, were the words: 'Lacks the necessary aptitude.'

*   *   *

Next, I applied to work in the Accounts Department where in a sealed, soundproofed glass room, lines of women operated National Cash Accounting Machines. These resembled huge typewriters. Wheeled trolleys containing great flapping orange cards were propelled round the place, and the idea was to take cards from the trolley and drop them into the fast-chewing teeth of the racing machine. This updated the

191

information thereon in small mean type, providing that the operator was competent and had some clue what she was doing. After I had catastrophically and erroneously applied all the wrong information to several trolley loads and lumbered the staff with weeks of corrective work, I was shown the door by a tight-lipped manageress. I knew what was coming. Over the relentless, furious din of machinery, I lip-read the familiar words: 'Lacks the necessary aptitude.'

I finished up in the Pricing Department where I could do little harm. There I was overseen by a slim, regretful woman with the curious name of Yendis. She explained to me in all seriousness that her father had longed for a son whom he would have named Sidney. Disappointed that his wife had been delivered of a mere daughter, he insisted that she be named Yendis, which is Sidney, reversed.

I quite liked the Pricing Department. I had a telephone on my desk that made me feel massively important. It was Extension 175 and I longed for it to ring, having cultivated what I believed to be a suitably upper-class telephone voice. 'Hextension wan-seven-faive,' I would enunciate, sounding impressive to myself and unutterably stupid to everybody else. The actual job was no more stimulating than all the others. Duplicated sheets circulated, upon which were listed new prices for items. I had to find the specific catalogue card from cabinets containing millions of them, cross out the old price and write in the new. It wasn't rocket science; you could do it whether or not you had a good headpiece.

At least I was freed from the daily visitations of Mr Tuck, who had proved to be less amiable than at first sight. He had gone away on holiday and to my surprise brought me back a gift, a Celtic kilt pin. I had no Celtic kilt but offered polite and enthusiastic thanks, after which he never spoke to me again. This was a small but depressing mystery, and I was glad to be working with Yendis who was consistent and easy-going. However, even as I sat in the Pricing Department admiring the weighty Bakelite of my very own telephone, change was a-comin' and hurtling down the track towards me at speed.

During the early Sixties, the Central Ordnance Depot at Didcot was integrated into the Central Ordnance Depot at Bicester as part of a major consolidation that I did not understand and never enquired about. Effectively the Didcot operation was moving to Bicester; Jean, me and everyone we knew were moving with it.

By coach, it was a distance of some thirty miles from Stanford in the Vale to Bicester, made far longer by numerous detours and circuitous perambulations to outlying villages, hamlets and cottages to pick up waiting employees. If we wanted to keep our jobs, we now had to catch the bus at 06.28am and this was very hard, particularly in the winter. Then a huddle of us would stand in the icy blast at the top of Joyce's Road where bitter winds howled across the bleak old airfield. The bus was notoriously unpunctual and closely allied to whether or not the young blade of a driver had managed to get out of bed. Every morning, hunched against the cold, our small frozen group gritted its teeth and waited for the ordeal to be over. It was the coldest I had ever been. Mum, kind and unselfish as always, got up first and cooked breakfast. It never varied and was always a frying pan full of sausages. Jean and I had no time to sit down and eat, having got up at the very last minute, so Mum would wrap a sausage up in greaseproof paper for each of us and shove it into our hands as we stampeded out of the door. It was hard to know whether to eat it because you were hungry or warm your hands on it because you were cold. As soon as we were on the bus we went back to sleep for the next hour-and-a-half. It was normal for us to be still wearing rollers in our hair. Leaving for work was early, cold, undignified and grim.

The Ordnance Depot at Bicester was enormous, covering an area of twelve square miles. It was inward looking and far removed from normal roads and streets, a world of chain-link fences, giant warehouses and military personnel. There was an enormous, complicated bus terminus where we disembarked from the Stanford bus and caught another to our actual workplace within the Depot. The place milled with people anxiously seeking their next transport; women fought their way along, wielding creaking gondola-shaped baskets containing their knitting and requirements for the day.

After an eternity, I arrived at my desk in the new workplace. It was not dissimilar to the last, being a huge office divided up into sections rather like classrooms, with the executive officer sitting at the front of each one, like a teacher. Ours frequently questioned me as to whether I was having 'the same old trouble' with boys. At the time, I thought this showed a fond paternal concern.

Once again, I found myself filling out catalogue cards, laboriously writing down all the details about pieces of equipment. Some of the descriptions were of mild interest. We dealt with specialist uniform items including the 'scrambled egg' gold braids that embellish the headgear and chests of very high-ranking officers, and lavish items of insignia embroidered with threads of precious metal. Despite these glimmers, it was still a desperately dull job; the only difference was that now it took a lot longer to reach.

I met countless people while at Bicester, but two men in particular had a significant effect on me. One, named Gordon, was intensely irritating, being a man in his fifties who had been handsome in his youth but could not accept that he had now gone seriously to seed. Gordon had once been in the RAF somewhere equatorial. He never failed to pause at my desk and whip out a faded photograph of himself wearing enormous tropical shorts, while half obscured by palm fronds. 'Yes,' he would murmur, nodding suggestively, 'you would have fancied me then, wouldn't you?' 'Not if you were the last man up the Orinoco, Gordon,' I thought confidently, viewing the photograph for the umpteenth time. He spoke with nostalgia and affection of his days in the RAF. They were the best time of his life, he said, the best years he had ever known. His faded eyes clouded with wistfulness. What a life that had been for a young man with vigour and curiosity, what an inspired and far-reaching decision it had been to join: the colour, the travel, the sheer joy of those times, how they had enriched his life. On and on he would reminisce. I listened, and though I had heard it all so many times, I must have quietly noted his feelings and enthusiasm.

On a more mundane note, Gordon also used to exhort me to have all my teeth out and be fitted with NHS dentures like him. 'Marvellous!' he would clatter, strands of saliva trembling between his upper and lower set. 'They're marvellous! No more trouble, no more toothache! Don't hesitate, book up straight away!'

'No thanks,' I thought, 'I'll gnash on with what I've got.'

Gordon visited often; his trousered crutch and the pocket containing the photograph would suddenly manifest themselves beside me as I sat writing, and my heart would sink.

I also met a Welshman from Mountain Ash who was a lifesaver to me. His name was Tony Davies; he was cleverer than I was and went on to become something important in taxation. Crazed and obsessed with rugby, he disappeared on beer-sodden weekends to support his team, before returning to live in a men's hostel named Rodney House, grim accommodation provided by the Depot for transient male employees. I was seventeen by then, and he was a couple of years older when he came to work alongside me and transformed my dull days. Bright and funny, he made me laugh and through him I met other young people, friends of his also suffering the meagre comforts of Rodney House. There were a lot of older people in our office, backward-lookers like Gordon and sour old men whose conversation consisted of filthy jokes, but Tony and I were young and had the same interests. We were besotted with the Rolling Stones and raved about their songs especially 'Time is on My Side'. He lent me an LP by an American singer/songwriter called Bob Dylan. I took it home and played it on my own in the front room, and it was as if he was talking to me. I was getting on less and less well with Dad because I wanted to go out with my boyfriends and he wouldn't hear of it. Now, suddenly there was Bob Dylan on 'Times They Are a'Changing', singing that our parents could not control us any longer and should stand aside. The song spoke to me, it bolstered me up; Bob Dylan knew how I felt.

I bought my first LP or long-playing record, 'The Freewheelin' Bob Dylan', and looked jealously at the pretty, long-haired girl clutching his arm on the cover. I sat listening to it hour after hour in the chilly front room after work. It must have been hurtful to Mum, who used to come in and say, 'Why don't you come and sit by the fire with us?', but I was so inspired by the songs, I had never heard anything like them. My brothers had brought home Lonnie Donegan and his skiffle songs, which were light, foot tapping and a bit of fun, but Bob Dylan's lyrics seemed insightful to me; they chimed with things that were happening in my own life at that specific time.

Hearing 'To Ramona' I didn't think Bob would approve of me spending my life filling in forms all day at Bicester, which was in sharp contrast to Dad telling me I had a damn good job and should stick with it. Neither, after I had listened to 'It Ain't Me Babe', did I feel enthusiastic about drifting into some boring, half-hearted marriage because I couldn't think what else to do. Bob seemed to me to be a voice of defiance and uprising. I admired his opinionated outlook on life and I also found that if I was particularly moved by one of his songs, it made me want to write something of my own. From someone with the gift of the gab I had paid good money for a guitar more suited to the back of the fire, and had also equipped myself with a copy of Bert Weedon's guitar tutorial, hilariously entitled *Play in a Day*. With the flesh of my fingertips thickly rutted and grooved by constant repetition of the chords G, D and A7, I tried at first to copy Bob Dylan and his protest-song style. It was desperate. I wrote emotion-drenched, toe-curlingly awful drivel, which mercifully never saw the light of day. After a time though, I abandoned those embarrassing attempts to ape Bob, and started to write more in a style of my own, about things I actually knew about. At seventeen, I came up with my first complete song. It was entitled 'It All Belongs to Me' and concerned loneliness. It was tripe, of course, but at least it was my own original tripe.

38

LEAVING HOME

In addition to the boring job, life in Stanford was dire as well. I couldn't think what was wrong with me that I felt so dissatisfied. The things that everybody else enjoyed doing didn't seem to suit me. I wanted something else, something more, but I did not know what was available or how to access it. My life had been lived within tight, unadventurous boundaries. Nights out at the village pubs left me utterly deflated and depressed and this in turn made me feel disloyal to my family and friends who liked going.

A village night out invariably meant sitting in one or other of the local pubs, according to their fluctuating popularity. Mum, Jean and I usually went to The Horse & Jockey or The Anchor and were often joined later by Dad coming on from

The Red Lion. For a time the licensee of The Anchor was a burly, curly-haired ex-Metropolitan police officer called Charlie who ran the pub with his blonde wife Margaret. Charlie had been on duty during a notorious gangland shooting on a London rooftop. At the slightest expression of interest, or none, he would whip out and proffer round the ancient police ID card he carried that night. It was a grim souvenir, the front slashed diagonally by a rust-coloured bloodstain.

As women, we seldom patronised The Red Lion because there was a feel about it, a kind of unwritten rule that it was more for the men. We went to The Cottage of Content only to buy a bottle of lemonade, or tobacco for Dad. We never went to The Marlborough or The Prince, both of which, sadly concluding that their wartime, soldier-filled heyday was over and unlikely to come back, closed their doors and became private homes.

By law, all the pubs had to close at 10.30pm but on certain nights, say if there was a darts match, a licensee could apply for an extension, which enabled him to stay open for an extra half-hour until 11pm. This seemed to me to cause jubilation out of all proportion to the actual event. I couldn't help it: I didn't like the pubs, they seemed to sap my energy, and the prospect of sitting there on a hard chair, drinking sickly-sweet pineapple juice while being glowered at by ole gaffers in dark corners for an extra half-hour left me cold. Nothing ever happened. No music played; it was only in the Wantage pubs that you might find a jukebox to play your favourite records and enliven the place, and then only if you could afford to feed it with coins.

There was no tasty food for sale, just crisps and

peanuts, for pubs offering the stringy delights of chicken-in-the-basket were still far away in the future. I didn't like beer; it was cold and sour and there was too much of it in the thick, clunky glass. The same old people seemed to talk to each other in the same old clichés. Somebody would say, 'Dead tonight, ennit?' and somebody else would reply, 'Thass a fact.' It was enough to make you weep if you were young, curious and burning with energy. I was tormented by the certainty that something fantastic, something exciting, colourful and romantic was happening somewhere but I didn't know where it was. I didn't know how to get there.

Nobody new and electrifying ever breezed in the door. The only time this varied was once in Wantage when the pubs were suddenly flooded with good-looking blokes. There had been a murder; they all turned out to be detectives.

To me, at that time, the village pub meant utter predictability: the same old routine, footsteps ringing on cold floors, freezing toilets with the windows open, the desultory thud of darts striking a dartboard, fags, beer, piddle, and me feeling inwardly desperate, thinking, 'God Almighty, *surely* there has to be more than this.'

My jaw would drop as we walked home up the village street and Mum would say cheerfully, 'Well, that was a good night!' I would gulp and think, 'A *good night?* How can it have been? Nothing happened! Nothing ever happens!'

The gloss had even worn off my boyfriend Pete. He would take me out a couple of times a week and together we would sit in a bare, cheerless pub called The Star, in Faringdon. It was usual for us to be the only people there. A couple of hours would pass in the small cold room, its walls yellowed with nicotine. Occasionally a shattering thing would happen: someone else would come in. It was deadly. Pete and I ran out of both conversation and steam. Mum would ask me brightly when I came in, 'Did you have a nice time?' and I would say I had, but I hadn't really. None of it was enough.

39

FATHER BEHIND THE WHEEL

Meanwhile Dad was learning to drive. This was a startling development much welcomed by Mum who saw it as a means of lifting their horizons, a chance to finally get out and about. Now, in the village, it was not so unusual for families to have a car, and an increasing number were to be seen parked on the grass verges down Vandiemans Road. Outside No. 16, alongside Tony's Ford Popular in Ambassador Blue, a new vehicle appeared. It was Dad's van, a beige Austin A35 bought from my brother Roger.

Dad was not a confident driver. One of the main struts supporting his decision to learn to drive at all was the determination of his friend Jack Dibden to teach him. Jack lived further down Vandiemans Road and while Dad had been a sergeant in the Grenadier Guards, Jack had been a regimental sergeant major in the Royal Corps of Transport and a paratrooper. He was unfailingly polite and smartly immaculate, his civilian attire polished, pressed and knife-sharp. Jack resolved to get Dad, then aged fifty-one, through the driving test at whatever cost. Unsurprisingly, having been an RSM, Jack's method of tuition featured more stick than carrot and involved close-up, parade-ground-type bawling at high volume. In the closed confines of a car, you learned or went deaf.

Mum used to cry with laughter. 'He certainly got the right one teaching him,' she would gasp, doubled up and mopping tears from her face. 'I heard'n shout "Balls!" at Father as they drove past!'

That Dad passed his driving test was a huge tribute to Jack. Prostrate with the nerves he could never overcome, and with runnels of sweat trickling down his face, he took it six times and failed. Jack brooked no talk of defeat and upped the volume of the bark; Dad passed at the seventh attempt. Thereafter Dad was a regular if unadventurous driver.

'Well, Mother and I've certainly done some motorin' today,' he would greet me when I came in.

'Oh?' I'd say. 'Where d'you go then?'

'Charney Basset!' he'd say. 'To the Chequers!'

The pub at Charney was about two miles away.

40

THE ORIENT COMES TO WANTAGE

At about this time the first-ever Chinese restaurant opened its doors in Wantage and doubtless wished it had kept them shut. Locally it was a sensation; the populace was agog: *a Chinese restaurant*! The

Orient fetched up in Wantage! Swirling through the enlightened alleys and streets went false rumours of restaurant freezers brimming with Alsatian dogs, monkeys and people's disappeared tabby cats. No ginger tom went AWOL without townspeople nodding sagely towards the Chinese restaurant; they knew what they knew all right.

Still, the grub was dirt cheap, cheaper even than the fish and chip shop in Mill Street or the coffee bar along Grove Road. On Saturday nights, the queue snaked all along the pavement. I only went once but, on that night, the courteous, industrious Chinese waiters were insulted at every turn by yobs, as if those at the bottom of the heap, the constantly kicked, had gleefully discovered someone even lower down the social scale to kick for themselves. I hated it. The food with the tasty, unfamiliar crunch of bean sprouts was lovely, but my enduring impression was of the sneering, contemptuous attitude towards the Chinese.

Soon Chinese restaurants were appearing in all the local towns, flourishing and spreading despite the initial racism they encountered. For a treat, my brother Tony took Mum to one that had newly opened in Swindon, and there a curious incident occurred.

They had their meal and Tone smoked a fag, after which they stood up and made their way to the counter to pay. Hearing shouts behind them, they spun round to see that a Chinese waiter was angrily brandishing a blazing tablecloth, and shouting that Tone's discarded cigarette had caused the incineration of the fine linen cloth. That would be £5, thank you very much. Shamefaced, though unconvinced of his guilt, Tone paid up. Naturally, this incident completely ruined the little treat. However, in conversation with his mates at a later date, he was stunned to be told the same story; in the same restaurant it seemed that his mate had unwittingly set the tablecloth on fire. Why, he had been made to pay £5 in compensation! The two men gaped at each other as the outrageous truth dawned. They had been done! Trussed up like a turkey! This scandalous story reverberated round No. 16 Vandiemans for decades after the event.

41

TIME TO GO NOW

At work one day in Bicester, a small brown envelope was dropped on my desk, which, when I opened it, proved to be the results of the two English O-level exams I had taken in Oxford. I had passed them both. Furthermore, I had been given an award to be presented by the Lord Mayor of Oxford for the Best Civil Service Student and for drama. I was astounded and speechless. Me, the duffer who had failed the eleven-plus! From only a one-day-a-week day-release course, I had gained two of the five O-levels people hoped to get after several years' study at The Elms. I was so happy. My bosses were pleased with me, I received pats on the back to which I was unaccustomed, and I was staggered to realise that, truthfully, I had done it without that much effort. It was uplifting for me, a lovely thing at a dreary time.

In other respects, the map of my life appeared flat and lifeless. If I had conducted an appraisal, it would have looked like this. I was seventeen. I hated my job writing out descriptions. The weekly dance at Wantage had grown tame and repetitive. My friends had started to acquire serious boyfriends but Pete and I had drifted apart. I thought a great deal of Tony Davies because he was different, a real friend who was informed, funny and clever, but he didn't want me as a girlfriend; we lived miles apart and anyway he was small; I towered ludicrously over him like a giant. At home, my relationship with Dad, already aggravated by his iron rule, was increasingly strained. I smoked heavily, never had any money and was brassed off.

Things came to a head with Dad when I started to go around with an older man from Wantage. It wasn't one of my better ideas. The man had been dumped by his girlfriend and was dark and bitter. Quite late one night we were in his car saying a tender goodnight while parked outside Vandiemans Road. I was keen on the man and we were chatting in a promising sort of way. Because he was older I was doing my best to seem sophisticated and worldly-wise. Suddenly I heard the window of Mum and Dad's bedroom clang open with such force that it hit the wall. The whole street pricked up its ears.

'PAM?' bellowed Father from across the road. 'PAM, IS THAT YOU?'

I wound down the window. 'Yes,' I said, sullenly.

'WELL, BLOODY WELL COME ON IN THEN!' bawled Dad, nearly falling out of the window. His great voice reverberated back and forth across the dark street. Neighbours listened agog behind their closed curtains. So much for being sophisticated and wordly-wise, I was being

205

ordered out and shouted at like a dog. Afraid of the very real possibility that Dad would bring a pickaxe handle down on his head through the car window, the new boyfriend roared off into the velvet night. I came indoors humiliated and angry. At the first opportunity, I told myself, I was going.

At work there was a terrible development; Tony Davies told me he was leaving. He could not have known what a blow this was to me. He was like a lifeline at that time, the one person I could talk to, who liked me and thought I was something special. He couldn't stand the boring job either and was going to work his way along the south coast and think what to do with his life. Initially he went to work in a Bedford brickworks, driving a forklift truck. I bought him a silver St Christopher to keep him safe. When he left Bicester, I felt truly desolate. It was awful, as if the sun had gone in and was never coming back. It wasn't something I could cry about, or wail or make a fuss. I was just filled with a sense of utter loss, like grief.

At that time, I read very little. Someone had lent me *Katharine* by Anya Seton, and I read *A Stone for Danny Fisher* by Harold Robbins, which I found lying around at home. More usually, I read the tosh-filled romantic magazines entitled *Valentine* and *Roxy* that were filled with cartoons and formulaic love stories.

One day in one of those magazines, I saw an advertisement for the Women's Royal Air Force. There was a happy-looking girl of about my age, dressed in a smart uniform, smiling against an enticing background of good-looking pilots and aircraft pointing dramatically to the skies. I looked at the advert for a long time.

I supposed I could do worse. Three of my brothers had enlisted after all. They had gone off to do their National Service and come home looking substantially more attractive in immaculate uniforms, bearing thrilling gifts and treasures from far-distant places. They had travelled widely and it hadn't cost them a penny; indeed, the services had paid them. They had made good friends. Dad, who had been in the Grenadier Guards for many years, always said that a stint in the army helped you sort out the decent blokes from the other bastards. Then there was Gordon. Admittedly, he was less persuasive but he constantly claimed that his time in the RAF had been the high spot of his life.

I sent off for the brochure. Back it came full of photographs of delighted-looking young women doing all manner of interesting jobs. There was not a catalogue card to be seen. They were air traffic controllers, dental nurses, musicians in the RAF band and girls receiving important-looking messages on teleprinters. Some strolled glamorously in the tropics, immaculate in crisp uniform dresses with epaulettes. I decided to take my investigations one stage further, and visited the recruiting office in Reading on the train. There I was interviewed by a broad man named Sergeant Cooper. He sang the praises of the WRAF and thought I would do very well. There was travel, variety and company of my own age. Would I like to take the entrance test while I was there?

I said I would. It was a multiple-choice test paper. The only people in the room were Sergeant Cooper and myself. If he noticed me struggling, he would wander past and generously wave a stubby finger over the right box. Unsurprisingly, I achieved a very good mark for which he warmly congratulated me. This scene had all the elements of a farce.

He asked me what kind of things I liked doing. 'Drawing,' I said, meaning the drawing of people, animals and cleverly shaded fruit. 'Well,' said Sergeant Cooper, 'as it happens, you've got a good enough mark to work in one of our drawing offices as a Plotter, if you should decide to go ahead.'

I went home on the train deep in thought. A Plotter. A Plotter in the WRAF. Leaving aside any negative Guy Fawkes connotations, it could mean travel, colour, excitement, boys and the thrill of the unknown. Nothing mapped out. A Plotter.

I told Mum about it. She was immediately on my side as usual. Whatever we wanted to do, she supported and helped us. 'I don't blame you!' she said. 'You give it a go if you want to; you're free as a bird!'

Dad was aghast. His doom-laden pronouncement still echoes across half a lifetime:

'You be throwing away the BEST YEARS OF YER LIFE!'

This alarmed me, but I didn't feel Dad was particularly qualified to criticise my decision. Hadn't he lied about his age and joined the Grenadier Guards at a ludicrously young age himself? Anyway, and more to the point, they didn't *feel* like the best years of my life! My job was excruciatingly boring, the hours were long, Tony Davies had left and I was going nowhere. I read and re-read my brochure. I decided to join the WRAF as soon as I was the minimum age of eighteen.

By this time I had moved to a different part of COD Bicester, into a new office with the picturesque address of C2 (Snout), so called because the new office had been tacked snout-like on to the end of an older block named C2. My eighteenth birthday came; I handed in my notice and told everyone I was leaving.

Jean meanwhile had fallen in love with a soldier named Malcolm Hall. He came from Salford and they were planning to marry. This made me feel the loss of Tony Davies even more; I was not at all confident about the decisions I had made and felt desperate to talk to him. I decided to pay him a surprise visit at his home in Mountain Ash, Glamorgan.

There was a café on the main road in Stanford. It was named The Waverley Cafe, but was always known as Maud's because it was run by a large ponderous lady called Maud and her less ponderous sister. There were a few tables and chairs, and stale-looking cakes under a glass dome. Sometimes a lorry driver would be reading the paper at one of the tables if you went in, but not very often.

Occasionally we bought sweets there; Maud had a good selection lined up on the shelves in stout jars, but the business of purchasing them was agonisingly slow. Maud demonstrated none of the briskness seen in Mrs Miles's sweetshop near Campdene. First, upon entering the shop, there would be the initial long wait for beslippered Maud to appear, then the laborious taking down of the jar, unscrewing of the lid and the forcing apart of sweets, which had stuck together in clumps. This was followed by the careful weighing into the shiny oval tray of the scales, the transference into a white paper bag, a fussy folding over of the top to form little ears, and finally the long-winded calculation of the cost. It was easy to lose the will to live.

In addition to this sprightly enterprise, Maud also acted as an agent for the Black and White Coach Company, and it was to her I went to arrange my trip to Wales. She said I would have to buy a ticket to Aberdare then take a local connection to Mountain Ash. I handed over the fare. I took a Friday off work, dressed up smartly and blithely set off. In due course, I was deposited on a long, sloping pavement in Aberdare and from there I climbed on the waiting bus to Mountain Ash.

I have never forgotten that bus because to my surprise, miners began to get on and take their seats. Their faces were grimed black with coal dust, they wore big miners' helmets and when they spoke to each other, it was in a strange new language I had never heard in my life. They were like a different species. I was wearing a new red coat, and they smiled at me in a lovely bashful way, their faces black, the creases white, and the eyes blue. Everything about them was intriguing and strange. I was only a few hours from Maud's café but I could have been on a different planet.

I would have liked to know those nice-looking men and their community, which accepted and carried out so enormous and dangerous a task. I wonder what became of them when the mines were closed, when whole streets were boarded up and the valleys fell silent.

I found my way to Tony's house on Campbell Terrace and knocked on the door. His mother answered it. Straight away, she asked, 'Are you Pam?' I said, 'Yes, I've come to see Tony.' I didn't see then how presumptuous it was, just to turn up clutching a return bus ticket for the next day, but if

210

his parents were indignant they didn't show it. Tony eventually came home from the pub and nearly died of shock when he found me with them in the little living room. I saw him anyway, and talked to him about my plans. As far as my WRAF decision went, I don't think it was much help, but it did make me see what he had realised long since: that there could be no resuscitation of our former easy friendship. It belonged to a period now irrevocably past. I had loved being with him and learned a lot from him, but events and distance had wound us up; they had set us on differing paths.

Additionally, although coalmining was in terminal decline by that time, my journey into Wales gave me a brief glimpse of a people, their way of life and living language that I am glad to have seen before it changed.

In C2 (Snout) a collection was held for me. Rather unsportingly, I was told afterwards that it amounted to £12, more than anybody else ever. It was well known that I liked writing, so as a leaving gift I was presented with a Sheaffer fountain pen. It was turquoise, of excellent quality and cutting-edge design. Filling the pen did not involve the normal internal rubber tube. Instead, on turning a particular screw, a blunt hypodermic-type needle extended from the nib and was supposed to suck up the ink. Unfortunately, it sucked in vain; I could never get it to work.

I was very fond of my workmates and friends at Bicester, and I felt well liked in return. I regaled them with tales of the Wantage Hop and the shortcomings of my endless cavalcade of boyfriends. I could always make them laugh; they looked on me as a bit of a card, and enjoyed sending up my obsession with Bob Dylan: 'But the bloke can't *sing*!'

There was little sense of devotion to the work from anyone, as far as I could see, and I made no secret of the fact that I found it insufferably boring. I was slapdash, easily distracted and loud, but I think I was looked on as someone engaging and funny, someone who cared about people and brightened up the days. They approved of me and I liked the feeling. It was going to be a long time before I felt so secure again.

42

THE WOMEN'S ROYAL AIR FORCE

It was April 1965 when Margaret, the landlady from The Anchor Inn in Stanford, took me to London and put me on the train for Grantham in Lincolnshire. A seasoned Londoner, she had taken pity on me, nervous and clueless as I was about the workings of big London railway stations.

Alone and clutching my suitcase, I got off the train at Grantham and was mightily relieved to be directed to a waiting air force coach. A straggle of other bewildered girls appeared on the platform and made their heavily laden way to the vehicle. Finally, when the train had no more girls to disgorge and the platform was quite deserted, a uniformed female driver started the coach engine and drove us to RAF Spitalgate, a few miles outside the town. This was a basic training establishment where large gaunt barrack buildings of blackened brick stood morosely among the trees. It was forbidding, unwelcoming.

I was shown into a long barrack room with ten or a dozen other newly arrived girls. We stood shiftlessly and waited. If I was expecting any warmth or welcome, I was disappointed. A female corporal swept in. 'Put your stuff down and *get outside*!' she snarled. There were one or two murmurs of 'Charming!' from the travel-weary, ill-assorted group as we shuffled outside. I didn't really know what I was doing there; I had just let things drift along. Suddenly I was being shouted at in a strange building in Lincolnshire although I hadn't done anything wrong that I could see, except turn up.

We were stationed at RAF Spitalgate for six weeks, and much of the first week was spent criss-crossing the gigantic camp, collecting enormous amounts of equipment from widely separated places. In the clothing stores, I waited in a slow-moving queue beneath a large, rather dated, poster warning against loose talk. It depicted a person in RAF uniform propping up the bar of a pub, but protruding from the shirt collar was the toothy, gross-looking head of a donkey. Underneath was written 'THE JAW OF AN ASS CAN SLAY A THOUSAND MEN!' Shuffling along, and once past the donkey, various things were slung energetically at me across the broad wooden counter: a great bale of blue clothing including a greatcoat, a mack, numerous skirts, jumpers, cardigans, PE kit, hideous black lace-up shoes, a button-stick and a gigantic beret. Although we were quick to ridicule the old-fashioned design of everything, I was secretly pleased when the regulation leather shoulder bag was hurled at me. It was the nicest one I had ever had.

All of this and more had to be taken back to our living accommodation. I had been allocated a bed halfway down the long barrack room, which had perhaps ten beds down each side, twenty in all. Each 'bedspace' had a plywood wardrobe and bedside cabinet; immensely thick buff-coloured lino covered the floor. The room was completely open with no provision for privacy at all. Grouped together in a cold, tiled, echoing area nearby were the lavatories and washbasins.

We were made to do a lot of PE, which was unheard of for me. With my new companions I jogged round the perimeter track of the airfield with my lungs on fire, coughing frenziedly as a result of a surfeit of cheap fags. For the first time in my life, I felt genuinely, ravenously hungry and the food, good and plentiful as it was, tasted incomparable. One day we were loaded into a Bedford truck, taken ten miles from the camp and deposited on the roadside clutching Ordnance Survey maps. Never in my life had I considered walking ten miles; the idea was laughable. Neither had I ever tried to read a map, let alone rely on one to find my way home. When our footsore group eventually straggled back in through the camp gates, I went to our barrack room, lay down on my bed and went instantly to sleep.

We had absurd inspections that it was impossible to avoid. Laid out upon the bed, every last item of equipment and clothing had to be placed in a certain meticulous order. Having previously left all menial tasks like ironing to Mum, I now had to iron my own shirts. It was so difficult. Pressing one part only put creases in another. If shirts were found wrinkled during the inspection, they might be flung rudely out across

214

the floor, and the perpetrator of the crime made to iron their shirts every night for a week. These people had daunting powers over you.

We had to clean the place and a cumbersome, archaic implement known as a bumper was provided. Used for polishing the lino, this was a weighty rectangular block attached to a broomstick by a kind of hinge. Dusters, or quite frequently sanitary towels, were placed beneath the block, then with aching arms the contraption was wrenched back and forth across the floor until a dull, reluctant shine grudgingly appeared.

Worse, we had to shine the loathsome black lace-up shoes using a system known as 'spit and polish'. A feminine-looking WRAF corporal came in to give us a demonstration. Using a duster, she hooked a knob of black boot polish out of the tin and rubbed it in small circles into the shoe. So far so good, we watched politely. Next and with some relish, she hawked up a gob of spit and fired it at the side of the shoe on top of the polished area. Taking up her duster, she rubbed the spit daintily round and round for a ridiculous length of time. Finally, she held up the shoe and pointed out the minute area she had been working on, which had now achieved a different texture, more like patent leather. Our job was to make the whole surface of the shoe look like that, she informed us pleasantly. We were incredulous, thunderstruck. It was going to take untold boring hours. It was going to take *days.*

Girls cried at night. You could hear the telltale watery sniffing all round the room. The days were packed full of activities so that by bedtime, you were numb with exhaustion, but homesickness was rife and raging. You were not forced to stay,

215

however. During those first weeks, you could go home at any time, but it branded you a failure; you had to face the anti-climax of a tail-between-the-legs return to the home from which you were so recently and optimistically waved off. In my case, there was also the matter of the £12 Sheaffer fountain pen. How could I go back? Going home was complicated.

We had to learn to march. On the parade ground we were taught how to stump up and down in a blue rectangle of women, all stepping in time, all with the thumbs placed uppermost on our hands like robots, heads up, not looking to left or right. At the time, I quite enjoyed it. Now, the idea of turning people into unquestioning automatons makes me more thoughtful, but I didn't ponder on it at all then. When the band played, it was lovely to swing along, not unlike dancing. We were out in the fresh air and newly fit, at the start of an adventure.

The attitude towards us softened slightly after the first three weeks, veins of kindness began to thread through the day and a few treats were laid on. I went on a free bus trip to Leicester and bought a new LP, *Another Side of Bob Dylan*. One evening an Avon lady came and talked to us about skin care. She started her talk by saying, 'I have not washed my face for ten years!' As we reacted with squeals of surprise and distaste, I suspected that she had said that *quite* a few times before.

We spent a lot of time in classrooms, where we were taught about Hugh Trenchard and the founding of the RAF. Useful instruction was given on first aid, and a cadaverous doctor came in to enlighten us on the symptoms of syphilis and gonorrhoea in the event that we had 'run a risk'.

We were cheerfully given procedures to follow in the event of nuclear attack, always assuming we hadn't been vaporised. The piling of mattresses against cellar doors, and the hoarding of tins of corned beef and baked beans was recommended. A film of an actual nuclear explosion was shown so that we would know what to expect, first the shock and then the blast. On the screen, a grotesque circular ripple shot out from point zero, the doomed land undulating like water, as a slow mushroom cloud formed above. We were unconcerned. Safe in our cellars we would lie on mattresses munching corned beef, laughing in the face of annihilation.

For unfathomable reasons we were ushered into a room full of tear gas. The centrepiece was a rusted cylinder; gas hissed from the valve. We were given some kind of protective mask to wear and made to trundle round in circles. At a pre-planned signal, we had to remove our masks and continue to trundle while exposed to the tear gas. It was certainly unpleasant, but we felt brave and heroic: we had been exposed to *tear gas,* and survived! We revelled in the praise we were now starting to receive from our corporal. I couldn't wait to write home to Mum about my exciting goings-on. It was already a far cry from the unadventurous card writing at Bicester, the doleful, disappointing evenings down the pub. I was being gassed! Furthermore, we were now allowed to use the NAAFI! This was the Navy, Army and Air Force Institute, which exists to sell goods and provide recreational establishments for the armed forces world-wide.

Going to the NAAFI was a privilege and greatly appreciated. We could get out of our uniforms and look like young women again. There was a coffee bar and, best of all, a jukebox! We played Neil Sedaka's song 'Happy Birthday Sweet Sixteen!' over and over again, and danced in the limited space. There were no boys, which was a setback, but being in that sociable environment fostered a sense that things were improving, that perhaps it had not been a catastrophic decision to join after all. Things were coming right!

I am sure it was all carefully managed as some laid-down way of forming a disparate group of people into a functioning team. First, those in authority were horrible to us, which made us band together, then bit by bit the figures in authority grew kinder, which made us like them, then treats and privileges were gradually added to lighten the mix. Also, momentously, we had stopped being at the bottom of the heap. On first arriving, we could see several other intake groups who were better at everything than we were. They could march, they could run, they knew the ropes. Now, to our shameful joy, we could see nervous new girls getting off the same bus from the railway station. New intakes as bewildered, as crucified by homesickness as we had been! How timid and uncertain they looked, standing in their sea of scuffed suitcases. We felt superior and made sure we looked down our noses at them.

I did have a low point when I decided that life in the WRAF, however it might unfold, was not for me. I can't remember what brought this on, but I had decided grimly to give up, endure the humiliation and run home to the love and warmth of my big loud family in Stanford. Sadly, it was all over as far as I was concerned.

Perhaps this falling away was expected by those

218

in charge. Perhaps there comes a stage when any little community in the process of formation tires, flags and starts to doubt itself, because at that precise moment, a treat was laid on. It was a trip to the splendid swimming pool at the RAF College, Cranwell, a few miles away. A bus drew up at the kerb ready to take us. I had planned to quietly pack my things and slip away. The bus idled outside; my friends dashed about gathering their swimming kit and I started to falter. Well, why not? I'd just go for a swim as it was on offer, then push off home the next day.

The swimming pool was the most spectacular I had ever seen. Having only ever visited the soupy charms and beetle-laden waters of Wantage swimming baths, this was luxury indeed. It was huge, a vast expanse of pure, sparkling water in a warm, lofty building. We swam and swam. At last, loose-limbed and exhausted, we climbed back on the bus and were driven home through the darkness. I remember leaning my head back against the plush headrest, looking out at the night-dark countryside and making the decision to stay. The life would be unpredictable; I did not know where it might take me. I knew I would be looked after, fed and clothed. I would meet countless new people and go to places I had never seen before. Surely, that was better than running home in tears, back to some clerk's job where the days would be laid out in dreadful predictable order year in, year out. What an abject failure I would look if I did that. Perhaps I was vain, but it mattered to me that people had thought me bold and adventurous when I left home. No, I wasn't going back. I was beside myself with homesickness, but I made up my mind to stay.

*   *   *

At about this time I heard from Dad in a touching way that brought home to me what an unusual person he was. Tall, hard and immensely strong, he had big labouring hands that were coarse and neglected, ingrained with grease and soil, deeply split and nicked by ancient, slow-to-heal cuts. But he could draw. In biro down the margins of newspapers or on the back of cheap envelopes, I would find perfect little sketches of goldfinches, pheasants or pansies with exquisitely detailed faces. I always thought my own ability to draw came from him.

At Spitalgate, for the first time in my life he sent me a letter. It was impossible to mistake his handwriting; beautiful old-fashioned copperplate script laboriously learned one letter at a time in the squat stone confines of Uffington School. I opened the envelope in mystification.

It was almost, but not quite, a letter of apology. Dad said that he had been very sorry to see me go, and his tone was regretful as if he blamed himself for me leaving home. I read it with a kind of outrage. He had always been so tough. I knew how he worked, that he took up an immovable stance and never faltered, so the last thing I expected was this climb-down. It wasn't his fault. Though we had certainly clashed over whether I was allowed out to dances or could officially have a boyfriend, the stagnancy of village life and the monotony of my work at that young age would have driven me to leave home anyway. I didn't like the crestfallen tone of the letter; it was as if I'd won something for which I had not competed. Later I talked to Mum

220

about it. 'Oh yes,' she nodded in a telling sort of way, 'he felt it when you went.'

At the end of our six weeks at Spitalgate, there was a grand passing-out parade. We were all dressed up in our best uniforms and natty hats, the sun shone and the band played the RAF March Past. I officially became Aircraftwoman Ayres, a preposterous title as I had never been anywhere near an aircraft. The day was bittersweet because our group had become tightly knit. Together we had endured indignity, limping the ten miles home, jogging in our very own cloud of frosty breath round the perimeter track, reassuring each other that our ill-fitting, rasping uniforms looked all right even though they didn't. We had sympathised with each other when we failed inspections and were made to lay out acres of equipment all over again or if, for some trivial offence, we were made to polish gloomy corridors with the detested bumper. We had heard each other's stifled sobs at night as we all yearned for our homes, however modest. As intended, it had brought us together as a close group, and now we were to be scattered.

43

RAF BRAMPTON AND BASSINGBOURN

Brampton Park in Huntingdonshire is an estate of about 125 acres, first recorded in the twelfth century as being held by the picturesquely named William the Sokeman, and thereafter having a varied history. It was once the home of a Lady Olivia Sparrow, going on to become an institution for people with stammers and, later still, a home for evacuated babies entitled the Sun Babies Nursery. In 1942, Brampton was activated as First Bomb Wing Headquarters and, in 1955, the decision was made to make RAF Brampton a permanent establishment.

I arrived in 1965. The wide gateway looked forbidding with its guardroom, roadblock and chain-link fences. It looked like a place that couldn't possibly have anything to do with me. I approached with great timidity, half expecting to be shot. It came as a mild surprise that my name was on their list and they let me in.

That it had once been a beautiful park was clear; ancient trees towered over lawns now sullied by charmless, flat-roofed barrack blocks. The staccato movements of grey squirrels could be seen, animals that were still considered unusual and enchanting at that time.

RAF Brampton had extensive sports grounds but no airfield. It had a large NAAFI and cinema. There was a small, cheaply built church clad rather unsuccessfully with fibreglass. It was supposed to look like stonework but this had begun to fray and loose sections flapped in the wind.

There were two WRAF accommodation blocks, Barratt Block and Welch Block and I was to live in Barratt Block in a room containing four people. My first conversation was with two older girls who were sitting on one of the beds. They were pouring quinine from a bottle into a teaspoon. Intrigued, I went over to have a look. Seeing that it was quinine, and as naive and gullible as ever, I was quick to warn them. Did they know, I asked earnestly, that in some quarters quinine was taken in order to *get rid of a pregnancy*! Their eyes

222

widened with mock surprise. 'No!' they exclaimed. 'Surely not that! It couldn't be! And there they were, thinking it was for bad feet!' They chortled together and turned back to their measuring. It never once occurred to me that they might be taking it to abort a baby.

For the first few weeks, I was based at RAF Brampton and travelled daily to RAF Bassingbourn in a packed air force blue minibus. This journey took about an hour and was strangely depressing, something to do with the endless straight roads, constant damp mist and the sight every morning and evening of the grimly named Caxton Gibbet, where once offenders in high-strung cages turned in the wind. Secured by the head, they could never rest their agonised legs as they slowly starved to death or wretchedly froze.

The reason for my daily commute was to attend a six-week course intended to train me as a Plotter of Aerial Photography. It was totally beyond my grasp. I couldn't do the work.

RAF Bassingbourn was a bleak, unsheltered place. Set in vast expanses of tarmac were huge khaki-coloured hangars, and their brooding presence formed a backdrop to the wide, mist-shrouded runway. Based at the airfield was a squadron of Canberra bombers and this lent the place a sense of businesslike briskness and movement. In twos and threes the aircraft would suddenly appear and noisily arc across the sky showing their underbellies; the roar of their swift take-offs and landings punctuated the day. I identified them straight away as Canberras. I recognised the distinctive wing shape because once at Campdene I found a red plastic one in a box of cornflakes.

In comparison to this real working airfield, RAF Brampton seemed quiet, sedate and almost hospital-like in its green, acorn-sprinkled grounds. At Bassingbourn, there was the noise, smell and activity of aeroplanes. I could see the ponderous fuel bowsers, the complex facilities and the glimpsed glamour of pilots. This all made me feel that I was a genuine part, however miniscule, of the RAF.

As far as I was concerned, the actual course was dreadful. It was far too advanced for me. Months before, when I told Sergeant Cooper in the Reading recruiting office that I liked drawing, I hadn't meant this technical kind, which presupposed some firm grasp of mathematics and geometry. I floundered uselessly. I could tell that the sergeant instructing the course had written me off as a duffer, and he was absolutely right. My heart sank as I was ignored in favour of the bright ones.

I wrote a song, 'The Bassingbourn Blues'. It had a reasonable tune and I played it on my guitar to the mild amusement of my friends. Though my ballad is lost and gone, a lonely snippet floats back across the deserted airfield:

> *Roll on the day when we can safely say*
> *With pride: 'I swept the whole of that runway.'*
> *Give me a broom on a frosty morn,*
> *With TAG on my records form,*
> *So I won't have these Bassingbourn Blues.*

TAG stood for Trade Assistant General, which was a euphemism for a person who had failed to gain any qualifications at all. TAG meant you were a no-hoper.

A kind young man, a fellow student, took pity on me. He was bespectacled, clever and from Brighton. With his help and patient explanation, and by learning to recite blocks of text I did not understand, I blundered through to pass the final exams. For the next four years this saddled me with a job where, most decidedly, in what was becoming a hauntingly familiar phrase, I lacked the necessary aptitude.

Having 'qualified' as a plotter, I was gutted to discover that I could not change jobs. Plotters required a fairly high level of security clearance; obtaining it incurred considerable expense, which the RAF was reluctant to waste. I imagined shifty figures on an hourly rate creeping round The Anchor discovering my dark secrets. But the facts had to be faced. Far from furnishing myself with a new, interesting job as I had hoped, by scraping through the exam I had made matters worse. I was not allowed to change jobs, so for the next four years I would be stuck in one I didn't like and couldn't do.

The course ended and I came back to live permanently at RAF Brampton. I worked in a highly respected establishment known as JARIC, short for Joint Air Reconnaissance Intelligence Centre; its symbol was a cunning-looking lynx above the legend 'Nil Lyncea Latebit' (The lynx never sleeps). It was perceived to be a place of high excellence, to which I brought exceedingly little and certainly nothing lynx-like.

At Brampton, for the first time in my life, I realised that I spoke with a pronounced accent, which was going to lay me open to constant ridicule. At home in Stanford, we all spoke in the same way; we saw few incomers. My beloved granny Ada, my Grampy Bill Ayres, Mum, Dad, my aunts and uncles and my brothers and sister all spoke with the same regional dialect, typical of the Vale of the White Horse. It was authentic and ancient, the sound of home, peppered with unselfconscious expressions, which I never heard anywhere else. Mum didn't always say 'Go and have a look'. Instead she would say 'Go and have a kite round', referring to the graceful birds of prey that wheeled so high, whose vision was so impeccable that they never missed the tiniest thing. Dad wouldn't always say he was going to the toilet or lavatory; sometimes he would 'nip out the dyke'. Dyke meaning ditch, this harked back to times when peasants relieved themselves in fields and ditches like animals. Hawthorn berries were *pegahs*, ants were *emmets*, bullocks were *sturts*, and the list went on.

I never used those terms myself because I recognised them as archaic, but my pronunciation of anything at all marked me out. One day at work, I was thirsty and asked one of the young airmen to pass me the jug. 'Pass the what?' he repeated loudly. 'Pass the *what*?' All round the office, ears pricked up ready for a laugh. Everybody said I pronounced it as if there was an 'r' in it, like 'jurg', but if that was true I was unaware of it. Then it was open season; everybody joined in. 'Give her the jurg! Pass that woman the jurg! Give her a whole jurgful!'

I laughed it off, but, in my heart, I wished I had some other kind of accent. This seemed to be the worst sort, which, without people actually knowing the first thing about you, would nevertheless mark you out as a smock-wearing yokel, a carrot-cruncher, swede-basher, grass-chewer, ditchdigger, shit-spreader, cheese-roller, cider-swiller and village idiot all rolled into one. 'Ooh-arrr,' people croaked gleefully whenever I opened my mouth, 'oooh-arrr!'

As I settled into a daily routine, gloom and doubt spread over me. Each morning I rose up from my bed in one corner of the rectangular room and went to wash in the cold cheerlessness of the concrete-floored ablutions area. When dressed and ready, I bade the quinine-drinkers an indifferent goodbye, walked over the road and ate breakfast in the grimly named mess. With blue-uniformed crowds, I then walked up between the sports field and a row of married quarters to JARIC, which was situated in a heavily guarded and fenced compound. At midday, we came back. After lunch, we returned. At the end of the working day we came back again. Like the proverbial fiddler's elbow, we went back and forth in a blue surge between the mess and the office. That was the day and if you wanted entertainment at night, you could drink cheap beer in the NAAFI. I looked at the situation with grave unease. This was going to be my life. The transient stages, RAF Spitalgate and Bassingbourn, were over. This was the finished product and I didn't like it at all. Each day I sat at a high draughtsman's desk beside a barred window. Through the glass, I could see traffic speeding along the A1 and I longed to go home. I felt as if I had come to a brick wall, a place from which it was impossible to progress.

*   *   *

It was a relief to get back to No. 16 Vandiemans for occasional weekends. There was much interest in

227

my doings, and exclamations of approval at my smart uniform, but the journey to get there was lengthy and cumbersome. Sadly, it was no longer possible to take a train home and alight at nearby Challow Station because the previous year, on 7 December 1964, it had closed down. Along with countless other beautiful but unprofitable country stations, it had become a victim of the Beeching axe. My uncle, Sam Loder, and all the good men who worked beside him to tend the railway at Challow, Denchworth, Baulking and Uffington, were moved on and dispersed. That permanent way-gang who straightened the rails with crowbars and shovelled granite chips under the shifting sleepers no longer patrolled the line, nor would they ever do so again. However, the trains that passed through Challow had cast their spell on Uncle Sam's eldest son; my cousin Oliver became and is still today a train driver.

With the demise of Challow, the closest station to Stanford in the Vale was now over fifteen miles away at Didcot, and on many uncharitably cold Friday nights Tony journeyed out in his Ford Popular to pick me up, take me home and ship me back again when the brief weekend was over.

Back at work, the bespectacled young man who had helped me get through the course at Bassingbourn had also been sent to Brampton and we started going out together. He took me to the camp cinema, which I had never had the nerve to venture into on my own. The film was *Lawrence of Arabia* with Peter O'Toole and I was delighted by the tremendous scope of it and the unforgettable score. My boyfriend was bright and liked to visit libraries and bookshops. I went with him, but I had never entered these kinds of places in my life. I didn't know what to look at, and was impatient to leave. One rainy day on one of our outings to Huntingdon, he took an umbrella and the lurking quinine-drinkers spotted him. Back in our miserable room, the two of them nearly had hysterics. Fancy choosing him! He was a *posh boy*! What a twerp he looked, carrying an *umbrella*! I sat on my side of the room and squirmed with embarrassment and uncertainty.

I went to Cambridge with my boyfriend and we sat beside the River Cam at King's College. I had never seen a place of such calm beauty. I looked enviously at the students who seemed so purposeful; who looked no older than me, but who nevertheless had a fixed and admirable goal. They studied in the sunshine on the banks of the Cam, and slipped through that ancient environment like blood through veins, giving it life and colour.

I felt at a complete loss. Of my own free will, I had chosen a weird path, the life of a servicewoman, and was now confronted by the prospect of four joyless years in the same place with no hope of advancement. One day at the back of King's College, Cambridge, the young man asked me to marry him and I said yes. I knew in my heart that it was a bad decision taken for all the wrong reasons. With a leaden heart, I received the congratulations of friends and family.

*　　*　　*

In May 1966, back in Stanford, Jean married Malcolm Hall, the soldier she had first met at COD Bicester. The wedding took place on a wild and blustery day at St Denys Church, and I was one of the bridesmaids. In the photos, I am standing very close to my sister so I can discreetly hold her veil in place and stop it billowing away over the churchyard.

The village hall reception was enjoyable while being typically modest. Catering was provided by The Co-op in the form of a much-appreciated ham tea at eight shillings a head, after which Jean and her new husband went on honeymoon for a week to Newquay in Cornwall.

I remember going back to No. 16 Vandiemans at the end of the wedding day, and standing in the bedroom that Jean and I had shared for so long. My sister had gone; her bridal dress was discarded and thrown over a chair, collapsed into its own lavish folds. Seeing it gave me a feeling of deep sadness. Of the two of us, I had been first to leave the family home, yet I selfishly hated to think she would no longer be there to come back to. She was inexpressibly dear and I had always looked upon her as somehow exclusively mine, but she had moved on, she belonged to somebody else. Now, with her husband, she was prudently saving to buy a home of her own, a little house that wouldn't be anything to do with me at all.

My own fiancé was downstairs waiting for me to go back to Brampton, but I knew my engagement was a terrible mistake. I had begun to have vivid dreams where I fled the church in my full bridal regalia before the shell-shocked congregation. My wedding was not going to happen. I had to get out of it but I didn't know how.

Back at Brampton, I gave it a go. For some reason I have long forgotten, we were walking along the A1 beside continuous thundering traffic. It was wet; filthy spray was being thrown up from the highway. Over the deafening racket, the conversation went like this:

Me: I'm afraid I don't want to marry you. I want to call it off.

Him: If you don't marry me, I will jump out in front of the next lorry.

Me: Oh, all right then, I'll marry you.

On this shaky basis, the relationship was lurching forwards when the RAF unwittingly intervened, and my fiancé was posted to RAF Khormaksar in Aden. The engagement died a troubled and lingering death. I felt chastened by the experience and was genuinely sorry for the whole episode, but the longed-for freedom was intoxicating. At eighteen years of age I should never have relinquished it, but I had been low and lonely, my judgement clouded.

After a while, things began to perk up at Brampton. The two women in our room, to whom I had confidently offered advice about drinking quinine, left. I was never so glad to see anybody go. I must have seemed unbearably prim and prudish to them, but Mum had instilled in Jean and me a keen sense of modesty, and I did not know how to be anything else. I had never heard rough talk about sex; it made me cringe. They seemed very promiscuous to me. Both of them worked in catering. 'If ya love 'em, why not?' they shouted cheerfully in my direction amid much obscene gesturing with carrots. I nearly died of embarrassment and they, cackling with laughter at my discomfiture, propped each other up for fear of falling over.

One night I misguidedly accepted an invitation to go with them to a dance at RAF Alconbury, a station in the control of the United States Air Force. The place seemed utterly foreign, a small but resolute microcosm of the American way of life placed down in the UK. Once in the dance hall, my two companions disappeared completely and left me to it. I felt alarmed and out of place. This hall had none of the rustic innocence of the VC Gallery in Wantage. An American much the worse for drink came up and asked me to dance. I was nervous of his unfocused eyes, and declined. Later a nice, friendly one asked me and I accepted. At this, the first one staggered back and shouted abuse at me. I fled out to the car, feeling totally out of my depth and isolated in an alien environment. Determined not to go back into the frightening dance hall, I resolved to wait in the car until my companions came back, however long that might take. I was relieved eventually to find our car in the darkness of the car park, and I gratefully wrenched open the back door.

In the gloom, I could make out the bare pumping buttocks of a man above a woman's pale spread legs. I just couldn't believe what I was looking at. They were sprawled, grunting across the back seat. The man snarled at me like a dog and I hurriedly closed the door. Having no other way of getting back to Brampton, I hung about the car park until the end of the miserable, interminable night.

I was glad to see those women go. They seemed to me to be part of an old, rough mafia that was in the process of breaking up and falling away. After they left, two new girls moved into our room. They were young and unthreatening, and like me they were just looking for a change of scene and inexpensive travel. The atmosphere lightened in

232

more ways than one. I started to look more closely at what RAF Brampton had to offer and someone asked me to go to the BPN. I'd never heard of it and asked what it was. 'Oh, it's the radio station,' they replied, 'the Brampton Park Network.'

Under the tall trees, beside the fibreglass-clad church and surrounded by squirrels, there was a flat-roofed radio station. Inside, people were preparing programmes or talking confidently into a microphone in the soundproofed studio. They were actually *broadcasting*! I was impressed. People were friendly and used Christian names; there was less adherence to rank. For once, I didn't feel as if I had turned up in the wrong place.

I met a young man named John Stubbert, from the gloriously entitled village of Morley St Botolph in Norfolk. John was an airman working in photography at Brampton, and he had a keen interest in amateur dramatics. At that time, he was taking part in a play. He wondered if I would like to go along, watch the rehearsal and carry on afterwards to the NAAFI for a hot dog. I said yes.

The cinema where I had seen *Lawrence of Arabia* also doubled up as the theatre. It was small but lovely, with lit dressing mirrors round the back of the stage. The rehearsal got under way and I sat down in the auditorium to watch. The play was *Haul for the Shore!* by Jean McConnell, a comedy in three acts set in Cornwall. As time went on, I sensed a rising impatience among the players, who kept glancing towards the door. They were irritated because the WRAF officer playing one of the significant parts, a 'featherbrained young person' named Polly Ipplepen, had failed to turn up. I overheard resentful mumblings: 'Social life too busy again I suppose' and 'She could at least have let us *know*!'

I saw the producer go over and talk to John, whereupon the pair of them approached me as I sat on my own in the plush seats. They explained that a member of the cast hadn't shown up, and wondered if I'd mind reading in. I was self-conscious but happy to help, and having been given a script went up on to the stage and launched off into the young Cornishwoman's first speech. I was aware of a dumbstruck silence falling over the gathering. 'What an accent!' somebody commented. 'What a *perfect* accent!' *I* knew it wasn't Cornish of course, but had realised by then that most people found it impossible to place and wrongly identified it as 'West Country'.

This approval was deeply gratifying to me. I was so used to hearing my speech lampooned and ridiculed, it was almost unbelievable that here was a situation where it was exactly what was required. My accent was spot on, a desirable attribute! I basked bashfully in the sunny, appreciative thanks from everyone and went back to Barratt Block feeling uplifted and happier than I had been for many months.

I don't remember making a conscious decision exactly, but a certain feeling seeped into me that I should do other things. I was resigned to achieving no satisfaction from work because it was mathematical, difficult and unsuited to any abilities I had. I resolved to cast about for activities outside my ill-chosen job, anything that would give me new experiences and some sense of progress.

I knew that it probably seemed a puny achievement to anyone else, but passing my two GCE English O-levels in the Civil Service had been immensely pleasing to me, so I put my name down to take some more. The RAF was helpful and encouraging in any further education endeavour. I chose social and economic history; I thought I would care more about how people coped with daily life than dates, battles and reigns. I also opted to do the English General Paper, assuming it would be an easy one to pass, as you only had to write three essays and use effective English.

The notice board in Barratt Block was the thing to keep an eye on for any upcoming activities. One day there was an invitation to anyone who would like to take part in the Remembrance Day Parade at the Cenotaph in London. I thought this fitted my criteria; it was something new and different, which would take me somewhere I hadn't been before, so I applied. Shortly afterwards I was told I had been accepted and that on the specified date I should make my way to RAF Uxbridge in Middlesex to train for the big day. Clutching my rail warrant, I gratefully left our office with its barred, prison-like windows.

RAF Uxbridge didn't look too promising. It was home to the RAF Regiment, and they too were preparing for the Cenotaph Parade. Men of enormous stature marched up and down the parade ground, their monumental feet crashing down in unison on the frozen ground. The little group of WRAF girls looked puny and insignificant by comparison. It was freezing cold and we wore our blue greatcoats, which greatly restricted arm movement and made it hard to swing along. We did the best we could and shone up our buttons to look good for the important, televised ceremony at the Cenotaph.

One evening at Uxbridge, I was stunned to be

called to take a telephone call. This was unheard of. When I picked up the phone, it was John Baker, the producer of *Haul for the Shore* at Brampton. He explained that the woman playing Polly Ipplepen had now dropped out of the play completely; they had been left utterly in the lurch and would probably have to cancel the show. He said that I was the only possibility. Would I ever consider taking on the part, although it was substantial, there were only ten days left in which to learn it, and bearing in mind that I wasn't even *at* Brampton but away in Uxbridge? He could lend me his tape recorder, he added rather lamely at the end.

I was ecstatic. What a challenge. I said yes and the script arrived by first-class post. By day, I practised for the Cenotaph and at all other times I learned the play. I know it was just a corny old-fashioned comedy in a tiny theatre no one had ever heard of, but it seemed so important to me. I had failed at every job I tried, but what little performance I had done had always gone well. I felt as though I had finally been given a chance to shine, and I was determined to give it my best shot.

The Remembrance Day parade was memorable and lovely. We were taken by bus from Uxbridge, and stepped off into the smart grounds of Wellington Barracks in Birdcage Walk. Large groups of servicemen and women milled in front of the fine cream buildings; everyone had to set off at the right time and in the right order. It was a colossal feat of organisation and much more exciting than I had anticipated. The immense significance of it struck me for the first time, the reason why we were all there. It was to thank and commemorate all those who, like my poor Uncle

236

Oliver in his gruesome burned-out tank, were never able to come home and be with their loved ones. The band started to play the RAF March Past and our little group representing the WRAF, including the fabled actress Aircraftwoman Ayres, marched smartly out and set off towards Big Ben. I had never seen it before in my life.

We were positioned close to the Queen at the Cenotaph. I was very much in awe of authority; I had been told not to look at her so I didn't. In my peripheral vision, I made out a black shape that stepped forward and bent to place a wreath, but I was a good aircraftwoman. I never looked.

On returning to RAF Brampton, I concentrated on the play. This caused some friction in our room because the other girls liked listening to the radio first thing in the morning, but learning the lines was so important to me that I put my borrowed tape recorder on as soon as I woke up. This caused something of a clash. One of the girls, usually quiet and mouse-like, exploded at me and shouted, 'Oh, really! Can we please have ONE THING OR THE OTHER!' I was shocked. What a Philistine! Fancy not realising the crucial importance of me making a decent fist of Polly Ipplepen! I selfishly rehearsed on anyway.

The plays put on by the RAF Brampton Theatre Club only ran for two nights. The arrangement was stiff and unbending; other ranks came on the first night and officers came on the second. I have forgotten everything about those two nights but this: they laughed at the play and they laughed *particularly* at my performance. They laughed and laughed. I came off stage at one point and the producer was waiting for me behind the set before I went back on seconds later. 'You're playing a blinder!' he hissed at me. I had never heard the expression before and had to ask another actor what it meant. I was reassured that it was all good. Those two nights were sensational to me. I felt happy and excited; after so long in the doldrums I had at last found something I could do and loved doing. I could that tell the audience were waiting for me to go back on stage, that my timing and 'Cornish' accent had them on my side. I felt that thrilling wave of affection that flows back from the audience when things go well. I was soaring with happiness and overjoyed as though I had crashed through some gloomy barrier into the light.

To my surprise, as the cast took their final bow at the end of the second night, our Squadron Leader from JARIC, a man who seemed to me of such terrifyingly exalted rank that I had rarely dared shoot him a sidelong glance, stood up and mounted the stage. An interested silence fell upon the audience. He said he would like everyone to know that Aircraftwoman Ayres had stepped in and taken on the part only ten days before. A great cheer went up, an actual gasp of admiration that I had learned the whole thing in so short a time. I was pushed bashfully to the front and stood there glowing as the audience clapped. Suddenly I was aware of it. I could feel it flowing through my veins. The first sparkling traces of The Necessary Aptitude.

*   *   *

Now two highly significant things happened. Firstly, there was an unbelievable change in the way I was regarded at Brampton. I had been the no-hoper. I knew that when someone brought a job

238

into our office the sergeant in charge would have a quiet word, saying 'Don't give it to Pam'. I was used to being ineffectual and bypassed. Now I was suddenly aware of being pointed out. People came up to me and said, 'I thought you were really good in the play!' On the normally weary trudge back and forth to JARIC, there was a look of recognition, people smiled and seemed pleased to see me. It was magnificent.

Secondly, the day after the play finished, that same Squadron Leader approached me in the drawing office. He came straight towards me and I stared at him nervously like a snake at a mongoose. I couldn't think what he wanted.

'The Commanding Officer would like to see you,' he said gently, 'you won't need your hat . . .'

I stumbled to my feet. Cripes. An informal meeting with the almighty Group Captain, the top man! What could it mean?

I was ushered along quiet unknown corridors, stopping before a grand, gold-lettered door. This opened to reveal a large, carpeted office and a man behind a desk who stood up. The scene was larded with grandeur.

On the tooled leather desktop lay a group captain's hat with its decoration of gold braid or 'scrambled egg'. A large photograph of the Queen looked imperiously down from the back wall. His wrist, as he extended his hand, was encased in a four-banded sleeve signifying the rank of Group Captain. To me this all represented importance on an unbelievable, massive scale, because I had no rank and was at the absolute rock bottom of the system. He shook my hand, smiled and spacing out the words said: 'I have never laughed so much in all my life.'

I was astounded to find myself sitting and chatting to the CO. I can't remember much of the conversation; I know he was charming and enthusiastic about the play, but I do remember this. As I stood up to leave, he said, 'And what is your ambition in the Air Force?'

I replied with no hesitation because I was dazzled by everything I had heard about the place: 'I want to go to Singapore.'

Shortly afterwards I heard that I had been posted to RAF Seletar in Singapore. It was a dream posting, a prize. It was the one everybody wanted.

It could have been a coincidence, possibly. After all, I had already applied to go, but I suspect that he put a word in for me. Otherwise, why would they have sent me? Me, recognised and shunned as the world's worst draughtswoman? I would have been the last possible choice.

Everybody else had heard the news before me. I was strolling down the buffered JARIC corridor when someone said, 'Oh yes, here comes Seletar Jane.'

'What?' I said ungraciously.

'Haven't you heard?' they said. 'You're off to Singapore!'

I assumed it was a joke but sprinted to the personnel office anyway. It was confirmed. It was true. At nineteen years old, I was off on a two-year posting to the Far East.

It is hard to overstate how distant and remote Singapore seemed to most people at that time. Other than by means of the armed forces, ordinary people did not travel abroad. Package holidays were a new thing, and only the brave few had ventured to try those inexpensive trips to places in

240

Spain and Majorca.

The Far East was different, a place so far, far away with a culture so utterly different to our own. Though something of the tatters of war still clung on, it had a tantalising glamour, raciness and desirability as far as I was concerned. I was much influenced by people I had met who had already been there. They shared a common longing and wistfulness for the place. Shaking their heads, they said *that* was living. Places like Brampton were just existing.

It was also something to do with going the whole hog. I had left home to travel, and, in the RAF, the Far East was about as far as you could ever go. It was the ultimate reward, a chance to see what so few would ever see, at least as far as we knew then. It had been hard to leave Stanford and all those I loved, but having made the break, I wanted the most exciting destination and now, by a means I never fully understood, I was going to get it.

I was posted to RAF Innsworth, which was a transit camp, arriving on 28 February 1967. Travelling by train, I passed through the Cotswolds and the Stroud valley where little terraced houses of enchanting golden stone clung to steep sunlit valleys. I was filled with a rapidly rising excitement. It was unbelievable. I was going to fly and I didn't know a single person who had ever flown. I was going to fly to the other side of the world.

I have few memories of my brief time at Innsworth. No advice was offered on how to cope with the vastly different climate we would be living in. There was little awareness of the dangers of excessive exposure to the sun, no mention of skin cancer or melanoma. I only remember one corporal advising us not to use standard Nivea cream to protect our skin from the sun. 'Otherwise,' she drawled, 'you're gonna fry.'

44

SINGAPORE

In March 1967, shortly before my twentieth birthday, I flew to Singapore International Airport, better known as Paya Lebar. My brother Tony took me to Heathrow in his Ford Popular, and Mum came as well to see me off. I was wildly excited and if Mum had misgivings, she never showed them. At the departure gate, she gave me a kiss and said, 'So long, old gal,' which was her customary farewell. Her eyes were odd and glittery; it never occurred to me that she might be fighting back tears.

I was directed on to a bus, which then travelled an enormous distance to reach the aircraft. At last, it pulled up alongside a Britannia of British Eagle, the company that provided all military transport to the Far East at that time. It was a chunky little plane bearing the airline logo, a flying eagle in the shape of a capital E. I walked importantly up the staircase and boarded the aircraft, hoping that Tone and Mum could still see me in this most glamorous and film star-ish of situations. Once inside the cramped cabin, I could see seated lines of families and single girls like me, going out to their various postings. It was deflating to notice that a high proportion of the women were crying and distressed, not at all excited and buoyed up as I was. Somewhat subdued, I took my seat for the journey. It was going to take twenty-seven hours.

I am sure everybody remembers the fearsome thrill of their first take-off. The incredible gathering pace, the sensation of being pressed back into the seat, of runway lights hurtling past and the final glorious transition from mad vibrating speed to the smoothness and lift of actual flight. It was unbelievable. I was on my way. It was incredible that I had been so lucky.

There were two stops, the first in Kuwait and the second at Colombo in Ceylon, now Sri Lanka. There was no security as we know it today. On landing, people got off the aircraft and wandered about until they were recalled. In Kuwait, I walked hesitantly out into the darkness and silence. High on distant derricks all around me, long horizontal flames flared silently out into the night sky. The warm air of the desert was thick with the smell of oil. For me, brought up as I was in the green countryside, it was an unimaginable scene, alien, frightening, mysterious. I stared at it in wonder.

The runway in Colombo was carved out of the red soil. It was encroached upon by palm trees, which I had never seen before, and there were thatched shelters where men lounged and smiled, showing spectacular white teeth. I stood in the brilliant sunshine and tried to buy souvenirs from them with the local money I thought I had been clever to obtain from the bank at home, but they were not interested and demanded dollars. 'Dollah, Dollah,' they insisted, shaking their heads, 'You give me dollah.'

As the end of the lengthy journey neared, the pilot made an announcement inviting us to look out of the windows and admire the lights of Kuala Lumpur. As I peered down at the lit city with its strange, foreign name, it suddenly hit me that I was thousands of miles from my home and everything I knew and held dear. It would be two years before I saw Stanford and my loved ones again. An enormous wave of homesickness engulfed me and I was in tears as we flew down the Malaysian Peninsula to Singapore.

The place smelled eggy. Warm and eggy like omelettes, as we stepped down from the plane. Travelling with us was a Flight Sergeant who had spent many years in the Far East. She took deep, happy breaths and announced, 'It's just like coming home!' That may have been the case for her but it was like no home I had ever sniffed. The heat, even so late at night, was overwhelming, the air warm, damp and syrupy. I had long hair and the heat and weight of it about my neck was loathsome. We were directed to a bus and driven through the wild clamour of the streets. Everywhere there were stalls illuminated by the white light of kerosene lamps, food stalls with hanging rows of flattened, boned-out piglets and chickens, textiles, clothing, music and cheap pictures fashioned out of straw, all amid the clang and bustle of a place that never slept. Smells of cooking from innumerable woks and the stench of refuse intermingled. I saw my first monsoon drains; deep, steep-sided concrete ditches at the roadsides built to cope with spectacular deluges that came in the monsoon season, but which at other times overflowed with foulness, with sewage, rubbish of every filthy kind and dead, rotten animals. I gazed out of the bus window, exhausted by the journey, half-suffocated by the intense heat, holding my hair up from my neck and watching it all like some garish, unreal parade. The bus drove through the gates of RAF Seletar and, in an instant, the clamour changed into serenity. The noise ceased. We drove along a smooth tarmac road with lawns extending away into the darkness on either side. There were monsoon drains but these were empty and clean. I had the impression of enormous trees and cool white buildings. The bus stopped at the WRAF Block and I went inside. That night I slept for the first time beneath revolving ceiling fans. They creaked and caused all of the curtains and hangings to constantly stir. At first, I found this continual subtle movement eerie and an irritation, but in time I came to love the rhythmic sound of the fans and the gentle motion of warm tropical air. It came to typify a place and period I truly loved.

45

DAYS OF MAGIC

I went outside into the bright sunshine and looked at my new surroundings. They were impeccable. Here the accommodation blocks were not dowdy, flat roofed and functional but had a cool, lofty beauty, white-painted with wide, airy verandas. They were surrounded by lawns, not the tender grass of home but buffalo grass, coarse and shiny like mown rushes. Planted into it were spectacular flowering shrubs, in particular hibiscus with big, flagrant blooms in colours of marvellous brightness. Here, shrubs with vivid leaves that I had only seen stunted at home as pot plants, grew to their full height, taller than a man. Frangipani trees, which before blooming reach out gnarled,

245

red-tipped branches like bleeding fingers, were in full flower with their lemon and white flowers and magical overwhelming scent. Above our building towered a tree that took my breath away, offering out huge red flowers like clasped hands. Stretching away in front was an immaculate oval sports field, marked out with pitches and a running track. Other white buildings stood gracefully around it and everywhere there were gardeners tending the grounds to bright tropical perfection.

We girls were enclosed in our accommodation block with chain-link fencing. The entire lower veranda was sturdily fenced and the sole remaining entrance conscientiously padlocked at night. I think the abundance of flowers around us served to soften the prison-like precautions.

Each room accommodated four girls. Spacious and lofty, they were fitted with two ceiling fans and louvred windows of slatted glass. A population of small lizards ran over the walls. Known as chitchats, they were welcomed because of their voracious appetite for mosquitoes but I was disconcerted when I first saw them patrolling the walls with their swift, jerky movements. Another hazard was the praying mantis. This large insect is bright green and shaped like a cricket bat. It has compound eyes and leans forward at a slight angle with two front legs clasped piously together as if deep in prayer. They were fond of wardrobes and it was not unusual, on reaching into a shelf, to find one perched solemnly on your underwear. Enormous ferocious-looking ants were to be seen everywhere, and any item of food inadvertently left out would soon call forth a marching procession of black ants to stump across the floor and up the table leg to carry off the booty. Another insect worthy of great respect was the woolly bug. Though scarcely visible to the eye, it ate woollen items. Piranha-like platoons of them would descend on any garment left in a forgotten corner, and eat it up within days. A few shreds would be discovered where it had once lain. I had an entire Air Force cap eaten by woolly bugs; all that remained was the badge. Thin, bootlace-like snakes abounded as well; they were startling and at night would whip sideways across the path before your bare, sandalled feet.

We were issued with our uniforms: pale, creamy button-through cotton dresses with belts and epaulettes. These were comfortable and I deemed them suitably glamorous and tropical looking, especially as the belt could be cinched in drastically to emphasise the waist and give an hourglass look. A blue Air Force cap at a rakish angle added a further nice touch, all of which was sabotaged by kiddie-like ankle socks and flat leather sandals. The spiflicating heat also meant that it was normal to be drenched in sweat, and to exhibit an enormous sodden patch across the shoulder blades at all times.

Once clothed, I was told where to report for work, and issued with a conveyance. A large bike. I was horrified. It did not fit with my stylish mental image of myself at all. Anyway, I got on it and, in the tremendous draining tropical heat, started pedalling.

RAF Seletar was very large and divided into East and West Camps. It was a working airfield; Andover and Beverley aircraft constantly took off or landed, and Wessex helicopters were parked shimmering on the tarmac. The bike ride to my place of work was of some considerable length, and though I left the WRAF block cool and freshly showered, I turned up at the other end red faced and exasperated on the hated bike, drenched in sweat and boiling hot. It was a picturesque ride though, through lawns, ornamental trees and tall, pleasing buildings for the maintenance and housing of aircraft. Every day I toiled past what seemed to me to be a rather pathetic scene. A row of decommissioned Gloster Javelin aircraft had been lined up on the grass and left to decay. I knew nothing about aeroplanes but I found their graceful shape poignantly beautiful. They were like darts. It was sad to see things of such power and potential rust and fall away.

My workplace was a building at the very end of the runway from which Andover aircraft in desert camouflage swept into the air perhaps thirty times a day. As a result people tended to converse in quick bursts. Beyond the perimeter fence the vegetation was lush and jungly, a burgeoning tapestry of mangroves, palms and innumerable vigorous plants I did not recognise. Our building was enclosed first by chain-link fencing and secondly by an enormous ochre-coloured blast wall of immense height and thickness, which excluded all sunshine. I do not know from what source the blast was expected, but we were ready for it if it came.

When I saw the drawing office within, my heart sank. Here, once again, was a room filled with tall draughtsmen's desks and high stools, with airmen casually referring to slide rules, a device whose secrets I could never unravel. I had come round the other side of the world, but the job hadn't changed. I knew I still wouldn't be able to do it.

I worked in a large rectangular room, with cold

248

red tiles on the floor and an enormously high ceiling. In one corner was a flight of steps leading up to an important-looking door. This was the single ladies toilet. Therefore, when it was necessary to use the facility, everyone could watch as you ascended the steps and could, if they were desirous, measure the length of time you were in there. To my mind, this always made a visit feel rather pressured. You couldn't stay long because everybody knew you were within. The fact that you might be suffering from the twin agonies of diarrhoea or constipation was evident for all to see.

Every day or so a small, monosyllabic Malaysian man wearing a pith helmet would enter the drawing office for the purpose of cleaning the ladies toilet. He would ascend the steps, open the door and vigorously whack in a bucketful of water. He then closed the door and left. Any female entering subsequently would find the cubicle awash and dripping.

I was friendly with a Tamil man called Samad who worked in our area, doing whatever jobs were required. One day I was astounded to see Samad up in the top of a nearby palm-type tree, brandishing a machete. He hacked away at the top, his legs tightly laced round the trunk of the tree, and eventually made his way down with a heavy bundle wrapped in newspaper. I followed him, mystified, as he carried the bundle into our drawing office and folded back the paper to reveal the contents. It was full of papayas, or paw paw as they were called there. With his machete, he cut them in half lengthways and flicked out the line of blue-black seeds. Everyone fell on the chunks of fruit, holding it in both hands, sucking and biting the perfect, peachy-coloured flesh. I had never seen it before but I took a piece and dived in. It was mouth-watering, perfectly ripe tropical fruit.

One day I had gone outside the office at lunchtime to eat my sandwich; I sat near a colourful bush with shiny leaves. A movement caught my eye and, turning to look, I saw a large chameleon in amongst the branches. His queer, thoughtful eyes studied me shiftily for a while, then deciding I was up to no good, he crawled further away into a part of the bush where the leaves were predominantly red. As I watched him, his green body became suffused with redness to match his surroundings and, in no time, he was completely red and colour-matched to his background. I had read that they could do it, of course, but to actually watch a chameleon change colour as I sat eating my lunch seemed miraculous to me, underlining how special the place was.

I never got up on time. It was always a last-minute panic to get to work and I rode my bike over the runway pedalling furiously.

Having left myself no time for breakfast, I was ravenously hungry and greatly looked forward to the arrival of the egg roti man. A local person, he arrived mid-morning selling hot dogs and egg rotis. All the young service personnel rushed out eagerly, though when I consider those hot dog sausages now, I am filled with queasiness. They were flavoursome but unaccountably gristly, filled with small, hard fragments of unknown origin and, it must be said, hair. The egg roti looked altogether more wholesome. This used the same type of long crusty bread roll as the hot dog did, but into its soft interior was enfolded a large omelette, spiced up in some garlic-laden way and lovely to eat. Either of

250

these dishes was highly restorative and after a visit by the egg roti man, life looked a lot brighter.

Adjoining our office was a cell known as the Rockette Room. This contained a monumental machine, an early form of photocopier. Shaped in part like a large mangle, it could reproduce large documents of the blueprint type. It had soon dawned on the Flight Sergeant in charge of the office that I was inept at being a draughtswoman, and while everybody was supposed to take a turn at supervising the Rockette machine, my turn seemed to be longer than anybody else's. I quite understood and didn't mind. There was an upside to working it anyway, as the little room was cold, air-conditioned and out of the oppressive heat. Also, if I was running the machine, I was not in fear of being approached by someone asking me to do a job that was beyond me, which was my normal condition. However, the Rockette machine was not user-friendly. To operate, it required large quantities of ammonia, notorious for its acrid stench. Choking clouds of ammonia fumes filled the cramped space, and unrolling a newly emerged blueprint released a shockwave. I would have to stagger outside and cough, and within the shortest period, the sagging operative would develop a pounding headache. I worked in there for months, lifting up knee-buckling weights of ammonia in white plastic carboys and sloshing it into the ever-yawning tank.

One day a freak accident livened up the daily routine. My friend Christine (who was a brilliant draughtswoman and given all the jobs) had a crowned front tooth. While strolling down the red-tiled floor of the office, she unfortunately tripped over the flappy sandals we were issued with, and embedded her front teeth in the bare knee of an unsuspecting shorts-wearing airman as he sat studiously at his desk. Though Christine extricated her teeth from his knee, it was observed that the crown remained embedded. It was later removed in hospital.

Another grisly scene springs to mind. Newcomers to Singapore always underestimated the fearful power of the sun. It was not like the sun at home; it could cause the most horrific burns after only a brief exposure. After I had been at Seletar for a few months, a Scottish airman I knew from Brampton was posted out to join our unit. He was a small, flinty Glaswegian named Bill, as hard as nails. Newly arrived, he came into our office for the first time and told me he had been lying in the sun. All morning he had lain out, he said, and it was fantastic. The next day he appeared briefly and wretchedly to tell the Flight Sergeant that he was reporting sick; his legs below his shorts were a ghastly blue. Great yellowing, water-filled blisters like polythene bags had formed down his shins; he held his blue arms away from his body in agony. He was hospitalised for weeks. Another WRAF friend Dawn fell asleep in the sun and was likewise in hospital for weeks suffering from burns.

We had sensational facilities at Seletar. Being fairly idle by nature, I could hardly believe my ears when I was told that we had servants. *Servants*! Two Malaysian ladies worked as *amahs*; they cleaned and laundered for us, charging 50 cents a frock. Each day, lengthy lines of uniform dresses flapped on the amahs' washing lines, drying speedily in the baking sun. It was lovely to be waited on; so very easy to get used to.

A beautiful swimming pool was provided and

252

much enjoyed by all the service personnel and their families. As a new arrival, it did not pay to be too sensitive; on first appearing at the pool in a swimming costume one could expect a loud chorus of jeers and hysterical laughter at the sight of such flawlessly white limbs. 'Moonie!' the sun-bronzed soldiers would bawl. 'God almighty, look at 'er! MOONIE!' It was an initiation handed out to everyone. It spurred the horrified newcomer on to acquire a tan quickly; to look like everybody else, even if it did mean agonising sunburn. For weeks after I first arrived, I wore a silk scarf round my shoulders under my dress to hold the coarse material off my permanently burned skin. Soon, I was mahogany brown and spared the shame of looking different.

Most weekends were spent lying on the coarse buffalo grass surrounding the pool. It was diamond-bright, twinkling in the sunshine and sporting at one end a complicated structure of high diving boards. The only discordant note was struck by several large fierce notices affixed just above the water line, which read: 'Do Not Expectorate in the Swimming Pool.' I didn't know what it meant and had to go and look it up.

This aside, everything about the pool was luxurious and delightful, apart from the journey to get there. As usual, I undertook this on my hated bike but at one point, the route became fraught with danger from an unusual hazard: a colony of monkeys. A section of the narrow road leading to the pool ran through a swampy area where they had made their home. At certain times of the year, the dominant male would be particularly protective of his females and would, it was claimed, rush out and claw the legs of passing cyclists. The monkey was alleged to be large with ferocious teeth; it was a terrifying prospect. I always pedalled up to the spot at breakneck speed then deftly lifted my legs up out of clawing range. I heard that sadly, on more than one occasion, the largest male monkey was shot dead by the military police. Despite my elaborate precautions, I never actually saw a fierce male monkey at all. In the end, I wondered if it was a kind of myth where the monkey grew larger and his teeth more bloody with each telling of the story.

One day in our drawing office the Flight Sergeant announced that there was to be a Swimming Gala at the pool, and asked for volunteers. A stony silence prevailed. 'You, you and you,' he said, choosing contestants at random. I was chosen as a 'you' to compete in the fifty yards breast-stroke. I turned up on the afternoon, did my best in the race and stepped up to receive my prize, a shield for third place from the Commanding Officer. I still have it today. I don't ever tell anyone that there were only three girls in the race.

We seldom swam in the sea. Most of the beaches I walked on were pleasantly sandy but narrow, and littered with debris from the palm trees leaning out drunkenly above them. You had to pick your way over dry, brown, insect-infested palm fronds half-buried in the sand. Local fishermen tended sharp-nosed little boats, and looked at us without expression as we passed. Vendors sold ice-cream flavoured with the malodorous fruit of the durian and on one particular stretch of beach we used to visit a spreading rambutan tree, which cast generous amounts of angry-looking, whiskery red fruits on to the sands. Having split open the hairy shell, the exposed rambutan was pale, glassy and lychee-like. For a long time after eating, shreds and fibres of the fruit straggled between the teeth, detracting from the beauty of the smile.

*   *   *

As for the real world outside the safe British feel of RAF Seletar, in my secret self I was quite nervous of it. The very foreignness made me feel at a loss. I knew nothing about the history or culture of Singapore, nor had I bothered to find any out. It was a place British service personnel hoped to be posted to because it was hot and you could have a good time; that was all I knew. Among my contemporaries, there was a general lack of interest in, and sense of superiority to, the local population. We felt like the top dogs.

Immediately outside the camp gates was a vibrant, dusty village called Jalan Kayu, which was always thronged with servicemen and women. To the left, across the stinking monsoon drain (don't look down) and up a debris-strewn slope there was an eating-house. Like many buildings, the walls only came part of the way up, leaving a wide band open to the elements at the top. Inside there was seating and a bar for cold beer and horrible tea, but we always sat at the tables and chairs outside. There, on a mobile stall, a local man would wield his wok over a noisy, roaring flame. He was graceful to watch, swooping and weaving from the waist, turning the food constantly, a sprinkle of this, a flick of something else from wet fingers dipped into little bowls. We were unadventurous and usually chose Nasi Goreng: a gargantuan plateful of fried rice studded with vegetables, egg and muscular curled-up prawns. Previously I had never seen any of this, never seen a wok. It was such an assault on the senses: the intolerable glare of the sun, the humidity and searing heat, the stink of the worst kind of refuse in adjacent monsoon drains, the mouth-watering tastiness of the food, the roar of the cooking flame and the mad clamour of shouting and haggling. Cars, buses and taxis poured past with associated clouds of brown dust, exhaust fumes and honking horns. There were poor, scavenging dogs, which it did not pay to look at. Eaten by mange, they were raw, crusted and skeletal. It was unthinkable to touch them. Amid all this, we tucked into our food.

The village lined both sides of the road as it rose up out of Seletar Camp. A succession of little shops bordered the sidewalks, and included countless tailors, sellers of electrical goods, furniture and pirated music. Much of this trade was aimed at the families living in married quarters nearby. An amahs' market was held on Monday evenings, when vendors set up kerosene-lit tables down either side of the street. Different music blared from each one; the racket was daunting. Each stall was filled with the garish and the gaudy and I bought armfuls of it like a magpie to send home. Mum received black velvet wall hangings printed with Chinese-looking birds on pink-budded branches; one hung proudly in the lavatory at No. 16 Vandiemans for decades. I sent her and Jean ill-fitting dresses, silk cushions, silk spectacle cases in the most violent of colours, cards of cut straw depicting houses on stilts called *kampongs* set against florid sunsets, pagoda scenes painted on bamboo rolls and shoulder bags decorated with varnished melon seeds.

One savvy trader had organised a supply of

Mary Quant cosmetics, which we young women flocked to buy. It was the Swinging Sixties, the era of Twiggy and the Rolling Stones. We might have been in the Far East but we didn't want to be laggardly where fashion was concerned so we sported the iconic Quant flower design on our make-up and ordered daring mini-dresses from the tailor.

We often took a taxi into Singapore city from the rank in the centre of the camp; there would be brief haggling over the price of the ride before setting off. Many of the cars were in an advanced state of neglect and it was not unusual during the journey for vehicle parts to drop off and cartwheel into the verge. Several roads within the camp were rather incongruously named after streets in London, Park Lane and Maida Vale for example. Shortly before the entrance gates there was an area of very beautiful homes occupied by high-ranking officers. White and airy, they were set into the lawns like elegant jewels. Haughty wives would look down from the verandas, amahs scurried about their housework, and all was set beneath ornamental trees of undreamt-of beauty. Then our taxi would pass through the entrance gates and out into the dust and jostle of the outside world.

At that time Singapore city was inescapably filthy. I was repulsed by the habits of people in the street; by the way they would spit phlegm or, covering one nostril, shoot the contents of the other out on to the pavement. It was revolting. Lee Kuan Yew, the extraordinary first Prime Minister of the Republic of Singapore, would prevail and change all this beyond recognition but not quite yet. Of all the sights in the city at that time, the Singapore River haunted me most. Unutterably polluted, the vile stench that rose up from it in the shimmering heat was indescribable. The ruined water was blue-black, and did not flow. Instead, laden with refuse, it rolled along like treacle; slowly, with a ghastly thick viscosity and rubberiness. I peered down at it from the busy road bridge while holding my breath. I was used to the clarity of the River Ock babbling its innocent way through Berkshire and beyond; I had never seen a waterway so befouled by man.

There were places in Singapore city that it was considered essential to visit; Change Alley was one. This was a narrow, merchandise-cluttered passageway leading off the waterfront. To enter it was to be immediately assailed by vendors of the most insistent type. All manner of goods were flapped in your face and promises: 'I give you good price! I give you best price!' shouted by frantic, dancing people.

An extraordinary array of faked merchandise was on sale. The most costly and exclusive makes of leather goods, handbags and luggage had all been copied in cheap brittle plastic and were available to buy for a pittance. Branded watches and jewellery, every item counterfeit, were aggressively shaken before your eyes. It was almost impossible to get along; the vendors brought you to a standstill. Once, in desperation I bought a smart-looking cigarette lighter. It worked for the first few times then one day when I lit it, a ferocious hissing flame shot up a metre into the air, narrowly missing my nostrils. It never worked again. It was one of my typically good buys. Another was a fake Singer sewing machine, old-fashioned and colossally heavy, which I bought and laboriously carried home at the end of my tour.

Never in its short life before I hurled it into a skip did it work properly. Many of my friends were altogether more informed; they knew what to buy and, having obtained great deals on cameras, whooped to each other about their Minoltas and Leicas. I never had that forward-looking resourcefulness; I found cameras and photography complicated and impenetrable. Once, when I took a photograph of my friend Christine outside our office, she asked if she could take it to her Camera Club as an example of what to avoid. I had composed my picture in such a way that a palm tree behind her grew vertically out of the top of her head as she stood cackling with laughter. It was a gem.

Once the frenzied delights of Change Alley had been exhausted, Bugis Street was the next destination considered to be essential viewing. I found the place and its purpose baffling; it made me uncomfortably aware of how green, prudish and totally unaware of a great swathe of human behaviour I was at that time. I had gone there one evening with a boyfriend; we had a meal at one of the outdoor restaurants. It was a notorious haunt for the most flamboyant of transvestites, where they met and paraded in gaudy, outlandish clothes, their faces caked with make-up, their long hair coiled and lacquered into elaborate styles. When it was gently pointed out to me that they were men, I couldn't believe it or begin to understand why they would want to do it. I had a lot to learn.

In our office, I overheard a lot of talk among the servicemen about the events of the night before. One man in particular was ribbed because of the prostitute he habitually used; she was considered by his mates to be elderly and cheap. 'She does whatever I want,' he used to say defensively, 'and she's pleased to see me.' There was a lot of bravado and talk of 'exhibitions' where in certain clubs a man could have sex with a prostitute while being cheered on by his mates, or where luckless young girls had been trained to draw unlikely foreign bodies into the vagina, or where there were displays of bestiality. It conjured up a pretty grim picture. None of the older men spoke to me directly about these things but I knew a young Geordie soldier called Alfie. We were the same age and he used to talk to me about what was on offer in a matter-of-fact way that was not salacious.

Other things I just overheard. There was a coffee-break room where the servicemen got together to play darts, where I might be in the corner making my coffee while they were talking about the weekend. They were nice men for the most part who did not come across as depraved. There were hardly any women for the single men to have normal relationships with, many were lonely and bought sex where they could.

A particular minibus took patients suffering from venereal diseases to a specialised clinic at one of the major military hospitals. None of the men wanted to be seen on the bus because their condition would immediately become public knowledge and, awaiting them at their journey's end, was the agonising treatment, which, I was informed but never chose to verify, involved the urethral dilator, an umbrella-like scraper device, which was inserted into the man's urethra, opened and withdrawn.

*   *   *

In Singapore, I saw things I had never even dreamt about. I was a blank canvas, bigoted and unworldly. A friend took me to see the dramatic sweep of the newly built National Theatre, doomed to premature demolition by lack of air conditioning and design faults in the cantilevered roof. I gawped at it, and gawped again at the impenetrable scenes from Chinese mythology portrayed in Tiger Balm Gardens, where paint peeled off violently coloured plaster figures and tableaux. I didn't know what to make of it. I sent photographs home to Mum of me looking prissy, holding my sturdy brown leather handbag in both hands beneath pop-eyed Chinese dragons and towering pagodas.

Early in 1968, I was taken to see Thaipusam, a Hindu festival celebrated by the Tamil community in honour of Muruga, the Tamil God of War. For many days preceding the actual festival, devotees are prepared by fasting and meditation to carry a *kavadi* or burden. They might do this so the God would hear prayers for, say, a terminally ill child or other stricken loved one. The *kavadi* can be something simple like a container of milk, but others are enormous canopies borne over the heads of the devotee and supported by skewers *inserted into their flesh*. It was searingly hot on the day I went, and the air in the dusty residential street was filled with the smell of incense. At intervals, a crowd had gathered round one of the devotees being fitted with a *kavadi* and I made my way to the front. I was shocked to see pointed metal rods like knitting needles being pushed purposefully in double rows into the abdomen and back of the burden carrier. When the canopy over him was fully supported by rods, he put out his tongue and a thick skewer was forced through it from the underside. He did not cry out or bleed, but shuffled from side to side rhythmically, his brown eyes vacant, entranced. It was extraordinary, unforgettable, a mystery.

Sometimes in Jalan Kayu, it was possible to see a Wayang, a travelling theatre of shadow puppets originating in Indonesia. The company arrived and set up their stage on the baked, dusty roadside. The production was accompanied by loud, enthusiastic Chinese music, and the roars and appreciation of the gathered crowd as good triumphed over evil reminded me of our responses to an English pantomime.

It was a sensational time and place to be young. We had all we could wish for, a pampered and protected existence, sunshine, young men for company and an endless succession of interesting things to do. One friend belonged to the Seletar Yacht Club and asked me to go sailing on an Osprey, though I had never sailed before or even considered it. I was uncertain when invited to step into the trapeze, a strong harness slung low about the hips that enables a crewman to lean horizontally out over the water to counterbalance the boat. To my surprise, it was breathtakingly exciting, the water warm and unthreatening, and I felt strong, fit and tanned as we cut through the Straits of Johor at high, cracking speed.

I was invited to a barbecue and dance on a nearby island named Pulau Blakang Mati. Now I can't remember who organised it or why, but we went by landing craft, a great joyful gang of us filled with anticipation, down deep in the high-walled utilitarian vessel, deafened by the harsh, machine-gun-like rattle of the engine. On reaching the island, a great blazing fire was lit; there was food and music. I remember dancing on the beach with my friends, the moon shining a bright path across the darkness of the sea, and feeling so full of happiness I could have burst with joy.

I thought about the endless boring evenings I had spent in the chilly pubs in Stanford on winter nights. The craving I had felt there for colour, excitement and variety, when after some dull darts match and a buckshee cheese and pickle sandwich I had asked myself the desperate question over and over: 'Is this *it?* Is this *all there is?*'

I thanked God I had found the courage to bail out; that my rash leap into the dark had paid off a thousandfold.

Years later, I discovered that Pulau Blakang Mati had a bloody history; the name translates alarmingly as *Island of death from behind.* This is thought to be a maritime reference to a sheltered area at the back of the island where no winds blew to fill sails, where boats consequently became becalmed. However, during the Japanese Occupation under the Sook Ching Operation, Chinese men suspected of anti-Japanese activities were brutally killed and the beach at Pulau Blakang Mati was one of the killing fields.

*   *   *

I did one awful thing in Singapore, which I have always felt ashamed of. At home in Stanford, once the family were out at work all day, Mum got herself a little job as a cleaner and kitchen-helper at nearby Buckland House, a beautiful Georgian stately home in 150 acres, which was run as a hall for one of the universities. The place was brimful of students, and teams of women from surrounding villages went by minibus to cook for them and to clean their rooms.

Mum found it exhausting. After the meal had been served in the refectory, there was apparently only very limited time for the women to clear up, wash up and pile out of the door. Mum would come home still sweaty from the scramble. 'My God!' she would gasp. 'That was a belt-up tonight.'

Dad was old-fashioned in his outlook and took a dim view of her working. It was too much for her he said, but Mum was resolute. 'I gets a bit of money of me own,' she would announce firmly, in a way that was non-negotiable. For her it was a longed-for transition to a dignified state, that of earning her own money after decades of complete dependence on her husband, when if money had not been forthcoming she and her six children would have gone without. Finally, she had some small control, and she put up a fierce fight to keep it.

In Singapore, I enjoyed designing my own dresses. It was creative and enjoyable; everyone did it. You visited one of the numerous little tailors in Jalan Kayu, accepted the proffered cold drink and chose an attractive fabric from the bolts of cloth stacked to ceiling height behind the proprietor. You then drew a design on a piece of paper according to your artistic ability, offered your various protuberances to be measured, argued about the price, placed the order and came back a week later to pick up the finished mode. Once I designed a humdinger.

Kaftans were all the rage. With no thought of the religious sensibilities of those around us, we wore them perilously short like a pelmet. I

264

designed one in beautiful silver-grey material, with grey-and-silver braid to trim the wide cuffs and neckline. It was unique, bang up-to-the-minute and racily short. I adored it. All I needed was somewhere to wear it.

It was customary for certain visiting British ships docking in Singapore to hold a dinner on board and invite WRAF girls as guests; all was very seemly and polite. A Merchant Navy ship called and a nicely worded invitation appeared on our notice board inviting us to attend. I had never visited a ship before, let alone *dined* on one, so a few of my friends and I accepted and transport was duly arranged to the quayside. I wore my new dress and went to stupendous lengths to look smart and attractive.

Once on board I began to wonder if I had made a mistake. The dinner in the officers mess was dauntingly smart, the table laid with beautiful crystal and silverware. It was not what I was used to. I became nervous because I had wanted to make a good impression, but now felt in danger of being laughed at as the girl who didn't know which knife and fork to use. Of course, Mum taught us table manners at home but they were simple rules, appropriate for our somewhat lowly social position. We always said 'Please' and 'Thank you', we knew not to grab or lunge for things, we didn't eat from our knives, we didn't talk with our mouths full and those of us who wore glasses never polished them on the curtains. However, her tutoring did not extend to cover a posh dinner such as this with *white-jacketed stewards*!

I was seated next to a very amiable young man indeed, handsome and striking in his dark uniform. He was friendly, fair-haired and easy to talk with. I

265

began to relax. He asked me about myself, about where I came from.

'Stanford in the Vale,' I told him brightly.

'Fancy that!' says he. 'I was at university near there.'

'Really?' I said with interest, my silver fork paused in mid-air.

'Yes, in a place called Buckland,' he went on pleasantly. At this point, his expression clouded with perplexity and thoughtfulness as small, remembered fragments began to come together. His face clearing, he asked excitedly:

'What did you say your surname was again?'

I could see the way this was going and didn't like it.

'Ayres,' I mumbled as incoherently as possible.

'Ayres?' he almost shouted in disbelief. 'Did you say your name was AYRES?'

I put down the silver fork and waited as if for a blow.

'*DIDN'T YOUR MOTHER USED TO BE A CLEANER?*' he asked.

I looked down at my smart new dress and around me at the grand table with waiters and stewards, the soft lights and twinkling crystal. I thought that admitting Mum was a humble cleaner would make me seem out of place, someone unworthy of being present in such lovely surroundings. I did not realise that the truth was the exact opposite.

'No,' I said. 'No, that wasn't my mother. It's a very common name. It must have been someone else.'

Somewhere far away, far from Tengah and the sea, and the little waves that lapped the bows of the ship, out along the Bukit Timah Road towards

Serangoon, an old cockerel stirred, stood up on his perch and crowed before settling back to sleep. He crowed once, twice, three times.

I should have said proudly, 'Yeah, she was a cleaner. She was a cleaner because she wanted the independence of earning her own money. And when she had earned it and saved it, when the work was too hard and she couldn't keep it up, do you know what she did with it? She went to Courts in Swindon and bought us a new three-piece suite so her family would have somewhere new and presentable to sit. She was a cleaner, she was grateful for the chance to be a cleaner and she was worth ten of me.'

That's what I should have said.

46

BEGINNER ON STAGE

I had started performing in a small way at Seletar. I met Geoff, who sang in folk clubs and wanted someone to sing a Flanders and Swann piece entitled 'A Song of the Weather' with him at Seletar folk club. I had never sung anything in public before. Geoff and I arranged to sing alternate verses and then both shout 'Bloody January again!' at the end. Having once agreed to do it, the fear I felt was out of all proportion to the small-scale nature of the event. Crippled by stage fright, and so breathless with nerves I could hardly gasp the words out, let alone imbue them with lightness and mischief, I stood behind Geoff as he sat with his guitar on the tiny stage. We gave a tremulous rendition of the song, which was sparsely clapped. He never asked me again.

RAF Seletar also had a theatre club. Having discovered it, I went there every night and, as a result, my love of performing greatly intensified. This was to change my life in every possible way.

Like so much of Seletar, it was beautiful. Just a short walk from the main road and tucked in close to the church, the club stood bathed in sunshine. It had a proper, professional-standard theatre with high airy roof, raked seating in the auditorium, good dressing rooms and a clubroom with a bar. Arrangements of rattan furniture and glass-topped tables filled the room and extended outside. Placed beneath shady awnings, they looked inviting and comfortable.

The club took its role very seriously. Plays were chosen by a committee, and no-nonsense auditions were held. Before long, I was cast as the scatty maid in a farce by C.R. Dyer entitled *Wanted—One Body*. I wore a skimpy yellow nightdress and jumped in the air a lot. You might say that I made the part my own. To my delight, the same thing happened as at Brampton. I was very well received, as was the whole play, and I went from being an utter nobody straining round the place on my bike to the girl who had been so funny in the play. Everybody started being nice to me; at work I was forgiven for being useless and, once again, I saw the extraordinarily affectionate way in which a clown can come to be regarded. It was mesmerising and, before long, I decided that I would do my best to become some sort of actor when I went home. I began to write to drama schools in England and to pore excitedly over each prospectus as it arrived, only to feel deflated that so much emphasis was placed upon classical drama, which I did not feel drawn to at all. I just had a longing to be funny, to make people laugh. Reading the various prospectuses, my ambition began to seem insufficient and puny. Nobody taught what I wanted to learn.

Additionally, after a time I began to realise that the parts I could play in any production were pretty limited. I was cast as the concierge in the farce *Boeing Boeing*, but my French accent was embarrassing, I couldn't shine and fell flat in the part. I wanted to succeed as an entertainer and from somewhere had acquired a steady conviction that I could, but the problem was clear: I did not have the right things to say.

Every Friday we had a club night at Seletar, which I looked forward to as a combination of lovely things. The weekend was upon us, we sat outside on the rattan chairs under the great nearness of the moon, a makeshift entertainment was put on and the *satay* man came. Now *satay* can be bought in the supermarket but then it was exotic and gloriously foreign. The *satay* man dispensed long wooden skewers with a highly seasoned, meaty brown nugget on one end. Before eating, it was dabbled in the accompanying puddle of peanut sauce. It never bothered me that the meat could have been absolutely anything.

We would then take up our drinks and file into the auditorium. One by one people would get up and perform something, possibly a serious speech from Shakespeare to make us think, a couple of people acting out a Peter Cook and Dudley Moore sketch, a one-act play, anything. The atmosphere was companionable and friendly. Anybody could take part and I sat in the theatre burning, raging, to get up and have a go.

A popular book at that time was a compilation of entertaining snippets entitled *Verse and Worse*. I searched through it repeatedly, desperate to find something that suited my voice, something I could put over despite having a dense country accent and, more importantly, something that I found genuinely funny. I could find very little. At last, like a ray of brightness beaming through the cobwebbed gloom, the answer occurred to me. Why not try to write something myself? Something tailor-made? Not some speech borrowed from a posh, drawing-room comedy in a world I knew nothing about, but something uniquely my own, the voice of Stanford! It was worth a go.

I wrote a piece entitled 'Foolish Brother Luke', sparked off because I overheard a comment about someone eating a banana in its skin. For the sake of an accurate record, I reproduce it below.

Foolish Brother Luke

And as the cock crew, brave undaunted sound,
Rocks from off his head were seen to bound
And at the hour of dawn by luck or fluke,
Arose the form of Foolish Brother Luke.

Now Foolish Brother Luke, he had no sense,
He never listened to his good parents,
But places rough and low did oft frequent,
On alcohol and sordid pleasure bent.

One day Alas, he met his Waterloo,
For Luke he had no sense like me or you,
There he sat upon his own dustbin,
Eatin' a banana, in its skin.

Sittin' on a bin across the road,
There lounged the form of Schemin' Annie Toad,
She knew he had some money, cause she'd seen,
Him in the dirty places where he'd been.

Pattin' all her curlers into place,
And rubbin' cochineal upon her face,
She crossed the road to Luke and said 'How do,
Foolish Brother Luke, I fancy you!'

He choked on his banana, and he fell,
From off his bin a-cryin' 'Bloody Hell!
At last it's happened like I knew it would,
Come inside and have some . . . Christmas pud!'

For Foolish Brother Luke was not so soft,
He'd pondered long up in his bedroom loft,
He knew she had some money, cause he'd seen,
Her in the dirty places where she'd been.

But what Luke did not know, poor foolish lad,
Annie Toad was mistress to his dad
What Annie did not know by luck or fluke,
Was that her mum was not averse to Luke

Annie Toad had blackmailed poor Luke's dad
To name her in his will and so he had,
But Luke to Annie's mum had done the same
So who, or why, or what was there to blame?

And so they wed, the gay misguided pair,
Throwin' all their money in the air,
But yet, a word of warning needed here . . .
They were struck by lightning.

Please don't judge it too harshly; it was my very first attempt at a performance piece. I wrote it to proclaim on Friday nights in Seletar Theatre Club and it went down very well, although the audience was understandably poleaxed by the final line. I felt relieved, immensely so. I wasn't going to spend any more time searching through other people's efforts for something to say; in future, if I wanted something to perform, I was going to write it myself.

Another idea struck me. A friend of mine at the club constantly repeated the same phrase: 'Well, this is the thing you see.' What made him keep saying it I don't know; nerves perhaps, or shyness, but it was deeply irritating. My opening gambit to him could have been anything at all, but his reply would always begin with the same old 'Well, this is the thing you see'. I steeled myself for it. It became infuriating enough to be funny in a perverse sort of way, and I wondered if I could get some humour out of the awful predictability, out of the fact you knew it was coming. I wrote it up and fiddled about with it, emerging finally with an effort entitled 'Like You Would'. This was a better piece to perform, less long-winded and eliciting more laughs from my Seletar audience. I was pleased with my hobby. Life was jogging along very nicely indeed.

*   *   *

The armed forces did not like their servicemen and women to be bored; an assortment of sports and activities was constantly on offer. In line with this, one day applications were invited for a course in Jungle Survival. This immediately appealed to me and I put my name down. Already I could see myself, sweat stained and heroic in the stifling heat, slashing my way through dense thickets with a coconut in one hand and a machete in the other. The great advantage of being hopeless at my plotting job was that any application by me to go somewhere else was granted with relief by my bosses. I was given permission and set off for RAF Changi and the School of Jungle Survival some twenty miles away on the east coast.

I remember the school as thatched buildings in a compound encircled by thatched walls; here and there were clumps of dry, rasping bamboo. As soon as our small group sat down in the classroom, a large liquid-filled jar was placed before us. It contained leeches. 'You'll spend a lot of time picking these off your legs,' announced the instructor matter-of-factly. I looked at them with revulsion. Long and slug-like, they were suspended in the water, their blackness only alleviated by two white fangs like little hard triangles in the mouth.

Outside we constructed various sorts of shelter from great big leaves or layers of little ones. It was exciting; I felt like a pioneer and looked forward to the actual trek in the more jungly parts of Johor. Alas, I was unable to go. As the date approached, I was admitted to the sick quarters with tonsillitis and a temperature of 104. Frog-like, I sat in bed nursing massively swollen glands while enviously picturing my friends wading through the jungle with leeches excitingly attached.

There was another snag to being hospitalised. I had acquired a couple of boyfriends with one not necessarily being aware of the other. Being confined, I could not escape when they both appeared at visiting time and sat sizing each other

273

up from opposite sides of the bed. Each one wanted to be the last to leave; they glared at each other as the hours passed. It was awful. For some reason, Singapore and my tonsils did not get on. On several occasions, I was admitted to the sick quarters, shuffling in with a ferocious temperature and agonisingly swollen throat. One of the scant advantages to this situation was that one of the boyfriends lent me a tape recorder of gargantuan size, complete with headphones and several tapes of *The Goon Show*. I found them hilarious and sat shaking with laughter. It was a sad little ward, often occupied by the silent, grey-faced wives of RAF personnel, grieving women who had suffered miscarriages and who, suddenly, could no longer look forward to the arrival of their baby. The sight of me in my nightdress cackling with laughter must have been the last thing they needed.

I have forgotten what I learned at the School of Jungle Survival. I can no longer build a waterproof shelter out of leaves or offer advice on the disengagement of leeches from the calves, but something I saw there has stayed with me my whole life. One day, crossing the compound, I looked up and saw on the horizon the brutal bulk of Changi Jail. British-built, the gaunt shape rose starkly up out of endless greenery. I had no clue what it was, but the sight of it actually frightened me. It was so enormous, so monstrously different from the gentle little buildings nearby, and it seemed to exhale a sense of ghastly foreboding and menace.

There, after the fall of Singapore in 1942, the victorious Japanese army crammed 3000 civilians into space for 600. Though not routinely used for military prisoners of war, the name of Changi Jail came to stand for all the prisoner of war camps in that area at that time, and for the barbaric cruelty that prevailed in them. Its name is synonymous with the suffering, starvation, overcrowding and disease endured by prisoners both in Singapore, and by those who were sent out from it to wretched deaths as slave labourers on the Burma Railway, and heartless destinations elsewhere.

One day I went to Kranji War Cemetery, which is on the north coast overlooking the Straits of Johor where I had sailed in the Osprey, delighting in my youth and fitness. I had never been to a war cemetery before. Kranji is the final resting place for Allied soldiers who died during the Battle of Singapore and the Japanese occupation of 1942–45. I walked among the immaculate white headstones, reading the heartbreaking inscriptions. Some of the boys were only seventeen. I was twenty years old; they hadn't even lived as long as me.

*   *   *

My initial interest in going to Singapore came about because I met a bold, confident, funny girl called Annie Cummings in 1966 at Brampton. Newly returned from a two-year posting to Seletar, she dazzled me and I longed to be like her. By comparison, I was a jelly, cautious and nervous, afraid of the consequences of things. She had a way of grasping life by the scruff of the neck and shaking every opportunity out of it. While in the Far East, she had travelled alone to Vietnam, Laos, Thailand and Cambodia, ecstatically soaking up the sights and the culture. She was knowledgeable as many travelled people are

275

knowledgeable, and afraid of no one. She laughed at the high-ranking officers I was so cowed by, and they laughed back. A young man I had been infatuated with for two years, whom I pined over daily and hoped might one day notice me, saw her and was immediately besotted. His aloofness evaporated; he watched her with cow-like, tragic longing and was pitifully tongue-tied in her presence. There was a certain satisfaction in this for me. I knew how he felt; I had felt the same about him. Seeing him now stripped of his superior manner and prostrated by unrequited love was a great consolation to me. It evened things up. He lost some of his gloss.

Whatever I did when I was in Singapore, I was conscious that it fell far short of what Annie Cummings would have achieved. I could never have been courageous enough to set off to neighbouring countries *on my own* like her. Yes, I was brave by the standards of people I had left at home in Stanford, but measured by another yardstick I failed to take advantage of my geographical location; I was too frightened of leaving the safe Britishness of Seletar to explore in the true sense.

On a rare philosophical note, I have found that this situation recurs in life; lurking in the background at every triumph is an Annie Cummings figure who did it before you and twice as well.

I did, however, apply for some flights. You could let it be known that you would like the experience of flying and the two requests I made swiftly resulted in invitations. The first flight was in a great, square-bellied Beverley aircraft that was dropping supplies 'up-country' on the Malay

Peninsula. Good-looking aircrew strapped me to the strong interior ribs of the aircraft (this had a certain dark appeal) and we were off! Once over the dropping zone the mighty back door was opened to reveal a bright wheeling rectangle of sunlit vegetation and blue sky. Below us was a group of tiny figures in a lime-green clearing; massive roped crates were shoved out of the back of the plane to take their chances as they plummeted down. It was very exciting.

I asked if I could have a flight in one of the Wessex helicopters, and again an invitation was quickly forthcoming. I was given an olive-green flying suit to wear, a thing of unbelievable glamour with clear-fronted map pockets down the legs. A colossal helmet was planted on my head and I was strapped into the open doorway with my map-pocketed legs dangling over the side. The rotors of the Wessex started up, the noise grew tremendous and the aircraft lifted off ever so gently from the ground; I was charmed. In this hovering position, the nose dipped down and the tail raised up. Suddenly, to my consternation, the thing shot forward at speed and I squeaked in alarm and excitement, unaware that a mike was incorporated into the helmet and the crew could hear me. 'Are you all right?' asked a languid voice in my ears. 'You haven't fallen out?'

I was so happy. I was happier than I had ever been in my life. The days were packed with sunshine and interesting activities of every sort. My tightly constrained life in Stanford and my Bicester job looked almost frightening in retrospect; a joyless, grey treadmill, which had squandered years full of potential. In Seletar I walked down to the theatre club in the evenings to meet my friends, and in my heart was a sensation of being utterly overjoyed, full and flowing with happiness. I had no clue that it was all about to come to an abrupt end.

*   *   *

I had long legs and could run. I represented the Far East Air Force at various athletics meetings, but was annihilated at the Dover Road Stadium by a phenomenal sprinter named Glory Barnabus. The capacity of the human body to acclimatise to radically different climates astounded me. When I first arrived and sat in the airport bus holding my hair up from the back of my neck in the infernal heat, the idea of *running* was unthinkable. Yet, after a year had passed, it seemed fairly normal.

Eight miles north of Kuala Lumpur lay the Batu Caves, an astonishing network of caves and caverns that tower to breathtaking, cathedral-like height, and are of immense religious significance. The main cave is lit by daylight filtering in from roof openings but underneath it is Dark Cave, two kilometres in length and utterly devoid of light. By unfathomable means, I was included in a party sent to map Dark Cave. This entailed a long road journey north up the Malay Peninsula, and the highways at that time were in a dismal condition. Only the tarmac crown remained intact; the sides had crumbled and fallen away, leaving a central carriageway the width of one car. The road was dusty and the traffic madly crowded like some hellish stock-car race. As we went north from Johor Bahru there was a collision behind us in the mass of speeding vehicles. Looking out of the back window of our car, I saw a billowing cloud of red

278

dust shoot up over the highway. In an almost leisurely fashion, a car rose into the air, somersaulting over and over before crashing down into the haze of dust and debris. People must have been dying but our driver did not falter: we sped on to Kuala Lumpur.

We were kitted up in boots, and helmets fitted with miners' lamps, to explore Dark Cave. I felt pioneering and bold but, once inside, my nonchalance evaporated. It is sobering to encounter total darkness; to be sightless in the silence with velvet blackness all around. However, on switching on our lamps and shining them upwards, we found the light reflected back in the eyes of countless bats clinging to every part of the cave roof, as if it was studded with tiny, lit-up marbles. Underfoot was the treacherous greasiness of *guano,* centuries of bat droppings coating the floor to a great depth.

The furthest I journeyed was to Penang in the north of Malaysia, travelling with a friend by sleeper train. It was the habit of the steward to knock gently on the door of the carriage in the mornings and leave a cup of tea with a plantain, or small banana, in the saucer. The train wended its way through a continuous landscape of rubber plantations pierced by high wooded crags. On all sides were rows of slim trees, precisely planted, each with a slanted cut chiselled out of the trunk and little attached tin cup to catch the white latex as it oozed forth.

Our destination in Penang was Sandycroft, a leave centre for service personnel and their families. Inexpensive and idyllic, it was positioned on the seashore with chalets, jolly sunshades and a swimming pool. The lurking presence of highly venomous stonefish in the balmy ocean was the only drawback. These creatures, near invisible in their wondrous camouflage, are exceedingly dangerous if accidentally stood on. Stark notices along the beach announced the likelihood of paralysis followed by death, which dispelled the holiday mood somewhat. I stood on something, I don't know what it was, and fled the sea with a weal of stinging white blisters encircling my foot. Fortunately for poetry-lovers everywhere, I did not die.

A popular excursion was to Penang Hill to the west of Georgetown. This old hill station was also once known as Flagstaff Hill because here the British flag was once routinely raised to signify the arrival of mail. On greased teeth and oily cables, a mighty funicular railway climbed to the very top, rewarding passengers with spectacular, far-reaching views from the summit. It was a happy holiday and, at its conclusion, we boarded the train south for Singapore and journeyed back to Seletar. On Monday morning, I cheerfully rode my bike over the runway to our office, and strolled in to work where a bombshell awaited. It had been decided that the place was overstaffed. Christine and I, the two WRAF plotters, were to be sent home.

My posting to Singapore had lasted about fourteen months, just over half the two years I had expected. I was having the most action-packed and glorious time. The last thing on earth I wanted was to go home to England. I was aghast, shocked, heartbroken. My boyfriend took me to MacRitchie Reservoir, which I loved, and I cried a lot.

I hated Christine because she had never liked being out there and was quietly delighted. 'It's all

With my new sister-in-law Cynthia, at the marriage of Jean and Ginge in St Denys Church, 1965.

My sister Jean and her new husband Malcolm (Ginge) Hall.

Taken for a WRAF recruitment brochure at RAF Brampton. I am being presented with a beribboned blank piece of paper.

Wearing tropical
uniform outside our
drawing office, Seletar.

Part of RAF Seletar camp.

At Tiger Balm
Gardens,
or Haw
Par Villa,
Singapore.

Running for
the Far East
Air Force,
Seletar,
Singapore.

On a Singapore
gun
emplacement,
looking for
Stanford in
the Vale.

With fag in Dark
Cave, Batu Caves,
Kuala Lumpur,
1966.

Playing my guitar
at Changi
Folk Club.

As Mabel Middy in the comedy *Wanted—One Body* by C.R. Dyer, Singapore.

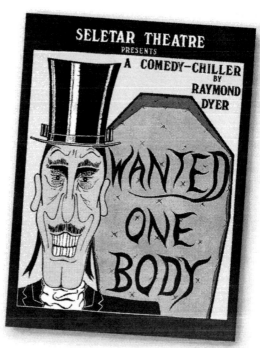

Programme for *Wanted—One Body.*

Seated next to the pipe-smoker, Smiths Industries of Witney.

Frozen but cheerful, Tryfan, North Wales

The folk singer. Note restrained collar.

My mother, Phyllis Evelyn Ayres, at Newquay in Cornwall.

Preparing to declaim in a Music Hall Night at Burford Grammar School.

My four excellent brothers. From left: Jeff, Roger, Allan and Tony.

The Entire Collection (Eight)
of
Masterpieces

by

Pam Ayres

(including 'The Battery Hen')

My first pamphlet *The Entire Collection (Eight) of Masterpieces by Pam Ayres*, printed in 1974.

Appearing on *Opportunity Knocks*, 1975.

so artificial,' she would say, 'It's just not real life.' This was a valid viewpoint but was precisely why I loved it so much; my own real life had been unutterably drab and this had been like stepping into the light. We had been friends but now we avoided each other and were monosyllabic.

I don't know why we were repatriated. I certainly wasn't much good as a plotter, but Christine was fantastic; people queued up to bring their jobs to her. We were just told that the MOD, as part of general cost cutting, had concluded that we had more staff than was necessary to do the work. That may well have been so, but the presence of WRAF girls must have been a continual headache to those in charge; it was costly and time-consuming to protect us, fence us in and provide a special, female-only NAAFI where we could eat and socialise. Moreover, one of the girls had recently been sent home. At that racially divided time she had fallen in love with a black man. Tiny, scandalised whispers circulated that she was having his baby and suddenly she was gone, whisked home, discharged and vanished in an instant. A WRAF presence meant that those situations would inevitably arise and have to be resolved; how much more straightforward to simply ship in identically qualified men. I could see all the logic of course, especially as my contribution to the work of our office had been a resounding zero.

In due course, a large wooden crate arrived to ship my belongings home. Seeing it, with its rough planks and rope handles, was like a blow, a gash. It confirmed the separation. I sadly placed into it a green-husked coconut signed with good-luck messages from my friends. Seasick, it would leak over my treasures on the way home.

I celebrated my twenty-first birthday at a riotous party given by the theatre club crowd. They gave me lovely presents including a St Christopher for a safe journey, and with my heart in my boots I prepared to return to England. My goods were packed. A soldier came, bound my crate with tight metal bands for its long sea journey home and took it away. I walked out of the WRAF block when the frangipani and hibiscus were in fierce bloom and went with my friends to Paya Lebar Airport and its wretchedly slave-built runway. I boarded one of the new VC10 aircraft and was astonished by the force as it roared down the runway and into the sky. At that time people could sit on the grass nearby, as there was no security. I waved out of the window to my knot of friends on the green embankment, but I knew they couldn't see me.

A golden, sunlit period had come to an end. I looked out of the window at the whole of the island of Singapore below the aircraft. I swore to myself that by some means or other, I would go back and in time I did, but by then all I held dear had vanished. The old scenes had been swept impatiently aside, and modernity reigned.

*   *   *

After refuelling stops at Gan and RAF Akrotiri in Cyprus, we landed at Lyneham and I looked back at the aircraft as I disembarked. It was called *Bounteous*. Mum was waiting with Tony and seemed overjoyed to see me. I felt awful, *awful*, and was wrestling with my feelings in the most terrible turmoil because *I didn't want to be there*. I loved Mum dearly of course, and all my terrific

282

family who gathered to welcome me home, but seeing them could not compensate me for what I felt I had lost. I grieved for my beautiful home on the far side of the world.

Our family often took a summer holiday in Newquay, Cornwall. Mum loved the place and adored every minute, revelling in the spectacular coastline, lavish beaches and buttery-yellow ice-cream. A holiday had been arranged as I arrived home from Singapore and, with typical kindness, I had been included. I found it desperately hard because I had seen and done such marvellous things while I was away. I loathed myself for my ungrateful, traitorous feelings but Newquay didn't measure up. Acclimatised to a country on the Equator, I was perished with cold and shocked rigid by the freezing temperature of the sea. Our family didn't have much money and had booked a cheap rented house with cheap beds and cheap nylon sheets. No amahs came to sweep the floor. I felt cut down to size, shot down, like some once-exotic bird whose fine feathers had fallen out, and which was now forced to waddle the grey streets, bald.

At night, we all went down the pub. And nothing happened.

*   *   *

Though I could not have explained it to anybody, I still felt my future was bound up with performing, so I decided it would be a good idea to visit a theatre. On enquiring, I found that Newquay had one called The Cosy Nook, and as none of the family was that keen to go, I booked a solitary ticket for the Variety Show that evening. It was a

283

walk of some considerable distance from our rented house to The Cosy Nook, and being a little nervous of walking home through the darkened streets after the show, and in the absence of a companion, I took the bread-knife.

When I arrived for the performance, the place looked utterly deserted. I proffered my ticket and went in; me and the bread-knife took our seat. The Cosy Nook looked shockingly empty and cavernous. No more than seven people were dotted about the auditorium. I had only ever seen packed theatres, either at the pantomime or for the small amateur shows I had been involved with. The poor Cosy Nook had 553 seats, but it seemed that nobody wanted to come.

The gallant cast came on and did the show. Their songs, jokes and routines vanished into the void; it was pathetic. They took a bow to the applause of seven people, and trooped gloomily off the stage. I went home thoughtfully. It was the first time I had seen this other side of performing. It wasn't all acclaim and applause then. This was enough to break your heart. It made me think dejectedly about my own grand ambitions to be on stage. Clearly, it could go the other way. You could finish up on stage all right but it could be the stage at The Cosy Nook.

47

IN THE WILDERNESS

I went home to Vandiemans Road when the holiday was over and, at the end of my disembarkation leave, travelled reluctantly back to RAF Brampton. I had asked to be posted somewhere, *anywhere* else, but Brampton it was, and I soon found myself back in the office with barred windows, which I had left so jubilantly fifteen months before. The transient population of the RAF had reshuffled and moved on, so now I didn't know many people and the once-vibrant theatre club was dark and closed. Thus began a long period in the wilderness. It would be six years before a great dazzling light came shining into my darkness.

I hated my job and was grief-stricken about Singapore. I became a bore. All I could talk about was the Far East, which most other people had not seen and weren't interested in. There was an expression in the services to describe nostalgic, backward-looking people. They were known as 'When I's' because they had nothing to say about the present or the future; they talked only about the past, 'When I was in Cyprus' or 'When I was in Germany'. I had become a morose 'When I'. Not wishing to remain one, I decided on further self-improvement.

Now having proudly passed four, I enrolled to take some more GCEs. I chose Geography and French and found myself sitting in a classroom beside a personable-looking sergeant. At that time I never believed in buying something yourself if you could borrow it from somebody else, and I kept asking for a loan of his ruler. I don't know if he read more into this than I intended, but one afternoon he asked me out and from this unpromising start I acquired a new boyfriend called Jeremy who had a Triumph Herald. We used to go out for nice rides to Grafham Water, the

285

tarted-up name for what had previously been drably entitled Diddington Reservoir, now much enlarged to slake the voracious thirst of Milton Keynes. Eternally hard up, I saw nothing untoward in wearing open-toed sandals in January; he was horrified and bought me a pair of beautiful furry boots in Huntingdon. Every time I see the town mentioned I get a warm furry feeling in the feet.

Jeremy belonged to a little performing group, which put on revues for local pensioners. It was called The Parkside Players and was run by a roguish bloke known to all as Dad Godfrey. I went along with my boyfriend to watch and before long was cast in a preposterously melodramatic Victorian sketch entitled 'The Grip of Iron' in which I was throttled on a nightly basis by an unconvincing cloaked villain named Russ. I had bought myself a better guitar by this time and written a somewhat risqué song entitled 'The Pregnant Again Blues'. Dad Godfrey heard it and put it into the show. Another girl sang a couple of songs from the musicals, Dad Godfrey played a topical calypso-type number, somebody said a few jokes and while it would not have won any awards, the pensioners had a nice enough evening.

I did not know what to make of Dad Godfrey. One night he asked me to help him put on an entertainment in the officers mess at Brampton. I took my guitar and went along. When I arrived he gave me sheets on which he had written new words to my song, and he asked me to sing those instead, just for that one evening. Ever gullible, I agreed. I sang the song including all the names and references he had given me, while not having a clue what it was really about. The men fell about with laughter at what were obviously inside jokes;

286

but it was an ugly sort of laughter I didn't like. It was an unpleasant evening, particularly as Dad Godfrey promised me £1 for going and only gave me ten bob, which was half.

My strangulating friend Russ was more youthful and fresh. He gave me a gift, a copy of the Flanders and Swann revue entitled 'At the Drop of a Hat' and I listened avidly to the witty songs. They seemed posh and some of the subject matter went over my head, but the clever selection and deft placement of words impressed me very much.

I did not feel the need to seek out any more folk singing after the tepid reception my efforts received at Seletar Folk Club. When, during that summer of 1968, a friend offered to take me to the Red Cow Folk Club in Cambridge, I agreed rather half-heartedly and ungraciously, not expecting much.

Once there I was knocked out, bowled over, besotted. We were in an upstairs room painted a fruity red, lit by candles stuck into bottles where years' worth of wax had run down the sides to form grotesque shapes. The place was jam-packed with young people amid a huge, buoyant sense of expectation.

Somebody enormous got up to sing; it may have been Noel Murphy with his great, wonderful Irish voice, I can't remember. People you would not have looked at twice out in the street got up and sang spectacular songs on different instruments or none. Some songs were rollicking, some funny, some poignant and beautiful enough to break your heart. There were brand new, freshly written songs and others as old as time. I couldn't get over the confidence, skill and boldness of the performers and the astonishing range of feelings they could make you feel.

That night I became an avid fan and came to love this bringing of people's talents to the forefront for the enjoyment of all. Here was an amazing tapestry of skills: people who could play instruments, had great voices or an encyclopaedic knowledge of songs and the ability to put them over in a hundred different ways. All those skills fused to benefit the crowd; they could laugh, be saddened or join in with some deafening, ridiculous chorus. My first night at the Red Cow pub in Cambridge was unforgettable. I couldn't wait to go again.

*   *   *

Back at Brampton as the cold winter came on, I applied for a detachment to RAF Rheindahlen in Germany. I had several reasons for doing this. Having returned to Brampton, I felt stranded, marooned; I couldn't settle down. Secondly, my sister Jean and her soldier husband, Lance Corporal Malcolm Hall, known to all as Ginge due to his red hair, had been posted to Sennelager near Paderborn in Germany and my sister was newly delivered of a daughter. I wanted to see mother and baby very much. In due course, the detachment was confirmed and I flew to Germany in thick snow at Christmas. There was a wild blizzard of snow against the aircraft windows as we tried time and time again to land. In the end, the pilot gave up, made instead for some distant airfield unaffected by snow and landed there. To get back, I endured the multiple delights of a freezing coach journey of many hours' duration in the small hours of the morning while starving

288

hungry. *'Wilkommen!'* I thought, as we finally drove into the gates of RAF Rheindahlen.

I worked in a huge building known as The Big House. On first entering it, I was taken aback to see German civilian women in grotesque masks accosting and flinging their arms round reluctant-looking men. I was told this was the observance of a custom, which said that a woman could choose any man, and he could not refuse her on that particular day. The women's masks were gruesome and hag-like; it was a strange introduction to working in a new country.

I liked being in Germany. We were close to the border with The Netherlands, and, in the pleasant town of Venlo, I shopped in a department store with the slightly unfortunate name of V & D. Invited to stay with a married WRAF friend living in Cologne, I accepted and stood on the paved street marvelling at the spectacular cathedral. I was also planning my trip to see Jean in Paderborn. All this was more like it. At twenty-one years old, I was getting around; seeing new places, meeting new people. Maybe I wasn't a 'When I' after all.

I was quite good at falling hopelessly in love with the wrong bloke; I did it all the time. Though I had left a perfectly nice boyfriend at home in England, I began to notice an attractive army officer who came into our office from time to time wearing a wide leather Sam Browne belt or a beautiful soft grey Crombie overcoat. With his shiny brown hair and dark eyes, I found him completely disarming, particularly as he was recovering from being injured, and limped. I imagined the weight of him leaning lightly on my arm. My letters to the perfectly nice boyfriend grew less frequent and more terse.

At work, I found myself constantly watching the door, hoping he would appear. If he did, then the contradiction and sheer awfulness of being infatuated leapt up. The moment he walked in and smiled pleasantly at me, I was robbed of any ability to act rationally. I went red. Not some delicate rose pink but a lurid scarlet, like eyes in a raw steak. Neither, if he had offered some pleasantry regarding the weather, could I have possibly answered him. I couldn't get my breath. My pulse raced. Any normal, even-toned speech was out of the question. I would have gasped at him wordlessly like a flounder. It was a kind of madness. I so wanted to impress him; instead I looked like a halfwit, like a boiled woman having a seizure. It was so unfair. To my dismay, during the three months I was there, he became engaged to somebody else. People congratulated him as the announcement appeared in *The Telegraph*. I was stricken, and for years, in a leather Sam Browne belt and soft grey Crombie overcoat, he limped through my fantasies.

My sister Jean was living with her husband and new daughter Stella in army married quarters in Sennelager near the town of Paderborn in North Rhine-Westphalia. A few months before my own arrival in Rheindahlen, I had taken it upon myself to squire Mum out from England to visit Jean, who was then seven months pregnant. This had been a classic case of the blind leading the blind as I steered the two of us inexpertly across Germany aided only by a phrase book, extravagant gestures and a sense of wild optimism. Remarkably, we arrived without mishap and it was lovely for the three women of the family to be together again. We had an interesting time, visited the sad, famous, Mohne and Eder dams which had been bombed in the World War II 'dam buster' raids, and explored the local area.

However, when the time came for Mum and me to depart, it was terrible to leave Jean to have her first baby so far from Stanford and the plentiful loving support of the combined Ayreses. It was heartbreaking for Mum. As the train drew out of Paderborn Station, she waved and waved to the forlorn pregnant figure on the platform, then collapsed back into the seat and cried in a defeated way that was utterly harrowing.

Therefore, as I now packed my bags in Rheindahlen I was very excited about seeing my sister again and exceedingly smug that I was going to be the first of our family to admire the new baby. I set off alone to Paderborn, a journey of just over a hundred miles, and was wandering around the night-dark streets in a baffled fashion when her husband Ginge loomed up and took me to their home in Sennelager.

Jean didn't look as I expected her to look. She was quiet, subdued, and different. Clearly, she was not very well. A gentle, reticent village girl, she had found adjusting to life in married quarters in Germany very difficult, and had come to feel increasingly isolated. She was delighted with Ginge, her husband, but he was a soldier who had to do what the army told him to do; he was often away. Having gone into labour, Jean had been taken the forty-odd miles to the British Military Hospital at Rinteln on her own by Land Rover. On arrival, all accommodation in the maternity unit was full, so she was left alone on a stretcher in a side room. Still unattended, she reached the final pushing stage of labour and had to shout and call for help. Shocked that she was so far on, and having no labour ward available, the midwives took Jean into a large, unheated room *with marble tables*, which she believed to be a mortuary or autopsy area. The baby was delivered in these freezing conditions. Ginge was away and unable to reach her until late the following night, by which time she was distraught.

On leaving the hospital, Jean felt increasingly ill and was diagnosed with flu. She began to feel exhausted and overwhelmed by feelings of dread; a constant fearfulness she could not explain. Unable to eat, sleep or relax and now with a baby to care for, my sister suffered from the worst sort of post-natal depression at a time when the illness did not even have a name. An army welfare official came to visit Jean and, ludicrously, recommended 'a nice meal out with her husband'. Of us two sisters, she was the one who had always longed for a baby, who could not wait to start a family of her own. The isolation and harsh conditions surrounding the birth had set her back, struck her down with a condition no one talked about, an illness that was written off as a kind of shameful inability to cope.

I was young and self-centred. I didn't really take on board what my sister was going through. One day there was a heavy snowfall; Ginge and I went outside and mucked about in the snow. At one point one of us fell over and stood up, face completely caked and covered in snow. We were doubled up and shrieking with laughter. Unbeknown to us Jean was watching out of the window, grief-stricken that an illness she didn't understand, and could not get help for, prevented her from joining in, from laughing in the snow with her husband and new baby.

48

LEAVING THE WRAF

As my three-month detachment in Germany drew to a close in March 1969, so too did my four-year engagement with the WRAF. I thought about staying on, but not for long. The prospect of spending any more years as a failed plotter was deeply unattractive; the only thing that would have persuaded me to stay was more overseas travel. I gloomily concluded that none was likely to come my way. During my four years in the WRAF I had received two much sought-after overseas postings to Singapore and Germany. Many of my friends had gone nowhere, remaining at Brampton throughout. Considering that the chances of being chosen again were therefore remote, I decided to leave and strike out at something new.

An RAF sergeant in our office in Rheindahlen, telling me he had a friend looking for a secretary, arranged a lunchtime meeting at a restaurant for the three of us. The friend, a substantially obese German, turned up in a vast Mercedes and for lunch bought me a plateful of black venison, the first time I had ever eaten it. Oh yes, he assured me, he was looking for a secretary and would provide her with a nice little flat in Dortmund. The work wouldn't be onerous.

I studied the flabby man as he shovelled venison into his chops. 'In your dreams, mush,' I thought.

My longing to be on the stage was ever-present but without direction. I frequently studied the prospectuses I had received from various drama schools in England. I liked the look of the Rose Bruford School in Kent very much, but felt I lacked the right sort of motivation. I had no desire to be an empty vessel, to inhabit characters and speeches written by somebody else. I wanted to be myself, to say things I had written *for myself.*

I arrived back at Brampton after three months in Germany and let myself into my room. With four years' service I now qualified for a single room of my own. Once in, I realised with disgust that I had forgotten to strip off my sheets before I flew to Germany, and the bed was as I had left it. After three winter months without heat, the bed was not so much damp as wet. Having no choice, I got into it. I felt friendless, adrift. I couldn't wait to leave.

The RAF provided resettlement courses to help prepare people for civilian life at the end of their service. In line with this, I began to pore over the courses available, and felt a great surge of interest when I saw one offered on Creative Writing. Approaching the Flight Lieutenant in charge of our office, I asked if I might be considered for inclusion, saying untruthfully that I hoped it would help me to write better business letters in the new secretarial jobs I intended to seek. Permission was given, along with a rail warrant to get me to Aylesbury and details of how to find a place nearby named Missenden Abbey.

I thought it was so beautiful. Built in 1133, it was a pale, gentle building with a castellated roof, set in soft lawns and seen through the flake-like horizontal boughs of Lebanese cedars. After the spartan nature of the RAF accommodation I was used to, my room seemed exquisite, the curvaceous arch of the window giving out on to wide, beguiling views of the garden. I was sold; I fell for the place.

A playwright named James Parish tutored our creative writing course; he had written three plays but was not particularly well known. I liked him. He was bald, rounded, elderly and pleasant. In a book-lined, ancient room, he taught our group of eight or nine and I was as happy as I had ever been. I felt in my element.

James Parish suggested interesting things. He handed round photographs of random subjects and invited us to write stories based on what we saw. I loved this; it was an opportunity to invent people and places and tension and romance, and I tore into it. Other people looked at their photos and groaned, saying they didn't know what to write. 'What are you doing here?' I thought crossly. 'Why bother to come?'

At other times, James would give us a first line to start us off and we would have to write it up into another story. He gave me an opening line about a circus, and I got cracking with a gripping account of two male trapeze artists who were both having an affair with the female trapeze artist, but the two men didn't know about one another's involvement until just before the show. Come the night of the grand performance in the Big Top, as the two men extended their dry, resinned hands to catch each other in mid-air, one, while emitting a maniacal cackle, let the other drop to the sawdust floor where every bone in his body was buckled and broken. I could hear the horrified gasp of the crowd! I could see the dark blood spread and soak the yellow sawdust! I was transported! What a story! The fevered scratching of my fountain pen could be heard all round the room. I glanced up and saw people looking at me strangely.

I could write a world and enter it; it became real to me. That course represented the first time I had been actively helped to do it, where everything was in place, the environment, tuition and atmosphere all conducive to people writing creatively and at their best.

I adored the course and did not want to leave. At the end of it, James Parish asked to see me for a chat. I went into the book-lined room. I was twenty-two and brash; he was elderly and thoughtful. I never forgot a word of what he said; it was immense and magical to me. I felt as if I had come home, had finally, after countless blunders, finished up on the right path.

He said, 'You know, Miss Ayres, that you are a writer. You already have a style all your own, which is remarkable in such a young person.'

He asked me what I intended to do with my life and I mumbled about my vague aspirations to go to Drama School.

'How much money do you have?' he asked.

'A hundred pounds,' I replied, pleased with myself. The sum of my savings seemed substantial to me.

'It won't last five minutes,' he said firmly, kindly. 'Let me give you some advice.'

He told me to go away and read. Read everything I could lay my hands on, but particularly Somerset Maugham. Go to the library, find the *Writers' & Artists' Yearbook* to see who was looking for what, and keep writing. He said perfectly seriously, 'You go away from here, read all you can, write all you can and *one day you'll be a somebody.*'

I staggered out of the book-lined room, reeling. What he said knocked me sideways. Me! Ole

Pammie Ayres from Campdene, a *somebody*! A new sense of myself was taking shape. I could dare to think that although I had not come from a scholarly background, from what I perceived to be a *writer's* background, perhaps that didn't matter. Perhaps you could be a writer, a performer, or the strange amalgam of both which I seemed to be, regardless of where you started from.

James Parish inspired me. I went straight out and bought myself a portable blue Brother typewriter, and from the library borrowed the *Writers' & Artists' Yearbook* and a volume containing several novels by Somerset Maugham. I started to write stories in earnest and to send them off like confetti to magazines. I sold nothing but built up an impressive collection of rejection slips, which I fixed to the back of my door with drawing pins.

The day came and I quietly left Brampton. The place was deserted; everyone was at work. My brother Tony came to get me; he put my luggage and my blue typewriter in the boot of his Ford Popular and took me home to Vandiemans Road.

I knew that joining the RAF had been an unusual choice for a woman to make, but not necessarily a bad one for someone in my situation. I had travelled widely despite having no money, been exposed to a thousand new situations I would never otherwise have seen and, as Dad had poetically predicted, learned to sort out decent people from the other bastards. I rued being a plotter and wished it had been possible to escape into some secretarial job, say, where my high standard of English would have stood me in good stead, and where I might not have been a laughing-stock.

I also knew there were many people who believed that the women's services were a hotbed of lesbianism, considered scandalous at that time, but I never saw anything to reinforce that. Everyone I knew was mad about boys, some of whom on occasion were courageous or frantic enough to shin up a girl's drainpipe, enjoy a night of unbridled passion and descend looking shattered in the morning. I never once saw anything I recognised as romance between girls. There was a car at one time, a Mini, which used to park up outside the WRAF accommodation. When I passed it, going for my tea in the evening, I occasionally saw an older woman inside with a much younger girl. The older person would have her arm laid casually along the back of the young girl's seat, and they would be talking. If I thought about it at all, I supposed they were just friendly towards each other, or were perhaps sisters.

*   *   *

Back in Stanford, to the whole family's pleasure and excitement, my own sister Jean came home from Germany at the end of Ginge's tour, and now she was pushing their little daughter Stella in a bobby-dazzler of a Continental pram. It wasn't the traditional hard-bodied, steely British type at all, but softly upholstered in a bright red padded fabric with a jolly parasol. Vandiemans Road was agog. One neighbour entered into the spirit of the occasion and sourly observed 'No good if it gets hit by a car'.

We were so glad to have her home. Jean would walk up to see Mum in the afternoons and in the sunshine they would set up a paddling pool in the garden for the baby. Away from the German garrison town, back with her husband in their Stanford cottage, and engulfed in a tide of love and goodwill from the family, Jean started slowly to recover from her illness. From seeing my dear sister in this situation, I learned never to underestimate how devastating post-natal depression can be, how it can take over a person's view of life and sap their energy entirely. Because of Jean's illness Ginge left the army, although it was a life he loved and one in which he was keen and successful.

Later Jean and Ginge had another little daughter, this time with a spectacular shock of dark hair. She was named Tanya and this time no trace of illness came to cloud the family's horizon. Jean was well and the little family flourished in their home with the view of White Horse Hill.

49

ANTI-CLIMAX AT CLACTON

I now decided to apply for a job at Butlin's Holiday Camp. Yes indeed, Butlin's must be the place to try because hadn't many great names in the entertainment business started their careers there? They certainly had: Jimmy Tarbuck, Cliff Richard and Clinton Ford to name but three. I wrote off for the job, and to my delight was offered the post of receptionist at Butlin's Holiday Camp, Clacton-on-Sea. Sadly, this meant I would be a Bluecoat, a member of the administration staff, rather than one of the Redcoats who were there for the entertainment and jollification of the campers, but I felt confident that it was only a matter of time before my talent was recognised and I was invited to make the switch.

I had to wait a few weeks for the job to start at the commencement of the holiday season, and for this short period, I received unemployment benefit or 'the dole', which was a few pounds a week collected from the local post office. I was taken aback to discover that this inflamed the Stanford postmaster to incandescent fury. He threw the notes at me with the contemptuous, lip-curling observation: 'Money for old rope!'

In April 1969, my long-suffering boyfriend took me in his Triumph Herald to the rain-lashed shore of Clacton-on-Sea. We parked outside the forbidding gates of Butlin's Holiday Camp in all its out-of-season desolation. 'I'm sure I'll enjoy my visits to see you here,' he volunteered with a joviality neither of us felt. Laden down with my suitcases and typewriter, I said goodbye to him and made my way across the windswept tarmac and blasted flowerbeds of the deserted camp.

I was twenty-two, but as I joined the straggle of inductees, I felt older than the others. There seemed to be a high proportion of university students looking to fill in their summer vacation, earn a bit of money and have a laugh. They had a lot in common with each other. Not having a university background, I couldn't think of much to say and felt the odd one out.

We all assembled and were addressed by a Mr Eccles who had the air of an exhausted man about to climb a mountain. He wearily explained to his new staff that for the first few days everyone would have to muck in, doing whatever jobs were

300

necessary to ready the place for the first intake of campers due in a week. After that, we would be given training in our permanent jobs, in my case as a receptionist.

For the second time in my life, I was issued with a uniform, which this time consisted of a blue blazer and white skirt. I held the skirt up dubiously. It was a rectangle of thin white cloth with tape attached to the top corners; you wrapped it round yourself a few times and knotted the tapes. Mine was stained and holed with caramel-coloured iron mould.

An identity card was issued to me and I was taken to the shared chalet that would be my living accommodation. Before I could protest, the young man escorting me heaved my bags showily up on to his shoulder, misjudged it and let my new blue typewriter in its smart case drop like a stone on to the concrete. There was a ringing impact. It had been pristine and factory-fresh; now it was busted and beyond repair.

Inside the cramped wooden chalet were four bunk beds; torn blue curtains sported little coloured yachts. It was freezing, there was not enough bedding, and on that first bitter night a violent wind battered the flimsy chalet, driving rain through the yawning gap under the door. In cold puddles, it lay on the rough splintered floorboards and in the morning, climbing blearily out of bed after a hellish night, I found both feet planted in water. I could not believe how awful it was, how bleak and comfortless.

Reporting to Mr Eccles, he gestured towards a colossal number of new slop buckets, strewn and scattered on the muddy lawns. 'Take those,' he said to me, 'and put one in every chalet.' I gawped at him. Chalets disappeared in every direction. There seemed to be thousands of them, untold thousands in girly-pink and baby-blue, lining both sides of the little roads. Some were single storey, some stacked two or three high with precipitous staircases up and down. My legs started to ache just looking at the job. That first day I trudged about laden with buckets and an air of gloom. The second night was equally grim and after another day of bucket-lugging, I told Mr Eccles I was going home. He looked at me with scorn and slung me my cards. My boyfriend, with his teeth gritted, turned up at the iron gates and as he drove me the interminable distance back to Vandiemans Road, I fancied I could hear the combined derisive laughter of Clinton Ford, Jimmy Tarbuck and Cliff Richard.

I knew I hadn't given it a fair chance. I knew, if I'd had a bit of determination, that the sun would have come out, the floorboards would have dried up and I would have got to know my room-mates. Doubtless, the holidaymakers would have streamed in, breathing life and cheerfulness into the huge, empty carcase, but I was too far gone.

I just could not summon the effort to do the whole thing again. By and large, I had enjoyed the WRAF though it had been difficult at first, but it was finished, I had resigned. This seemed like a shoddy, second-rate copy, a repeat performance but with dirty uniform and horrible, cheerless accommodation. I ran home, my plans in tatters, with no idea what to do next. Mum was pleased to see me, and listened to my woes in her easy-going way. 'Ah, something'll turn up,' she said comfortingly, dishing up an extra meal for me, 'and your old bed's still upstairs.'

50

MORRIS RADIATORS

Many men travelled from the Stanford area to work in the vastness of the British Leyland Motor Corporation complex at Cowley. As an employer, it was hungry and unloved. Word would flash round the village that workers were needed, that Cowley was 'crying out' for blokes. The jobs were seen as a sad kind of bargain. It was possible to make good money only if you could stand the fluorescent-lit monotony, the repetitive assembly work on endless, slowly inching car lines. The Cowley Works was a grim, dark-coloured sprawl unleavened by green leaves. Its sirens wailed and drab-dressed men in their teeming thousands marched into the maw.

By 1969 my brother Roger was married and living in nearby Wolvercote. He worked at Morris Radiators, a smaller, kinder-looking factory feeding component parts into the main Cowley Works. Pleasantly situated behind the expensive, tree-lined streets of Woodstock Road, it adjoined a wide sports field and maintained a garden.

Knowing I was in need of a job, Roger kindly spoke to the personnel officer Mr Maltby and I was invited for an interview. I knew nothing about the place or what jobs were available but having failed at Butlin's, my savings were running out and I urgently needed work. I assumed it would be light assembly of some kind in the factory. I had never done it before and didn't relish the idea much, but I loved my brother Roger a lot and it was a bonus that I would see him every day. I warmed to Mr Maltby; he was old-fashioned and paternal. After the interview, to my surprise and great pleasure he offered me a job as a clerk-typist in the office. This was far more than I had expected; it bolstered my Butlin's-bludgeoned ego. On seeing Roger, he told him I was a bright girl, capable of something more than assembly-line work, and this bolstered it even more.

I looked around for somewhere to live and found a bedsitter in Stratfield Road in Summertown. It was in a typically Thirties-built, semi-detached house adapted for letting, containing numerous bedsitters and one bathroom. During the time I lived there, my fellow occupants comprised one older lady training to be an auxiliary nurse, a cookery demonstrator for the Gas Board and a former monk who having fallen in love had left his Order and was planning to marry. My room on the ground floor was clean and cold and for some reason reeked overpoweringly of mothballs. I bought a bunch of blue cornflowers and stood them in the fireplace where they looked puny.

In my new office, eyebrows were raised that I had been taken on as a typist when I had no qualifications; I had only done a few evening classes, and then used my paltry skill to type my own stories. After my typewriter met with its fatal accident in Clacton, I had stopped doing even that. It became clear that I didn't really know how to lay out business letters properly. I was nervous and inaccurate, knowing I was an imposter among the other properly trained and certified typists. At lunchtime, I would sit by a pond in the garden and ask the gardener about plants. I did not make many friends.

Rather belatedly, I enrolled for a course in shorthand and typing at a college of further education on the Oxpens Road. It was hard to get there and back because I couldn't afford a car. Additionally, I didn't know the layout or names of the streets in Oxford, so despite much squinting at minute timetables I was hopeless at figuring out when the next bus was coming and where it might be bound. I spent a lot of time traipsing home through the draughty city clutching a typing book and an instruction manual for Pitman shorthand.

Alone in Stratfield Road in the evenings I sat on the floor, leant back on the armchair and did endless shorthand drills. It was vital in order to develop speed to pen the squiggles faster and faster so that in the end you could comfortably keep up with a normal person's speech. I actually found it fascinating that by making the marks heavy or light, and by their placement high or low on the printed line, they could be made to clearly signify swathes of text, which would have taken hours to write longhand. I bought myself a proper shorthand fountain pen with flexible nib sensitive to the slightest pressure. Finding shorthand ingenious and pleasing, I sat on the floor and became adept.

Mum had instilled into Jean and me the value of industriousness. It was unusual for us to sit around doing nothing. If we were inactive we would placate our consciences by picking up and doing some knitting. At Stratfield Road, I knitted a massive woollen coat, possibly because I was so cold. It was an enormously complicated garment, densely patterned in a mind-enfeebling Aran design. Having finally finished it and sewed on the carefully chosen wooden buttons, I tried it on, disliked it, and never wore it once.

More fruitful was my decision to join Summertown library and to start reading in earnest, as James Parish had advised me at Great Missenden. I read *The Hobbit* and *Lord of the Rings*. I also borrowed Ernest Raymond's extraordinary and harrowing novel *We, the Accused*, the memory of which stayed with me for a very long time.

I knew that at home in Stanford Mum was bored by the monotonous routine of life, and that she loved all new experiences. Now that I had a small Oxford base, I arranged a few outings. The plan was that I would meet her from the bus at Gloucester Green terminus, we'd do something interesting, she would stay overnight with me at Stratfield Road and I would see her safely back on the bus to Stanford in the morning. All looked set fair.

I was aware that Mum as a young woman had admired the glamorous, beauty-spotted actress Margaret Lockwood. Noticing that a play she was appearing in was about to be featured at Oxford's New Theatre, I bought two tickets so that Mum could actually see her favourite in person. Unfortunately, like The Cosy Nook in Newquay some time before, the great yawning auditorium was virtually empty. The play was long and thin, and Margaret Lockwood, though game, looked depressingly less dewy than in her heyday. Finally arriving back at my bedsitter, Mum was horrified by the never-explained pungent smell of mothballs and couldn't wait to get outside in the morning to breathe free. It was not a resounding success.

On another occasion, Mum gallantly came back

and we went to see *Gone with the Wind*, a film she had rhapsodised about all through my childhood. When newly released in 1939, it was a groundbreaking epic of massive scope and scale, which rocked the world of cinema. Mum saw it in the freshness of her youth, when she had boldly left the hamlet of Baulking, and was newly arrived in London. Now in domestic service and living in a tall white house facing the Natural History Museum on Cromwell Road, she was spreading her wings. In a grand London cinema, she had fallen in love with the handsome Clark Gable, and had been overjoyed by the wonderful spectacle. The four-hour film had been an unforgettable experience, truly a high point in her life at a time when she was young, stunningly attractive and unencumbered.

When I saw that the New Theatre was having a special showing of the film, I moved swiftly to buy a pair of tickets and, on the night, Mum and I arrived early and eager. We could have taken our time. There was no queue, no crowd. Thirty years on, all euphoria had ebbed away, time had moved on, and the once-great epic was now half-forgotten. Mum and I filed into the now-familiar half-empty auditorium.

After the first three hours, we grew restless and shifted uncomfortably in our seats. Neither of us wanted to voice the awful truth: the film looked dated. Both the petulance of Vivien Leigh and Clark Gable's smoulder had lost their impact; they seemed old-fashioned and affected. The newer films that we had seen in the intervening period had conditioned us without our realising to expect more realism and technical perfection. Mum and I left before the end. I felt it had been a bad mistake,

307

and that seeing the film again had damaged something precious, which should have been left undisturbed.

We had one more evening out together at the New Theatre before I left Stratfield Road. I read that Ken Dodd was coming. Mum thought he was hilarious, and enjoyed his plaintive ballads as well. I knew that our first two outings had something of the damp squib about them but surely Ken would come through! This time the evening was going to be a triumph!

It certainly was. Mum and I laughed as we had never laughed before. We rocked back and forth, gasping for breath, tears rolling down our faces. On standing up to leave we felt weakened and ached from the onslaught. We never forgot the brilliant evening. It was fantastic on two levels: firstly, because I had never once seen Mum so convulsed with laughter; and secondly to see the sheer skill of the man. I could not get over the machine-gun-like rapidity of his routine, the absurd little one-liners and jokes that built up layer upon layer until the audience was clutching its collective belly, throwing its head back and roaring with uncontrollable laughter.

When Ken Dodd came back to the New Theatre the next time, I was first in the queue for tickets. I took an American friend who had never heard of the comedian. In the theatre, I waited eagerly for the curtain to go up, completely confident that the evening was going to be a knockout. When the show got under way, however, a cold, disappointing realisation crept over me. So much of it was the same. So many throwaway lines, ad-libs and one-liners, which I'd thought so spontaneous and off-the-cuff, were there just like before. I was naïve I suppose, but I felt so unspeakably disappointed. I was looking forward to an evening of different but just-as-good material whereas this seemed more of a re-run. My American friend, finding the comedy unfunny and chauvinistic, sat stony-faced throughout. We shuffled out flatly at the end and I considered this another example of an experience I was unwise to revisit. I also thought, as I mentally raked over the failed evening later that night, that it was unwise for a comedian to return to the same theatre two years later and do such a similar show. Surely, a paying audience, for their large outlay of ticket-money, deserved more material they hadn't heard before? I felt indignant on their behalf.

At Stratfield Road, my last remaining link with the RAF had snapped and fallen away when I broke up with my boyfriend Jeremy, the RAF sergeant from my geography class who had loyally trailed after me first to Butlin's at Clacton, then back to Stanford and now on to Oxford. We realised that there was no future for us; at that time, I had no hankering for a husband and children. All I had instead was a consistent and strong feeling that I had not reached the place where I was supposed to be. This was impossible to explain because I didn't know where that place was. Therefore, on 20 July 1969, two momentous things happened. My boyfriend and I sadly agreed to go our separate ways, and man landed on the moon.

As winter came on, the cold comfort of Stratfield Road grew chillier still. I had never run a home of my own before and was utterly clueless. I noticed with faint surprise and irritation that there was no handy tub of Vim in the kitchen sink

309

cupboard. Somebody had forgotten to buy it! After a time I realised it was me. Mum provided all that kind of stuff at home; I had just airily taken it for granted.

Still a heavy smoker, I never had money to spare. One evening I visited some friends who shared a flat along the Cowley Road and sat enveloped in the warm cosiness of their sitting room. By contrast, my bleak bedsitter was cold as a morgue. Oh yes, they explained, they had all clubbed together to buy a nice gas fire as it was getting so nippy. It seemed that everybody else had their lives organised; they saw what was needed and got on with it. Bored and frustrated in yet another lacklustre job, I seemed to be one of life's perpetual flounderers. One hopeful spark was quickly extinguished when I read about a theatre club in Oxford and rang the number eagerly. It was student-oriented, they explained apologetically, and at twenty-two, I was a little old.

*   *   *

It occurred to me in a defeated sort of way that I might as well rejoin the WRAF; in civilian life, I was going nowhere and felt as if I was neither fish nor fowl. I still missed Singapore and longed to travel the world. I was certainly not going back as a plotter, but I knew that some girls worked in the WRAF as air quartermasters, which meant they were aircrew, and their job concerned the correct loading and centre of gravity of aircraft. I did not know a centre of gravity from my elbow, but undeterred I sought advice from an RAF recruiting office in Oxford. I told the officer in charge that I didn't seem to be making much

310

progress in civilian life. He said sagely, 'Yes, it's a draughty old place out there,' before putting my name down for an aircrew selection test at Biggin Hill.

The selection process took place over three days and I booked them as holiday from my job. There were aptitude tests, comprehensive medicals and leadership exercises. On the first day, I was given a problem to solve. As I recall it involved several unlikely vehicles trying to cross the Sahara: a London taxi, a double-decker bus, a motorbike and sidecar and others. Each vehicle travelled at a certain speed and used a certain amount of petrol. Some could only go uphill and some only on the flat. Which one crossed the Sahara first?

I didn't have a clue. Once more, the two halves of my brain revolved in opposite directions as I studied the impenetrable facts. After the medicals came the leadership exercises. The candidates were divided up into syndicates; I was given two oil-drums and a selection of planks. The man in charge assured me that the floor of the hangar in which we stood was in fact shark-infested custard. I looked at him as if he was a halfwit. With the oil-drums, the planks and my native cunning I had to get my syndicate across the custard without their feet touching the floor. It was hopeless. At one point, I had four people clinging to each other, each with just one foot on the drum. By some miracle, I got through the three phases of the course, and went disconsolately back to the cold comfort of Stratfield Road.

*　　　*　　　*

One night soon after the Biggin Hill debacle, Dad

came to visit me in his van. As a linesman for the Southern Electricity Board, he had been regularly required to climb tall, creosoted poles to attend to the power lines above. The technique was spectacular to watch. Boots with immense downward-facing spikes were donned, and the linesman buckled a stout, specially made leather belt around the pole and his own waist. Leaning back into the belt to create tension, he would then purposefully stamp the spike on his boot into the wood of the pole, and walk his way to the top. There were no ladders, no hydraulic cherry pickers. Their equipment was spikes and a belt. One day something went wrong and Dad fell, injuring his knee. Although he underwent an operation to remove the cartilage, the joint gave him persistent pain and was always swollen up like a ball. No longer able to climb poles, he was switched by the SEB to a job as a maintenance man, tending its various sub-stations. He drove round them all and kept them smart by weeding, spraying, cutting back brambles and clobbering rabbits.

That day his work had brought him near to Oxford and he called in to see me before going home to Stanford. It was November, I was swathed in a red scarf and the bedsitter was freezing. This was the first time he had seen it and he was unimpressed.

'Whasswanna sit round 'ere for?' he asked with some incredulity. 'Whyever dussent thee come home longa us?'

I had no answer. I didn't really know why I was there myself. When I thought of our large, cheerful family in the warmth of No. 16 Vandiemans Road, it seemed so obvious. Dad was right. I packed in the job at British Leyland and went home as soon as I could.

Shortly after I was happily established back in Stanford, a letter came from Biggin Hill saying I had failed the aircrew selection test. I felt no surprise as I read the reason given. It seemed I lacked the necessary aptitude.

51

SMITHS INDUSTRIES OF WITNEY

I did not want to work in Stanford, in some pub or shop. Smiths Industries of Witney sent a coach round the village daily to pick up employees so, knowing that Jean had once worked there and liked it, I wrote off to see if they had any vacancies. I was invited for interview by Miss Olive Meades, the Personnel Officer, a woman of extremely old-fashioned and elderly appearance, which probably belied her actual age. Small and Edwardian-looking, she wore her long pepper-and-salt hair raised up and coiled repeatedly round her head with numerous escaping strands. At no time did I see her wearing make-up, her skin was downy and, in certain lights, bewhiskered. It was as if a mistake had been made, and a person from the wrong era had been planted down among the chimneys and angular factory rooftops of Smiths Industries.

At the interview we discussed Tolkien's *Lord of the Rings*, the shrub growing outside her window (a *Garrya elliptica*: *Garrya* from the person who discovered it, and *elliptica* from the shape of the leaf), and the meaning of the word 'viable'

313

(capable of sustaining life) after which I was offered a job in the Hydraulic Purchasing Department. This was another office job and I was delighted. All had fallen into place.

At the Witney works, Smiths made automotive products including hydraulic tail lifts, certain types of heater and precision fans for the movement of air. I was working for one of the buyers. The world of hydraulics was as remote and uninteresting to me as the radiators of British Leyland had been, but I was undeterred as I sat down at my new desk in the glassy, suffocatingly hot office. I had a job.

In front of me sat my boss Mr Pettifer, a man fond of making homemade wine, one batch of which exploded spectacularly in his front room. Immediately to my right sat a man who smoked a pipe: a sad, drooping-looking pipe, which was either alight or engaged in the long drawn-out ritual of being lit. My colleague favoured shag tobacco of the utmost strength and spent relaxed hours teasing out the shreds and tapping them fussily into the tar-caked bowl with his fingertip. Then, as a flame was applied, his cheeks worked hungrily to suck the burning mass to a white heat. Clouds of smoke crackled up like a bonfire, obscuring the view from the wide windows and wreathing me and the five male occupants of the office in blue, engulfing smoke. Nobody seemed to mind. Any timorous remonstration of mine elicited only the raising of a pitying eyebrow and the long blowing of a languid stream of smoke in my direction. I favoured an inexpensive but pleasant perfume called Sea Jade, which came in a shapely turquoise bottle from Boots the Chemist. Freshly washed and fragrant I would take up my position in our office in the morning, only to stagger out at night with my hair and every item of clothing, however intimate, rank and reeking of smoke.

This was an odd office, where people were bullied. Had I thought about bullying at all, I would have dismissed it as something children did to each other at school until corrected. I was so wrong. In that workplace grown men were bullied and humiliated, were called into the flimsy office of one of the managers and screamed at in a rising, demented fashion, while those in the vicinity feigned deafness for fear they were next in line. The victim would then have to walk out through our area, sweating and half-dead with shame. It was appalling. One of the constantly bullied, a nice man named Charlie, died early of heart failure.

The long bus ride from Stanford in the Vale to Witney did not normally yield much in the way of conversation. In the mornings, people were groggy, and many including me viewed the journey as an extension of the night and made a point of going straight back to sleep. I sat next to a pleasant, round-faced man named George. He had a large family, and on summer evenings they would wait for him at the end of their lane, the little boys obviously excited to see their dad, and a beautiful pink-cheeked baby girl named Janet sitting up expectantly in an old-fashioned, deep-bodied pram, which had seen better days. He always got off the bus and greeted his wife with an affectionate kiss. They looked a delightful family and he took great pride in them.

One day our bus passed a steam engine making its laborious way along the country road. I made what turned out to be a mistake by casually telling George that I liked them. I didn't know anything about steam engines, but recognised that to certain people they became much more than just a machine. They became things their owners genuinely loved, and upon which they would lavish hard work, cash and time. Also, they were nostalgic to me, remembering as I did the little farm belonging to Johnny Fowles opposite Campdene.

Every summer of my childhood, a marvellous transformation took place, which I watched from my vantage point among the Canterbury bells. One day the farmyard would be silent and deserted and the next it would be filled with action. The threshing machine had arrived! A large, vibrating, pinky-hued contraption, rectangular in shape and made largely of wooden planks, stood ready to shake the living daylights out of Johnny's wheat and barley. The steam engine that powered it was toweringly huge under its little roof-canopy, and it chugged all day with a lovely conversational rhythm while wreathed in puffs and wisps of steam. There must have been breakdowns and frustrations but my memory had pared everything down. All I could see was a scene of perfect rhythm, of fat, bulging sacks of corn being carried from the thresher and of a continuous rising mass of straw travelling up the escalator to be tossed in place by men with pitchforks, standing wide-legged on top of the burgeoning rick.

Transported by the ageless beauty of this picture, I told George that, yes, I was very fond of steam engines.

Now the floodgates opened. It so happened that George was fond of them as well. Inordinately fond. In fact, he had great albums full of photographs of them all annotated in white ink, giving the exact type and location. Not only that, but George knew another bloke who had even more albums of steam engines, and he had kindly said I could see his as well. My comfy early-morning snooze on the way to work became a thing of the past. Now every day George got on the bus with one or two ancient albums under his arm, and to this day I can still smell the damp mustiness and hear the crack of pages being opened, which had not seen the light of day for decades. George, a fervent enthusiast, was careful to explain each photograph, one at a time. Thereafter, whenever I saw a steam engine, I felt half-asleep and my nostrils filled with the smell of mildew.

I was friendly with Dorothy, another lady on the bus. Sadly she had lost her husband who had once worked as a local bus conductor. Her husband and my dad knew each other, but Dorothy's rosy view of their friendship did not correspond with Dad's. 'They was such pals!' she used to say. 'They got on so well, them two did, oh the *laughs* they used to have, yes indeed!'

I mentioned this to Dad one evening who considered it thoughtfully for a moment before offering his somewhat contrasting opinion. 'I hated the bastard,' he said.

All of the works-bus conversationalists were more cheering than one lachrymose employee who got on each morning at the top of Burford Hill. The manner of his arrival never varied. He would lurch down the bus, take his seat, fold his hands across his lap, sigh deeply and observe:

'One day more; one day less.'

*　　　*　　　*

A great thing about Smiths was that they ran a further education scheme at Witney Tech, so I

317

enrolled for shorthand and English. I still loved the delicacy and cleverness of shorthand; it was like a mysterious code only understood by relatively few. The English teacher was a likeable man named Murphy. I told him I was interested in taking English at GCE A-level and was surprised and excited when he said with great brevity, 'You'll walk it.' Other events crowded in though; I never found out if that was the case.

I also decided to apply for a driving test. I had taken and passed the RAF version in Singapore but this counted for nothing in the UK. My instructor there had been mightily aggressive, given to shaking his fist out of the vehicle window and bawling racial abuse at fellow drivers. He taught me never to change down through the gears as I approached a 'T' junction but instead to drive up to it at full tilt and only brake at the last minute. On booking a few driving lessons in Witney prior to the test, this unusual technique petrified the instructor and drained his face of all blood. I had to unlearn countless bad habits, and this was hard.

At that time, it was permissible to take the driving test in the undemanding traffic conditions of Witney, and this is what I did. I passed first time, having never encountered or driven on a motorway at all. Shortly afterwards I drove on the M1 to Leeds in the north of England and was terrified all the way, partly because, within seconds of joining the carriageway, a Ford Anglia immediately in front of me suffered a blowout. On its shredded tyre it snaked from side to side of the carriageway amid clouds of smoke and the stench of burnt rubber. It was not a good introduction. My conveyance was a fog-grey Morris 1000, the iconic rounded car favoured by vicars, cautious spinsters and Nurse Speed; I bought it for £50 from my brother Allan.

* * *

Living at home was lovely in many ways but certainly cramped my romantic style. The front room with its Dansette record player was available for courting members of the family but it was hard to be a smouldering temptress when at any time your brother might stroll in looking for his shirt. At work, I heard about a recently widowed lady who lived in a spacious property nearby. Lonely and nervous, she was seeking a tenant if she could find the right person. In the hope that it might be me, I applied, was accepted and moved in. It didn't really work. The lady was grief-stricken and lavished her love on numerous assorted cats for whom she regularly boiled up great saucepans full of giblets. This filled the house with the most revolting and stomach-churning stench. 'Oh yes . . .' she would murmur enticingly to one of the cats, 'you can smell those giblets, can't you?'

'Yeah,' I thought sourly, 'and so can I.'

An eerie thing happened in the house. One year after her husband's death, *to the very second*, his photo fell off the wall. It just crashed down on to the floor. She came to find me, aghast, and I tried to think of some reassuring words but could not.

52

EXTRANEOUS ACTIVITIES

Perhaps because I was brought up with four brothers, I always felt comfortable with men, perhaps more so than with women. At work, I built up a good group of friends, mostly single men from the offices around mine, and one day they invited me to go with them to see The Oily Cart. When translated I found this meant the D'Oyly Carte Opera Company, which was performing *The Pirates of Penzance* by Gilbert and Sullivan at the New Theatre, Oxford. I'd never heard of any of it, and hardly thought I would be the kind of person to enjoy an *opera*, but I liked the company of my friends and went.

It knocked me for six. This was another new world to me, musical theatre. I knew it existed but had never once seen any. I was entranced by the clever use of words, by the packing in and just-so placement of stressed syllables. 'I Am the Very Model of a Modern Major-General' was welcomed with joyous uproar by the audience and I came out intrigued and mystified. Once again I felt a connection to this clever use of words for comic effect. The impact of deftly delivered words on an audience was extraordinary. They could be thrilled, sobered, made to howl with laughter. I'd been so close to refusing the invitation, thinking in my bigoted way that opera, however light, wasn't for people like me. I was so glad I'd had the sense to go and investigate.

*   *   *

I also made friends with a single man at Smiths who liked walking. This was something I never did if I could help it; certainly, I had never met anyone who actually sought it out for pleasure. He was going camping to Grizedale Forest in the Lake District, and asked me if I would like to go with him. Despite not having heard of the place, I was intrigued and accepted.

Knowing nothing about weatherproof clothing I bought a jacket made out of white rabbit fur, which I hoped would be practical and inconspicuous. It was neither. I made the mistake of buying it from a shop we patronised in George Street, Oxford, where goods were cheap. The saleslady was one of the old school, highly skilled in fobbing off poor saps like me with the wrong thing. She kept reducing the price. In the end, I walked out carrying a garment I had no use for, firmly believing I had a bargain. I told my friend I had bought a white rabbit-fur coat in which to go walking. He said nothing but handed me a cagoule.

We left Smiths after work on Friday and drove for hours in dark, rainy weather, passing through the town of Hawkshead and eventually parking in a fragrant woody environment, which I could not see. Efficiently and at great speed, my friend pitched a small, limpet-shaped tent in the headlights, lit a tiny Primus stove, unpacked various containers and served a brilliant meal. I had never seen anything like it and was filled with admiration. Being an ignoramus, camping was always a concept I had jeered at: something pathetic to do with boy scouts and tripping over guy ropes. That night I slept in a sleeping bag for

321

the first time in my life. Rain pattered endearingly on the blue canvas of the tent and beyond was a dark enveloping silence. I was warm, dry, well fed and enchanted.

In the morning, the unfamiliar bleating of sheep awoke me and I made my way outside. I was greeted by the sweet, scented woodland of Grizedale, freshened by rain, sparkling in the warm sunshine and dotted with ewes and their lambs. My friend was cooking breakfast and brewing up coffee. I would never in my life scoff at camping again. Any holidays I had experienced in the past involved masses of paraphernalia: bulging suitcases, high-heeled shoes, hairdryers, make-up, unsatisfactory accommodation and greasy café food. This was a different idea, a paring down to the minimum, comfort, independence and freedom of choice reduced to a few well-chosen items carried on the back in a rucksack. It was so gloriously simple; I was smitten.

A dark, chattering brook disappeared into the shade of the forest and we followed it, treading softly on ground cushioned by generations of leaf-fall. Along the bank in ones and twos grew fly agaric mushrooms, bright and gaudy beneath their white-spotted red caps. I had only ever seen them depicted in fairytales. The lovely sights, woodland scents and soft velvet silences were intoxicating and ever-changing. In wintertime, I would see those same arching streamside ferns exquisitely frozen and entirely encased in ice.

Enthused by this undreamed-of kind of camping, I bought a tent, a low, two-person Marechal Pedestre, and started to go regularly with my friend to other rugged and windswept places: the Brecon Beacons, the Peak District,

Scotland and Skye. Although I was no climber, another friend proposed me for membership of a mountaineering club with good premises in North Wales and Coniston. Over many subsequent weekends, far removed from the world of hydraulic pumps, I experienced the satisfied weariness of looking back up some great hill and realising with incredulity that I had climbed to the very top. This new interest made me realise I could do more than I thought, and it opened my eyes to the bewitching beauty of my own country.

It also brought things to a head in the giblet-boiling household. I rented a bedroom and sitting room from the widowed lady and all was nicely carpeted and well presented. Returning from a trip to the Lake District, knowing that my treasured new tent though definitely not *wet* was nevertheless not exactly *dry*, and further realising that the most harmful thing I could do was pack it away damp, I draped it over all the good-quality furniture in the sitting room. It was not dirty or wet. I just wanted to give it a final air in the warmth.

I don't know why the lady went into my sitting room but I do know that upon entering she was horrified to see a tent, which she assumed I had put there to drip dry. When I came home from work both the giblets and my landlady were boiling. She was enraged that I had seen fit to *erect a tent*! Did I have any idea *how much it had cost* to lay that Axminster carpet? What was I *thinking* about? The subject matter widened as grievances crowded in, and as a parting shot she added that my camping companion boyfriend *stayed too late!* I should *get the ring on my finger first!*

She was a very nice lady. I had upset her, and clearly I was not the tenant she had hoped for. I started looking for somewhere else to live.

$$*\qquad*\qquad*$$

At work, garlanded with pipe smoke, I was bored stiff. My job was to make tea and type ill-composed letters to suppliers of hydraulic components. For respite, I walked at lunchtime, crossing the busy A40 and following the country road that falls away down to the village of Crawley below. A path appears and leads through the picturesquely named woodland of Maggots Grove to the valley bottom. Here the little River Windrush winds its gentle, reed-lined way to Burford and beyond. If I hurried, I could get down there for a few minutes and walk beside the water; it was like a balm. One day in the reeds, I saw the exposed backs of two pike sunbathing companionably side by side in the shallow water, as pike will occasionally do. Once I saw the grass-lined nest of a skylark.

Feeling increasingly dejected, I had started to daydream about just continuing to walk, to get far away from Smiths and what seemed the shambles I had made of my life. I had no money, no permanent home, another boring job and a certainty that at twenty-five years of age, I was going nowhere. However, indifferent though I was to the job, I was not keen to be sacked from it.

Smiths employed several people with odd names. There was a Mr Skinner, a Mr Hogsflesh and one of the bosses was lumbered with a name that I found hysterical: Claude Pratt. The Personnel Manager was called Mr Branch and one long, hot afternoon when I had nothing to do, I started to tinker with the name, endeavouring to compose a letter filled with tree-related words that

324

still read well and made sense. It was engrossing. I put together a fake communication giving somebody the sack, explaining that Mr *Branch* had finally *twigged* that now the *sap* was rising, he should try to get at the *root* of the problem, cut out all the *dead wood*, and while not *barking* up the wrong tree nevertheless turn over a new *leaf*, etcetera, etcetera. I had no thought of a recipient, but played with the words as an amusing exercise. A few other people joined in with suggestions and we all laughed. Someone then suggested that we send it to our great friend, workmate and D'Oyly Carte enthusiast, Dave, who we loved, and who had the most fantastic sense of humour. I thought it was a fine idea, forged the signature of Miss Meades the Personnel Officer at the bottom and sent it off on headed paper requesting him to move out of his Smiths-owned accommodation as soon as possible, thanking him in anticipation of his co-operation and hoping it did not leave him out on a limb.

In retrospect, it was an act of lunacy. Dave had two little children and the responsibility of his family on his shoulders. When he read the letter, he did not see the jokey terminology; he saw the headed paper and the signature at the bottom. He received it on his day off and immediately drove into work brandishing the official-looking document. I saw him stalk furiously across the car park. He stormed into his boss's office and slapped it down on his desk. 'I got your letter!' he shouted, angry and desperate.

Word shot round our office that Dave hadn't realised it was a joke. We looked at one another in consternation. I had constructed the thing and sent it off. All fingers in unison turned and pointed at me; I was going to have to own up. Within an hour, copies of my letter appeared on all the notice boards with a curt annotation to the effect that if anyone knew anything about the forgery they should come forward. I came forward. I told my boss that the ill-conceived joke was my idea. A message came back that I should attend the office of Mr Claude Pratt the following day and be in no doubt that the self-same Mr Pratt considered that the perpetrator of this scandalous forgery should be peremptorily dismissed.

Gawky and horrified by this unfamiliar castigation when I was used to feeling fairly well liked, I made my way through the crowded general office to the domain of Mr Claude Pratt like somebody going to the gallows on a tumbrel. Everyone was agog. What was afoot? I was dismayed by the speed with which the situation had ballooned; I couldn't believe I was about to be *sacked*!

I finally reached the office of Mr Claude Pratt and was shown in. I can't remember much of the conversation. I am sure he pointed out that the letter had caused shock and distress, and that the most serious aspect had been me cheerfully appending the apparent signature of Miss Meades. I said it was a ludicrous letter sent as a joke, which I never thought anyone could take seriously. I also pointed out that when the idea was first mooted, I was surrounded by a crowd of enthusiastic eggers-on, and that the speed with which they evaporated when the ordure hit the fan had been a salutary lesson. Mr Claude Pratt was very fair, accepted that it was a prank, said the matter would be taken no further and was now closed. As I opened the door of his office to leave, he asked, 'Who actually composed this letter?'

I said, 'I did.'

'It's very, very good,' he replied.

Thereafter I considered Mr Claude Pratt to be an extremely good egg.

I apologised to Dave, but it took a long time for us to recover our former ease in each other's company.

53

ARTISTIC ENDEAVOURS

I heard about a theatre club seeking members in Faringdon. Apparently, it was in the old Marine Camp at Butts Close, the very buildings made to stand in as makeshift classrooms when I was at school, and where I had nearly gone nuts trying to operate a treadle sewing machine in the needlework class. After the long intervening years, I made my way back.

Sure enough, inside the still fierce-looking chain-link fences and entrance gates crouched a black Nissen hut. Askew above the entrance hung a hand-painted sign that read 'The Little Theatre' and I rushed in. To my delight, I found that Bill Reeves, my favourite former English teacher, and his wife Nancy were members. I greeted them with great affection, joined the club, read at the next audition and was cast as a French tart. Given some vague tips by the producer about how to sound convincingly French, I only succeeded in sounding ludicrous. The big opening night came on apace and a great gang of friends from Smiths Industries decided to come and cheer me on. I was unconvinced that this was a good idea but they were adamant. My sister Jean came as well and that night in the Nissen hut tension ran high. The auditorium was tiny, the stage only a metre from the audience, but nevertheless like countless amateurs before us, we actors sat backstage and applied absurd, unnecessary quantities of greasepaint, including the obligatory, large red full stop on the inner corner of each eye.

I can't remember what the play was, but the success of it depended on the setting off, at a certain dramatic point, of a maroon, an explosive signalling device normally used to indicate distress or warning. If the maroon did not go off, the plot made no sense.

The maroon exploded early. A shattering report with no relevance to the story suddenly terrified the audience and paralysed their eardrums. The crowd from Smiths could be heard weeping with laughter. When the cue came for the real explosion, none came. We could only afford one maroon. Instead, the props person backstage hurriedly improvised a few knives and forks and dropped those. This sounded like the dropping of a few knives and forks and convulsed the Smiths crowd still further. The play staggered on until, as it mercifully approached its conclusion, the lights went out, plunging the Nissen hut into total, stuffy darkness. Electricians blundered about in the gloom. The Smiths contingent brayed with laughter; it was the best night out they had ever had. At last, the lights came on although a large proportion of the audience had gone home in disgust. The play limped to a close and we took a shamefaced bow to the wrong sort of applause. At the end, my sister said, 'Your red dress had great big sweaty patches under the arms.'

*　　　*　　　*

Smiths Industries had its own newspaper, entitled with great originality *SI News*, and this was published once a month or so. At about this time they inexplicably ran a poetry competition, which I entered, composing an ironic piece about why young women should choose to work in Engineering. It was a tongue-in-cheek account of the attractions that might tempt a woman into what was then very much a harsh male environment. Here are two lines I can remember:

> *Ladies do not hesitate, but take the primrose path*
> *Which leads beside the furnace and corrosive acid bath.*

There were about six verses altogether. I thought it was a good piece, and funny. Signing myself Alice Frick, I sent it off. Before long, I received a phone call from the editor's office to say I had won the competition! I was ecstatic, and when the next edition of *SI News* came round, I hurtled through the pages to find a funny poem of mine in print for the very first time! It was so exciting; I read and re-read it countless times. There it was, written in large letters and below in smaller print was the runner-up. That poem was very different from mine and began, 'When Pope in his Elysian fields . . .' I was so elated and gathered up numerous copies of the paper to keep.

Some time later, a young man named Martin came to work in our office. He had come from another branch of Smiths in Cricklewood, London.

'What were you doing at Cricklewood?' I asked him one day.

'Oh, I worked on the newspaper, the *SI News*,' he replied.

'Really?' says I, alias Alice Frick. 'I knew somebody who went in for that poetry competition they ran.'

'Oh my God!' says he, remembering. 'That poetry competition! We only had two entries!'

54

A CHANGE OF ADDRESS

One day a vacancy was advertised on the notice board. It was for the position of secretary to Miss Meades. As my secretarial skills were now more polished, I applied. I knew she was a different person, not at all run-of-the-mill. At my first interview, she had seemed well read and intensely knowledgeable about words and this was attractive to me, as was the fact that she did not smoke a pipe. I was offered the job and moved across the road into the Personnel Office. She informed me straight away that she had been aware of the business of the forged signature and no mention would thenceforth be made of it. Her archaic language intrigued me. Sometimes a visitor would arrive early for an appointment. 'Ask him,' she would instruct imperiously, 'to wait in the vestibule.'

During my time in that department, an interesting situation developed when a hot affair flared between one of the male bosses and his older, prim-looking and bespectacled secretary. Both were married to someone else. It was noticed that their door was always closed. Someone had heard the sound of muffled grunts within and shortly afterwards the secretary had appeared red-faced, with her towering hairdo listing to starboard. There was an almighty scandal and both were sacked. Some months later, I saw the lady working in a shop and there was something horribly sad about the situation. She had lost her reputation and a good job with status. I was an unwelcome reminder; she looked embarrassed and uncomfortable to see me.

Of the three personnel officers who dealt with staff-related matters at Smiths, I got on especially well with one named Tom Williams whose hobby was restoring Riley cars. Finding some pathetic old wreck behind the combine-harvester in the crumbling barn of a crumbling farmer, he would buy it, have it towed home and spend untold years turning it into a thing of extraordinary beauty, low-slung, potent and of impeccable pedigree. I was sad when he was offered a better job, and moved away to work near Manchester in a town with the unappealing name of Stalybridge. I wrote upon his leaving card:

> Stalybridge, O Stalybridge,
> Fair jewel of the north,
> Your oily charm reached out an arm
> And plucked Tom Williams forth.

At work I got to know another of the secretaries, a young woman named Elizabeth. She was privately educated and confident with a posh voice and a

Coutts chequebook. I found her terrifying and by comparison felt like a buffoon: ill-educated, rough around the edges and conscious of my Vale of the White Horse accent. This wore off, however, and we became friends. One weekend she suggested a trip to Modbury in Devon. A relation of hers, Hester, lived there and we could have a couple of days in the spring sunshine. I agreed and we travelled down the M5 in my failing Morris 1000, followed for much of the way by a dense cloud of smoke.

It was the first time I had stayed in the house of a stranger and did not really know what to expect. At home, in No. 16 Vandiemans, the house was full to bursting point; our three bedrooms were always stuffed with people. Visitors seldom stayed overnight but if they did their accommodation tended to be hastily assembled and of a ramshackle nature. Mother had a camp bed, which would be erected behind the sofa in the front room. Raised ten centimetres off the floor at most, its little folding legs were placed in such a way that the bed was ridiculously easy to capsize. If you got in too close to the top, the foot reared up and vice versa. A great deal of seesawing went on before the occupant settled down to sleep. My future sister-in-law, sleeping in the camp bed one night, woke up shrieking with fright, having been scuttled over by a mouse. Therefore, my expectations were not great when, with much backfiring, I drew up outside Hester's home.

The house was old and mellow, unshowy but filled with welcoming touches; fresh flowers set upon dark, polished wood. There was no camp bed askew upon the floor; instead, I was shown into the *guest room*. A window looked out upon the pastel colours of a Devon street and, beside the high, quilt-covered bed, a little bowl packed with primroses had been placed. It was so beautiful and friendly. I was such a duffer. Elizabeth pointed out a bay tree outside the front door exclaiming, 'Isn't it great? Hester doesn't have to go far to get her bay leaves does she?'

'No,' I said, 'she certainly doesn't!'

I didn't have a clue what bay leaves were used for. Neither did I know what Hester was doing when I saw her on Sunday morning in the big comely kitchen, briskly stabbing a huge leg of lamb and pushing in white slivers of garlic.

That weekend, along with Hester's children, we pottered along the Devon lanes where steep, canyon-like banks were studded with primroses like little lights. Nearer to the coast, we strolled eagerly over green fields to the sea. It was the loveliest weekend, where I learned something about hospitality and welcome. I was appalled to hear that soon afterwards Hester's kindly husband had suddenly died. Tragedy struck the amiable home and the children lost their father.

*   *   *

Elizabeth rented a flat in Witney but wanted to move out. Assuring her landlady that she would look for a suitable replacement, she asked if I would be at all interested. This was timely. I was ready to live independently again, liked both Witney and the flat, could afford the rent of £4 a week, and moved in as soon as I could.

No. 94 High Street, Witney, was the nicest place I had ever lived in. It occupied half of a large rambling house, which at one time had been a hotel. In those far-off days, horse-drawn coaches would have clattered over the cobbles and swept in through the central arch, but by 1972, the only thing under the arch was a low black door bearing the number 94 in polished brass.

Once inside, all was rich red carpet and black wood panelling. Up one flight of stairs was my new home. The small bathroom was positioned immediately over the archway and, from time to time, I mused that if the floor gave way I might appear on the pavement below still seated in the bath.

I had a huge sitting room, one wall of which was occupied by a monumental fireplace big enough to take a tree at a time. Since there were no longer servants to heave such timber up the stairs, the fireplace had been made smaller by infilling with square red tiles, leaving only a small, regular-size fireplace and basket at the bottom. It looked awful, a great generous feature meanly reduced to an eyesore. On the opposite side was a big, floral-curtained window looking out on to the High Street, and a little kitchen frequented by mice. The walls were painted green, the furniture was upholstered in a brown imitation leather called Rexine and the overall feel was fairly dark. Up another flight of stairs was my bedroom and here the floor sloped at such an extreme angle that walking up it required similar tactics to climbing a hill; you leant well forwards. It was a proper home though and I was glad to have it. It was also the home where all aspects of my life would change beyond recognition.

My landlady was called Mrs Harris and I liked her very much. She was small and portly, well dressed, powdered, behatted and possessed of an air of comfortable wealth and position. She always called me 'Pem' in a rather genteel, *refeened* kind of voice and had a way of spacing out words for maximum impact. Of a handsome remembered man, she would confide, 'Oh my dear! He—was—an—*Adonis*!'

Her husband by comparison was a tall, rather joyless man, stooped and of grim demeanour. His name was Glenn and his father was clergyman, naturalist and gardener Mr Ernest Harris who in 1936 wrote a book entitled *Wild Visitors to a Cotswold Garden*, based on his affectionate observations of the teeming wildlife in the garden at the rear of the house. Mrs Harris enthused to me: 'Oh my dear! Such a garden! It—was—a—*showpiece*!'

By the time I arrived, its glory days were long past. It was sad, neglected, let go in every possible way and abandoned to its fate. Yet it remained seductive; I often went there, intrigued by the still atmosphere, and by the clues and vestiges of beauty that remained.

The garden ran down to the banks of the River Windrush and the broken planks of a ruined boathouse. There were statues. The sinuous bodies of nymphs danced on beneath thick, engulfing greenery, their limbs chipped by vandals and time to expose the metal core. Once-beautiful curvaceous and shell-shaped ponds had been desecrated by yobs, filled with refuse and polluted by cans of petrol. Catastrophically, in their season frogs came back to their old home to mate; they could be seen in their scores forced to wallow in petrol-laden filth.

School parties used to visit the garden occasionally because it had once been a

335

fellmongers yard, where animal skins fresh from the slaughterhouse were brought to begin the process of tanning. Crude, rectangular pits had been dug in the ground for the steeping of hides. It was a strange, forgotten garden where shrubs, no longer trimmed or trained, grew rampantly to the height of trees. As if it could not bear to look, the sweetly named Windrush hurried past, swift and clear.

55

TWO BANGERS

I had car problems. My Morris 1000, already on its last legs, was never the same after being struck by a bus in the village of Bampton. Hurrying to work one morning I had overtaken the stationary vehicle. The driver claimed that he was indicating to turn right and he may well have been, but I didn't see it. As I drew level with the front, I hardly had time to squeal with terror as the enormous bus, towering above me, swung over and hit my car with an ear-splitting clang. The passenger door never closed again; the car was seldom so well ventilated.

The driver gave me the insurance details of the bus company in Witney and I went to see them hoping they would offer to repair my car, but when I stated my business nobody knew anything and the staff just melted away. In the end, baffled and out of my depth, so did I.

I needed a new car but was always depressingly short of cash; so were most of the people I knew.

Foolishly, I was still a smoker, which was costly, and I had no grasp of how to borrow money or how all that kind of thing worked. I had been brought up to be fearful and suspicious of loans and hire purchase, and although I had a bank account, I found the branch a frightening, alien place, which I had to pluck up courage to enter. The business of trying to find a replacement car or of funding expensive repairs seemed hopeless, out of reach. Instead, I combed muddy scrap yards in search of a Morris 1000 to cannibalise, found a sorry-looking black one in Wantage and bought the passenger door for a few quid. Some kind person hung it on the hinges and I was mobile again, though in a failing grey car with one black door I hardly cut a dash. I would look out of the driver's mirror on the road up to Smiths and see that all following traffic was obscured by white smoke. I was embarrassed by it. The car proclaimed my shortage of cash in a loud voice.

A solution of sorts was provided by my brother-in-law Ginge who offered me his car, a hand-painted turquoise and orange Ford Anglia with an ugly cut-in rear window. In turn, I sold my Morris to a man in the village who assured me of his tender, cherishing intentions shortly before annihilating it in the stock-car races down the old Faringdon sandpits.

As for the Ford Anglia, it was the worst car I ever owned. It had been souped up. Part of the souping process involved the removal of the normal steering wheel and the substitution of a tiny 'sporty' version fashioned from aluminium and set absurdly low between the knees. To the casual observer this gave the impression that the driver had his hands between his legs and was doing something faintly sinister.

This car also had a problem with the passenger door, but one that was much more lethal. It used to drift open. Upon turning right or nipping round a roundabout, the door would suddenly and silently swing wide open. Once it did it when Mum was in the passenger seat and I had to grip her clothes with white knuckles to stop her falling out on to the road. No cyclist would have stood a chance; he would have been wiped. I detested the car. It was ten times worse than the old one and I felt horribly dejected. The friend who had taken me camping to Grizedale Forest suggested a cheering trip to Norwich Folk Festival and I went like a shot.

56

THREE FOLK FESTIVALS

Norwich Folk Festival, held in the grounds of the University of East Anglia in 1971, was a revelation to me. We arrived and pitched our tent in one of the rows marked out on smooth, sloping lawns. It seemed that everyone had brought an instrument; there was music everywhere, good music played for the joy of it. Crowded into a tent nearby was a jug band. I'd never heard of such a thing, a *jug band*? But suddenly this gang of men all stood together in front of their tent and began to sing. I turned in amazement to listen. With their pints of beer, with banjos, guitars, concertinas, jugs of all sizes and mighty harmonising voices they roared out songs that thrilled my blood. I loved it. I couldn't get enough of it.

Several times, we bought tickets to see a performer, and while it was enjoyable to sit as a member of the audience and watch an act, those were not the experiences that stayed with me afterwards. I remembered the men and women standing about on corners or sitting on the sunlit grass, playing and singing the ancient songs of our country; songs of the fishing industry, of farming and soldiery, sea shanties from blood-soaked naval battles, tragic ballads of mining catastrophes, songs of the Plague, of hiring fairs, long-dead kings, ghosts, loves, legends, history and heritage all parcelled up and *sung*. It was a new world; it lifted my heart.

I went with my friends to folk festivals at Lacock in Wiltshire and Bromyard in Herefordshire. All had the same appeal; the unabashed spontaneity and joyfulness of dance and song, of food and drink, of youth, sunshine and friends held dear.

I started to think about performing myself, and tried to track down the words of songs I had fallen in love with and longed to sing: 'Lord Franklin', 'The Galway Shawl'. My shorthand was helpful. I had a high, reedy voice but could hold a tune, and I was able to learn complicated and lengthy songs without difficulty. At home in 94 High Street, I started to practise these songs seriously on my guitar. Mum, who in her youth had loved George Formby and the cheeky suggestiveness of his routines, had bought a ukulele but never learned to play. Seeing my interest forty years later, she gave it to me. I had it repaired and restrung in a brilliant music shop, which then flourished in Witney. I wrote a daft song entitled 'Oh Don't Sell Our Edgar No More Violins' and accompanied myself with a few chords on the ukulele. While not really believing that I would ever have the courage to use one, I started to build up *an act*!

57

A BLIGHT

At work, I was promoted. Being secretary to Miss Meades had its perks, inasmuch as I heard about job vacancies before anybody else. The position of Confidential Secretary to one of the managers came up; as far as secretarial jobs went this was the top of the tree. I applied and was accepted. Now I had trappings: my own office and one of the new breed of electric typewriters. This job concerned the maintenance of buildings and general fabric of the site. I spent my day typing letters about guttering, weighbridges and the safe working loads of gantries. Outside my window were two massive gasometers, which ponderously rose and fell according to how much gas the factory required to power itself through each day.

Despite the increased salary, I came to like the job less and less. No other women were employed in the silent, depressing office, just a group of men who struck me as rather lacklustre. There was certainly no questioning the loyalty of one of them, Harold, who once told me the jaw-dropping fact that he kept his pencil rubber in the darkness of a drawer so it would last longer and 'save the old firm a few pence'. My boss was a freemason; all week a succession of fellow masons would sidle into his office in a somewhat furtive and secretive way. The set-up had a queer atmosphere. I didn't like it.

Since leaving the WRAF, I had also started to get regular migraines. I went to the doctor in Faringdon and was given powerful painkillers, which proved useless. A deep, knife-like pain would develop in my left eye, with a correspondingly awful pain in the left temple and down the back of half my head into the shoulder. I felt poisoned and indescribably ill. It always made me vomit and I would take the washing-up bowl up into the sloping bedroom, and lie as motionless as I could on the bed when not throwing up into the bowl. This state would last for two or sometimes three days. The pain was appalling; there was no escape from it. I used to lie there and long to somehow vacate my own body, to just slip away and be pain-free.

At work, I soon found this was considered a load of old horse manure, and that the word 'migraine' was scorned everywhere as a euphemism concealing the truth: that you'd either had a hangover or had overslept. I grew to detest saying 'I've been ill with migraine', although it was perfectly true. One day my new boss said contemptuously to me, 'I suppose you've been out *shopping.*' I was filled with a sense of hot injustice: that I was saddled both with the migraines and with this reaction to them. I wished those people could have just one bout of it; then they would know how bad it was, and they would understand that you *could not* function.

These venomous asides from my boss offended me. I knew my illness was highly inconvenient to him but I was no liar; I would have been at work if I could. Another job came up; it was lower down the scale with less prestige and less pay but I didn't care. It looked a brighter option, in a busier office with other women, and I hoped the migraines would come less often in a sunnier, less sour environment. Unfortunately, it made little difference.

My doctor arranged for me to go to the Migraine Clinic in Charterhouse Square in London. The doctors there were gratifyingly understanding, and I left heavily laden with white boxes containing previously untried prescriptions. At that time there was an automatic barrier at the approach to the clinic, a red-and-white striped arm that rose and fell across the road. It seemed to have a mind of its own. As I walked unwittingly along, without warning the hefty barrier swept down into the closed position, whistling past my ear and causing me to duck. It must have missed the top of my head by millimetres. I mused afterwards that perhaps this was the last resort of the Migraine Clinic; if they couldn't cure you they fractured your skull on the way out. None of the different drugs helped me anyway. It was not until the miraculous advent of Sumatriptan a decade or more later that the illness was finally stopped in its tracks.

58

THE FOLK CLUBS

Back at Smiths, my next new boss was called Mr Ernie Skinner, Purchasing Manager. The letters he dictated drove me nuts, riddled as they were with old-fashioned clutter like 'thanking you in anticipation of your co-operation' or 'I fear I must crave your indulgence in this matter'. He unfailingly referred to me as 'Glamour' as I took dictation, typed letters, made tea and picked sodden cigarette ends out of his wet saucers.

If I had not joined the WRAF, I am sure I would have had none of my own teeth by this time. It had not been customary in our family to attend for routine dental check-ups and the dentist was still very much a figure to seek out in desperation when toothache was beyond endurance and extraction the only remaining option. In the WRAF, I had been made to attend for treatment, though I was so nervous that I was prescribed a sedative called Oblivon, which came in a turquoise, egg-shaped gel capsule. This treatment while I was stupefied undoubtedly saved my hitherto neglected teeth. However, I still dreaded the visits; the high, screaming whine of a drill deep in my molars was the stuff of nightmares. Despite this, once I was living in Witney I did have the sense to arrange regular dental check-ups. During one of them, a tooth that needed filling was identified and an appointment was made for 6pm on a subsequent day.

When that day arrived, I was cold with fear, watching the clock on Ernie Skinner's wall slowly count away the hours towards 6pm. I felt clammy and gripped by impending doom. Having no letters to write and no indulgences to crave, I began to doodle a verse or two about my fears, about my regret that I had not attached more importance to the wellbeing of my teeth when they were pearly and pristine. It began: 'Oh, I wish I'd looked after me teeth . . .' I arranged and rearranged it, and finished it that afternoon. I liked it. It ridiculed a

343

situation I was frightened of and made me feel a bit better about the ordeal to come. I learned it by heart and chucked it into the drawer at home where the component parts of my act were beginning to come together.

In the 1970s, folk clubs became popular and spread like a rash all over the country. All they required was a once-weekly meeting room, usually the back or upstairs room of a pub, a few floor singers capable of doing a short set each and the potential to take enough money on the door to occasionally pay one of the guest performers who made a living by touring the circuit. Many of these touring folk acts went on to have successful recording careers, and some, including Billy Connolly and Jasper Carrott, became enormously popular and worked for decades in mainstream entertainment.

The presence and popularity of folk clubs at that time was massively fortuitous for me. I wanted to be an entertainer but had no clue how to penetrate the business, how to make some kind of start. How could I assail such a fortress when I lived in a little market town and worked as a typist?

The solution for me, although I did not immediately recognise it as such, was the folk club circuit. The clubs were gloriously easy to find; there was one located in most villages, however remote. The audiences were friendly and supportive to new acts; puny-voiced newcomers would find their efforts gratifyingly bolstered by enthusiastic choruses swelling from the ranks. This was no stiff, paying audience waiting to get their money's-worth; it was a gang of like-minded enthusiasts, their edges softened by pints of beer, there to be with friends and to sing, either in fluid, intertwining harmonies that touched the heart, or in raucous support. The folk clubs were magic to me. They were my training-ground, providing a supportive, easy-going audience willing to listen and quick to applaud.

They were also easy to mock and much lampooned. Non-converts represented the folk singer as someone hirsute in rope-soled sandals bawling some incomprehensible and unaccompanied dirge while having one finger stuck in his ear. There was a little of that but not a lot.

I discovered that my local folk club was held in The Bell Inn, a thatched pub near the village pond in Ducklington, a few miles from Witney. It took place on Monday evenings. I started to go regularly and soon it became the undoubted high spot of my week. I came to know the performers; they were as varied as the songs. Trevor ran a Pick Your Own fruit farm, played variously sized concertinas and specialised in seafaring songs including the highly ambiguous shanty 'Fire Down Below!' Keith taught special needs children and sang luscious ballads such as 'The Death of Queen Jane'. Robert the jeweller sang, so did Bob the slaughterman, and in the end so did I, Pam the typist.

I desperately wanted to have a go and one night I stood up with my guitar and sang a terrified, croaking version of 'The Raggle Taggle Gypsies O'. Everybody joined in and the following Monday I was asked to sing again. That was how it began, with me contributing some well-known folk song or other that I had practised during the week in Mrs Harris's flat. I was happy to be one more floor singer with an average voice. The change came when I decided to lighten the mix somewhat and insert one of my jokey poems. I don't remember if it was 'I Wish I'd Looked After me Teeth' or 'The Battery Hen', but the reaction was highly exciting, people really laughed and some asked where they could get a copy! This spurred me on to write more because I didn't want to repeat the same old thing. A popular choice was 'In Defence of Hedgehogs', protesting about the numbers of dead, flattened hedgehogs I saw every day on the roads. I came up with another, this time a ludicrous love story entitled 'Not You, Basil!' The idea came from hearing my boss Ernie pick up his phone and exclaim, 'Not you, Basil!' I built up eight or nine on different subjects. I knew they weren't poems in the accepted sense. They were a bit of fun written in the hope of making people laugh, and they enabled me to fit words together like a jigsaw, which I loved to do. The term Pam's Poems tripped nicely off the tongue. Pam's comic verse or monologues might have been more accurate but were clumsy to say. Pam's Poems they became. I developed an act made up of my Poems, beautiful traditional songs like 'The Galway Shawl' and the few idiotic ballads I had written including 'Don't Sell Our Edgar No More Violins'.

I started to write every evening. I hurried home from Smiths, ate a crummy tea, gathered my pad and pen and entrapped myself in my writing seat, comprised of the brown Rexine armchair with an ironing board placed across the arms. This formed a usefully wide writing surface and I happily worked at my ironing board desk every night. The folk club gave me the things I had always lacked, a *reason* to write and a *use* for the material once I had created it. I set out to write any kind of funny stuff I could, for the audience at Ducklington Folk Club.

Meanwhile Mrs Harris had sadly lost her husband. She was lonely and took to calling me into her part of the house for a chat when I arrived home from work in the evening. I confess it wasn't always what I felt like doing; I was starving and wanted to kick off my shoes and relax. Her stories ('he—was—an—*Adonis*!') about smoulderingly gorgeous officers in the Blues and Royals had started to sound a bit familiar. I'd heard them before. She would airily wave a hand towards an ornate tin on the table between us and invite me to help myself to nibbles. I only nibbled them once. The tin was half-full of salted peanuts, all turquoise with mould. One chilly evening I discovered Mrs Harris crouched over a reeking paraffin stove. I didn't like the look of it much and implored her to be careful when moving around the room so that she didn't knock it over.

'Don't worry about that, Pem!' she reassured me feistily. 'If I knocked it over I've got a bucket of water right here to throw at it!'

I blanched, knowing this was the worst possible thing for an oil fire but Mrs Harris waved my fears aside and urged me to eat more nibbles. In reality, it was a sad situation because as I became busier and was increasingly out of the house, Mrs Harris became more lonely and in greater need of care. Later her daughter took her to live near her own family in Hitchen Hatch Lane, Sevenoaks.

An interesting development had happened at the folk club. A group of us began to be asked to leave our home base of The Bell Inn, and entertain at small local events. One such was a Young Farmers' evening at the village hall in the village of

Windrush. It was a massacre. The Young Farmers had drunk enormous amounts of beer and were in no mood to listen to touching love ballads about a shepherd swain, or to elderly sea shanties. Trevor stood and pumped his concertina over increasingly hysterical laughter and a rising beery chorus of jeers. In the end Trevor snapped, went red in the face and told them off for their rudeness when people had come along out of their own goodwill to try to entertain them. The hubbub died down to a resentful 'Who the **** does he think *he* is?' mumble. Into this bear-pit I went next, nervously declaiming on the subject of battery hens and squashed hedgehogs. Nobody laughed much. This was a far cry from the safe friendliness of The Bell, from our whitewashed clubroom with horse-collars on the wall. It was another side of entertainment altogether, the humiliating side that co-exists beside success through a paper-thin division.

One night at Ducklington Folk Club, I was astounded to be approached by a booker. He wanted me as a guest performer at his club up near Banbury, *what would my fee be*? I looked at him as if poleaxed. It was one thing to stand up in my own club among friends, but to go further afield as a *guest performer* meant you were up a notch, you considered yourself something more special, someone people ought to *pay to see*! I knew my embryonic act had been gratifyingly successful so far and that for most of my life I had longed to be on the stage. I was terrified but knew that if I was serious, I had to do it. I charged £12 and accepted the job.

59

A TEACHER

I had met a wonderful man at the folk club, and was in the happiest of relationships. Our backgrounds could not have been more different. He was Leonard Strauss from St Louis, Missouri, a Harvard-educated teacher working temporarily at a school in Witney. I had never met anyone like him. On our first date, we went blackberrying, brought our treasure back and made jam in the tiny, earthen-floored weaver's cottage he rented in Witney's West End. I did not know of any English boyfriend who would have suggested a spot of jam making; it would have been considered laughable; irredeemably soft and girly. Yet it worked for us, and in hot sunshine near the village of Finstock we picked our blackberries, laughed and talked.

He looked at things differently. In Chipping Campden, he pointed out the soft beauty of the honey-coloured stone houses, which I had looked at but never seen. He knew little tea-shops in Burford where we snuggled into corners; previously I had walked straight past them with my usual 'not for the likes of us' mindset.

I ate cheap pasties and burgers. He invited me to wonder what rubbish had gone into them to make them so cheap, and told me kindly that my diet was atrocious.

He was aware of the history of our area as I was not, of the great houses and those who had frequented them: Snowshill, Hidcote, Asthall Manor, the Mitfords and William Morris. I went with him to see Andrés Segovia play in the Sheldonian Theatre in Oxford. I had never heard of either. This beautiful, soft-spoken American was unintentionally a kind of teacher to me, because in a subtle and unpreachy way he introduced me to new ideas, and showed me the beauty of my own area.

Then, I found it difficult to talk to children in a meaningful way. I struggled to think of appropriate subjects and they soon lost interest in me. By contrast, his empathy with them was extraordinary. They loved him. He was genuinely interested in what they had to say and they could discern this. Knowing nothing about teaching, I only looked on as he planned class projects in the little weaver's cottage. One was a walk from Witney to Burford along the River Windrush, all broken up into manageable sections. He wrote to farmers along the way asking permission to visit them with the children, and all was set. As far as I could see this was just an interesting riverside potter, but his plans were imaginative and far-reaching. The children painted a map of their route, which involved measurement, geography and art. They noted, researched and documented the wildlife they encountered along the way. Farmers ushered them into their farms, explaining the activities going on in fields and barns. Finally, they wrote a song, wrote it themselves all about the River Windrush, singing the words and playing the notes on their instruments. I was bowled over. To be able to extract so much that was interesting and educational from a walk! To learn diverse things so enjoyably, from the happy exploration of a river.

He was a brilliant teacher loved by children and parents alike. Sadly, I think it weighed upon him that his own parents had expected his expensive, prestigious education to equip him for something grander, a weightier career in law or medicine. Teaching seemed to fall a little short, and was perhaps felt to be slightly disappointing.

In Witney, we shared our time between his tiny weaver's cottage in West End and my flat at 94 High Street. My landlady Mrs Harris adored him; he was very kind. One night a group of yobs freshly ousted from the pub next door broke the window of her ground-floor bedroom; she was terrified and called up to us in the flat in a panic. He went down in his reassuring way, carefully cut out and stuck cardboard over the broken panes and arranged for a glazier to call the following day.

We decided to set up a bird table, as he was not familiar with British birds and wanted to be able to identify them for his pupils. As my flat was on the first floor, this was tricky and involved the rigging up of a level feeding platform extending out from the windowsill. All went well and the crumbs I sprinkled out daily attracted a host of birds. One morning he crossed to the window to have a look and I heard him say breathlessly in his American voice, 'Oh my Gaaaad!' I hurried over. There, relaxing upon the table was the substantial bulk and fleshy red face of an enormous Muscovy duck.

I had a hankering to go to Paris and we booked a cheap flight from the grandly named Ashford International Airport. On a Douglas DC3 aircraft of startlingly battered and elderly appearance, we flew to an anonymous airstrip in a Parisian suburb, miles distant from the centre. The flight was short but it took half a day by bus to reach the heart of the city.

Because he had studied in Paris, Leonard knew

his way around and could show me all the landmarks. I marvelled at the idea that a person could step out into a foreign city and know it like their home, that even though they might originate from a place thousands of miles distant, they could be equally at ease in a different country, could know its customs and slip effortlessly into its language.

We climbed to the beautiful Sacré-Coeur basilica on top of the hill of Montmartre, admired the cathedral of Notre Dame and the Arc de Triomphe. Walking down the Champs-Elysées I was dejected to find it patrolled by chic, tiny-waisted, bomber-jacketed French girls walking arm-in-arm. They smiled coquettishly at my companion. This had the effect of making me feel insecure, elephantine and deeply unfashionable in my gaudy yellow mack.

On another trip, we visited Ireland. As we drove off the ferry in Cork, I saw anti-British graffiti for the first time. I was largely ignorant of the blood-soaked history of the place, fondly believing we were popular with all. I found the hate-filled daubs on bridges and walls deeply disturbing.

At that time I was besotted with David Lean's film *Ryan's Daughter*, particularly as it starred a limping army officer. We tracked down the school where it was filmed and I peered in through the boarded-up windows. As a backdrop, the Blasket Islands stood in their recently deserted beauty. Ireland in the early Seventies was considered poor and quaint. The countryside was made up of a profusion of tiny fields, the hedges ablaze with wild purple-and-red fuchsia. Sad little donkeys with overgrown, curled-up hooves dotted the paddocks and everywhere thatched crofts provided picturesque but primitive homes for their owners. Small trotting donkey-carts frequented the roads, bearing one churn of milk and the reclining carter.

The country exhibited a fascinating and deep religious faith. Nuns were to be seen everywhere, walking briskly on sandalled feet through the town or in strung-out groups along country roads. On Sundays, the churches teemed with people; massive congregations of smartly dressed worshippers queued to get in. Of the homes we stayed in, many displayed a luridly coloured image of Christ with an illuminated, pulsating heart.

We bed-and-breakfasted around Ireland and everywhere had placed before us great slashed loaves of soda bread made with coarse brown flour, buttermilk and bicarbonate of soda. Freshly baked, this bread was mouth-watering and fragrant. Overnight it grew rope-like, tough and chewy. We toured the sights, savouring in particular the view from our room in Clifden, which was dominated for the whole of our stay by a large parked hearse. We saw but were content not to kiss the Blarney Stone of Blarney Castle, and travelled to the wondrously entitled Macgillicuddy's Reeks. This range of hills is very beautiful but a team of ill-used, exhausted horses forced to carry tourists through the Gap of Dunloe dejected me and I couldn't wait to leave. We were silenced by the awesome Cliffs of Moher, attended a truly dreadful laid-on-for-tourists *ceilidh*, bought beautiful woollen tartan rugs from a hidden-away mill and came home happily with vivid, teeming impressions of the place.

Soon afterwards, two negative things happened. Leonard's time as a teacher in the UK finally ran out and, at the age of twenty-six, I was diagnosed with a lump in the breast. My doctor said, 'We *always* operate.'

I told Ernie Skinner I was going to be hospitalised and why. He was hideously embarrassed and announced that I should have invented some other, less personal, ailment to tell him about. This had never occurred to me. I had the operation and the lump was found to be benign. To celebrate, Leonard and I went out and bought an orange anglepoise lamp to illuminate my ironing-board desk. He knew I longed to be a writer and had already given me thoughtful gifts; a good dictionary and a *Roget's Thesaurus* (I'd never heard of it) destined to be in daily use for the next thirty-five years.

The grim day of his departure came inexorably on. He packed up his belongings, we cleaned and spruced up the interior of the house and he left to go back to America. With typical and extraordinary generosity, he left me his car, a little navy-blue mini. The tiny weaver's cottage with the fig tree round the door looked heartbreakingly empty and forlorn as we locked up and gave in the key to his landladies. I had been ecstatically happy there. I never once went back.

I was very low. I missed him in a hundred different ways. We had a plan in place for me to go to the USA, to visit him in Massachusetts, but it seemed so far off, so little compared to what we'd had. The recent operation had left me depressed and in pain. I remember sitting on the plush red stairs at 94 High Street after he had gone, feeling damaged and bereft.

*   *   *

Mum and the gang from No. 16 Vandiemans were going to Newquay for their annual holiday. Mum knew how I was feeling and urged me to go with them. I went but it was difficult. I had grown used to being half of a couple who were on entirely the same wavelength. I could not go back to the bleak business of sitting in pubs. One positive thing was that my relationship with Mum changed and shifted up a gear; she talked to me about Leonard, knowing how much I missed him. I realised that we were talking as two affectionate adult women would talk, not necessarily mother and daughter any more, just as two women who cared about each other, propping one another up in an age-old fashion.

60

A BOOK AND A BROADCAST

It was exciting that bookings for folk clubs were definitely on the increase. Though I was earning something like £40 a week at Smiths, I was now regularly charging £12 for a half-hour guest spot and it did not take me long to realise that one income could soon start to equate to the other. Moreover I loved the folk clubs and did not love Smiths.

I was booked for Len Harman's famous folk club in Turville, Bucks, where the audience sat on old car seats and church pews in a cow barn still stocked with cattle. A thoughtful group of heifers listened politely and attentively to the music, pausing only to moo and pass copious amounts of urine.

Sensationally, I was offered a spot in Towersey Folk Festival, which was considered one of the very best. It was there that I first saw Fred Wedlock perform his classic parody of Simon and Garfunkel's 'The Boxer'. Fred's version was entitled 'The Folkie' and described the hazardous life of a folksinger who, with his cheap plywood guitar and a playlist restricted to songs using only two chords, fled an Irish club in Kilburn with the imprint of a Guinness bottle stamped on his ear. Fred was magnificent; it was one of the best laughs I ever had.

To my growing excitement, I was finding that people wanted to buy copies of my poems. If a performance had gone well and they had enjoyed a good laugh, they then wanted something tangible to take home. I knew I should get them into print and take advantage of what could easily be a fleeting demand, but I didn't know where to begin. Having tracked down an address for the Poetry Society, I wrote a polite letter to the august body setting out the situation and asking for their advice. Receiving no reply, I decided to research the matter myself.

In the telephone directory, I found two printers in Oxford, the Church Army and the Oxonian. I typed out the poems, drew accompanying illustrations, made appointments to see both printers and set off. It felt very odd to be seeking to do business on my own account, but I felt determined as well. The Oxonian Press quoted me £60 to print 500 copies of what was not much more than a pamphlet. Leonard, typically, had left me some money to help me achieve my aim, so I agreed the price although it seemed astronomical.

I needed a wry-looking photograph to go on the front. The expression I wanted was a sort of tongue-in-cheek, I-know-this-isn't-*really*-poetry look, and I didn't have one. Deciding to get it taken by a professional photographer, I booked an appointment with Arthur Titherington in Witney, and found him brusque. I am ashamed to say that I talked airily to him about my jolly time in Singapore, unaware that he had suffered terribly there at the hands of the Japanese during the war. Later I read an article about him and learned that after Singapore he had endured three years of slave labour in a Taiwanese copper mine. By the end, this tall man weighed 5st 7lb; only ninety of his fellow 523 prisoners survived. He campaigned throughout his long life for an apology and compensation from the Japanese. I came to admire his bloody-minded determination and his blunt statement: 'I do not forget and I do not forgive.' I was very pleased that it was Arthur who took the photograph for the cover of my first 'book'.

The presses at Oxonian rolled exceedingly slow. After many exasperating weeks my poems were finally ready and, my chest filled with butterflies, I collected 500 copies in a string bag. They did not look entirely as I had hoped. The print was microscopic and the paper used for the covers the worst possible choice; the merest touch left a fingerprint of forensic quality. Nevertheless, I had them. Arthur's suitably wry-looking photograph was there on the front page beneath my suitably succinct title:

**The Entire Collection (Eight) of Masterpieces by
Pam Ayres**

Thereafter, following any performance that had gone half-well I would declaim:

If you liked my poems and you want to read some more,
I've got a book for forty pence; buy it at the door!

I would then sprint down from the podium, whip out the books and set up shop. It was heart stopping. People formed a queue, bought the booklets in twos and threes *and asked me to sign them*! This had all happened so suddenly and seemed utterly unreal. Yet I had proof that it was completely real. On my late-night return from each engagement, my normally empty pockets were full of money. Like a miser, I counted it up on the floor of Mrs Harris's flat. There were pounds and pounds. I could repay Leonard. I was incredulous.

I decided to try local bookshops although I had seldom entered any. I meekly approached W.H. Smith in Witney and the little bookshop halfway up the hill in Burford. To this day, I do not know where I found the courage. It was agony. Surrounded by shelves of fat, expensively produced volumes I proffered my thin booklet with its homemade drawings, and shifted from foot to foot as the proprietor leafed silently through the pages. I could have died with embarrassment at my own presumption. Yet every single shop I visited took my book. It may have been only one or two copies on a sale or return basis, but not one person turned me away. I had never felt so fragile, or found the asking of anything so difficult. I still feel touched and grateful that my small endeavour was not scorned, that I was given a chance.

*   *   *

At work, I knew a man named Bill Govier, a union official. At first, I didn't like him very much. I hated the way he wagged a finger at me if we passed in the corridor: 'Get in that union!' he would command in his bossy way. I didn't particularly want to join. I'd had to attend a few meetings and cringed when addressed as 'comrade' or 'sister' as if we were all Russian. It was like some corny old sketch except that it wasn't; people did actually stand up and harangue the crowd saying, 'If this ain't put right, comrades, I for one will be DAHN THE ROAD!' Anyway, I had to join; the unions were powerful and it was hard, unless you had a death wish, to go against them.

Bill Govier lived in the nearby town of Bampton, which had a strong community spirit; they constantly raised money to enable their elderly residents to enjoy a treat. As it was coming up to Christmas, a blowout for the pensioners was being planned in the form of a turkey dinner. Bill asked if I would take part in a fundraising show in the town hall and I agreed.

Immodest it may be, but I have to say I was a triumph. The audience laughed hysterically at my poems, and again I felt a quiet, thrilling sense of fulfilment that something I had devised, written and performed myself had genuinely convulsed the audience. It wasn't a feeling that made me whoop or jump up and down, but it was unspeakably lovely just the same.

At the end of the show Bill asked if I would like to go on BBC Radio Oxford and read a poem. I leapt at the chance: *would I like to go on the BBC indeed*? It was unbelievable. Bill said he had a friend who presented a poetry programme; he would ask him to give me a spot.

I went home filled with the excitement that now seemed to be my constant companion: a cavalcade of electrifying things was happening: the paid appearances, the sales of my booklet and now the possibility of a broadcast on the BBC! After years and years in the doldrums, my life seemed to be unfolding along a new and sensational path. The future, which had seemed wholly predictable, was suddenly filled with possibilities.

After a couple of days, my phone rang in Ernie Skinner's office. It was Bill. Radio Oxford was *on*! I was given a date and time to turn up. This was a huge step for me and I hoped against hope that they would not change their mind and think better of it.

Arriving at BBC Radio Oxford I climbed the stairs slowly, holding my breath, savouring the immense weight of the moment. The stairs were made of a pink aggregate that looked like the multi-textured meat and jelly called brawn. At the top, a large sign over the door spelled out the intoxicating letters: BBC. To me this had potent, undeniable magic. It was the top of the tree, the best you could get; the place where writers and people with abstract creative skills finished up and found their home regardless of what sad misfits they might previously have seemed. A place where a person might find they had *precisely* the necessary aptitude.

I was shown into a studio and sat down behind the microphone. The environment was awesome to me, the control desk and perforated soundproof walls. I could not begin to explain why, but it felt like the very heart of where I wanted to be, as though after all this time, I had finally arrived at the right place. The presenter gestured to me to begin and I recited 'The Battery Hen', an embittered account of the creature's life that was funny at first hearing, but which I hoped would also convey the revulsion I felt for the system. It did not take long to say. I got up, hoping I had made an acceptable job of it and drove back to work in Leonard's mini.

When 'The Battery Hen' was broadcast soon afterwards, the response was sensational. I was typing one of Ernie's cumbersome letters, thanking the recipient in anticipation of their co-operation, when someone very excited rang me from Radio Oxford and exclaimed, 'Your poem is on *Pick of the Week*!'

'Is it?' I said. 'Fantastic! What's that?'

I had never listened to BBC Radio 4 or even heard of the programme. The person explained that it was a round-up of all that was considered best on the BBC that week, so it was a massive compliment. That wasn't all. The poem was picked up by the BBC's *Farming Programme* and for unfathomable reasons was also broadcast coast to coast in Canada.

I was stunned to find that I had to put my shoulder to the door of No. 94 High Street and shove it open. Heaped behind was a mountain of letters which slithered aside. It was fan mail forwarded by the BBC! Scores of people from the UK and Canada had written to say how much they liked the poem, how it was funny and sad at the same time, how by the way in Canada, battery hens were known as caged layers. Everyone was asking where a copy could be obtained! The mail kept on

361

coming, and I arranged it in date order in buckets and washing-up bowls round the floor of the flat, in the forlorn hope of replying to everyone.

BBC Radio Oxford contacted me to ask if I had written any more poems. I told them I had 'I Wish I'd Looked After me Teeth', 'Like you Would', 'The Stuffed Horse' and various others. Emphasising how delighted they were that my first effort had been so well received, they invited me in to record the rest. I jumped at the chance and, at my ironing-board desk, importantly compiled a list of that part of my work, which I considered *suitable for broadcasting*!

Mike Dicken and Andy Wright of Radio Oxford recorded my first group of poems. They laughed a lot and the recording was hugely enjoyable. At the end of the session, Andy Wright said something to me that stood out in big, important words I would never forget. 'If you've got any more like that,' he said, 'we'll 'ave 'em!'

Andy Wright seemed to be the boss, and he asked me about writing more poems specifically for the BBC. I blanched, saying, 'I've never written to any kind of deadline,' and I hadn't; I just wrote pieces as and when a good idea turned up. Whether or not this would continue to happen seemed hard to predict. I felt afraid that agreeing to meet a deadline might frighten the tendency away altogether.

'What about if I give you six months?' Andy asked.

Six months felt like a different proposition. Six months was nothing like as daunting. I agreed to give it a try. The plan was for Radio Oxford to broadcast my poems in a little, weekly, one-off spot. I left the building feeling charged up, unable to believe what had just happened. Andy was going to send me a contract. I was *writing for the BBC*!

Mrs Harris was elated. As far as she was concerned 94 High Street clearly had a kind of literary magic about it, for not only had her father-in-law Mr Ernest Harris written his enchanting book *Wild Visitors to a Cotswold Garden* within its friendly walls, but a lady named Dora Saint had subsequently lived there too. Under the pen name of Miss Read she had written some of her highly successful *Fairacre* and *Thrush Green* novels, for which she was later awarded an OBE. Clearly, declared Mrs Harris, the spell had been cast again and I was the furtherance, the walking proof.

Once BBC Radio Oxford began to broadcast my poems weekly, demand for the booklet went through the roof. Breathless young men who had sprinted down the road from W.H. Smith appeared at the door of 94 High Street asking for more copies, as they had sold out and could not meet demand! I equipped Mrs Harris with a stack and, lonely no longer, she kindly dispensed them while I was out at work, taking the cash and telling callers at enormous length the entire literary history of the house complete with relevant dates, photographs, nuggets of extraneous information and offers of cake.

61

AN AUDITION

Through 1974, my second career continued to gather pace. I had a small, regular spot on Radio

Oxford, and was writing as much as I could. I was also performing in progressively larger places. Sales of the booklet were now measured in thousands and this last fact was particularly gratifying.

Before deciding to produce the booklet myself, I had contacted a few publishers in the doomed hope that they would fall over themselves to sign me up. I had used my normal optimistic scattergun approach and this was not at all scientific. I just looked into the front of a couple of random books, noted the publisher's name, rang them up, explained about the success of my local appearances and the demand for my poems that had ensued, and asked for their advice. I particularly remember the pronouncement of one dismissive lady. I don't blame her at all; I am sure she was busy with no time to spare on some rustic-sounding hopeful who was bending her ear. She said, 'Go home, dear, and forget all about it. As far as publishing the poems yourself is concerned, don't waste your money. *It'll never make your fortune and you'll end up using them to paper the walls.*'

Certainly, it wasn't making my fortune, but when I came home from the folk clubs at night and counted my booklet-sale money out into little towers of coins on Mrs Harris's floor, it gave me a feeling of incredible satisfaction and self-sufficiency. Here was money paid willingly by smiling people for copies of my own particular sort of daft verse, which I had written on my ironing board out of my own brain. My own brain, which had always seemed so turned-off and reluctant when faced with normal jobs and workplaces, but which leapt up with excitement at the chance of writing something funny. I counted my money. Had I wanted to, I could pay the rent and buy my weekly food shop entirely from the sale and performance of my own work. This was a massive change. It hinted at the thrill and dignity of independence, the possibility of not always having to type bad letters or clean up other people's fag ends, but of harnessing whatever odd ability I had been given, and of using it to make my own way.

*   *   *

Once again Bill Govier was organising a Christmas knees-up for Bampton's game senior citizens. I topped the bill in the little fundraising show and all went extremely well. After all the performers had taken a bow, Bill bowled up to me in a 'We're standing no nonsense' fashion.

'A lot of us here want to put you up for *Opportunity Knocks*,' he declared.

'Nope,' I replied ungraciously.

'Think about it,' he said. 'You just give it some thought.'

Over the next few days, I did. *Opportunity Knocks* was a long-running television talent show, which first appeared on ITV in 1956, then, with various channel changes, came and went until 1978. For much of its long run it was hosted by Hughie Green, a tall man with a mobile face and a vague transatlantic accent. He was famous for his catchphrase 'I really mean that sincerely, folks', which people tended to quote ironically when they didn't mean something sincerely at all.

The programme did a good, valuable job and was one of the few showcases on television where people could demonstrate their talents. All kinds of acts were given a platform and invited to show what they could do. Many of our popular entertainers, including Russ Abbott, Max Boyce, Tom O'Connor, Les Dawson and Mary Hopkin started on *Opportunity Knocks*. It was the foundation of all the TV talent shows that followed.

I considered the situation. There were things about the programme that I found deeply demeaning, particularly a notorious device known as the Clapometer. Though the winner was eventually decided by a weekly postal vote from the audience ('in your own handwriting for fairness, folks,' Hughie stipulated), there was also a toe-curling ritual at the end of each programme where the audience were asked to applaud each individual act while the volume of their applause was supposedly measured. This heralded the weekly manifestation of the Clapometer, a gigantic decibel meter alleged to gauge the loudness of applause in each case. It was wheeled out and the performer made to stand beside it while the audience clapped. A gigantic needle on the gauge wavered madly to and fro just as if, cynically observed some, a stagehand was wrestling with it round the back. Sometimes the audience didn't think much of the act and hardly clapped at all. It was heartbreaking to see the poor sap fighting to assume some dignified facial expression as the needle of the Clapometer scarcely quivered from its resting-place.

Did I want to put myself through that ordeal? To register zero on the Clapometer and become a laughing-stock? Emphatically no. Did I want to be ranked alongside certain other types of act I had seen on the programme, Tony Holland the Muscle

366

Man for instance, who sprayed himself silver and twitched his muscles to the tune of 'Wheels'? Or another jaw-dropping performer I had seen, a man who came on and to the accompaniment of pulsating music, beat himself on the head with a tin tray? Could I see myself in that line-up? Not if I could help it.

Nevertheless, some people like Russ Abbott had used the programme cleverly, not as an end in itself, but simply as a means to be seen, as a springboard to other mainstream work in the numerous rich folds of the entertainment business. Winning acts had undoubtedly achieved massive success, fame and fortune on a grand and glittering scale. I knew I was doing well around the local folk clubs and was successfully selling my pamphlet, but that could easily be viewed as small beer, as being a big fish in a little pond. It was a poser.

What if I just went for the audition? It would be fascinating to discover what a professional panel thought of my act. I needn't tell anyone I was going, just turn up and get the verdict. I had read somewhere that *talent shows relieve people of the burden of their own ambition.* A humiliating failure of an audition might do that, which would be unfortunate, or it might propel me to greater things as it had others. Either way it would give me an interesting professional evaluation of what I was doing. I contacted Bill and said OK, let's apply for an audition but do me a favour and keep quiet about it.

We had to send away for a form. When it arrived I scrutinised it, particularly the section entitled Brief Description of Act. After perplexed deliberation, I wrote the somewhat wordy but accurate: Writer and Reciter of Humorous Verse.

367

It didn't exactly trip off the tongue. I posted the form back thinking I probably wouldn't hear anything more about it. In this, I was wrong; a letter soon came back inviting me to attend for audition in Birmingham, a place I had never visited though I was twenty-seven years old. I booked a day off work.

One morning in April 1975, I dressed for the audition taking great care, putting on a pair of black trousers, a white shirt and highly fashionable red tartan smock. I loved it, but in retrospect must have looked about nine months gone. Arriving in the unfamiliar concrete canyons of Birmingham, I found my way to the hotel where the auditions were being held. The place was rather tired: it smelt musty and damp, and had seen better days. I was directed downstairs to a rather faded ballroom where flimsy gilt chairs lined the walls. The first thing to catch my eye was a large, rather hostile notice suspended from the ceiling by chains. It read:

ONLY SUCCESSFUL CANDIDATES WILL BE NOTIFIED BY LETTER

I suppose this was to discourage pushier acts from pestering the judges for an opinion of their chances.

Three people sat at a long table beneath the sign: a slight man flanked by two women. The man was Keith Beckett, the producer of the programme. His fellow judge was Doris Barry, who advised Hughie Green on theatre and dance matters and was the sister of ballerina Alicia Markova. The other was a secretary holding a stopwatch. A few hopefuls like me were gathered in little anxious knots around the room. Overall, there was a general feeling of nervousness and apprehension.

My audition was at 5pm in the afternoon, not a good time. A pall of cigarette smoke lay upon the air and there was the sense of it having been a very long day. I took a seat and waited. At one point, Keith Beckett got up and left the ballroom. Before doing so, he spoke quietly to Doris and gestured towards me. I lip-read him saying, 'I want to see *that one.*'

When my name was called I went up to the solitary stand microphone and recited 'Oh I Wish I'd Looked After me Teeth'. I did not expect to see any reaction from the judges, reasoning that they spent all day watching people trying to be funny and therefore would betray no reaction on their faces. I was genuinely stunned when they began to laugh. I felt great flickers of excitement. They were professional judges and they were *laughing*! The lady with the stopwatch even forgot to turn it on.

When I finished the poem, Keith Beckett asked me to wait behind until the end. Other acts then auditioned; there were musicians and a shouty singer. I was asked to come back up to the microphone. Keith asked if I had anything else.

'Yes,' I said, and did a long rambling story with a good end entitled 'Pam Ayres and the Embarrassing Experience with the Parrot'.

When I had finished it, he extricated himself from his seat at the long table and walked over to me. I watched him warily as he approached, and had no idea what he was going to say.

'Who writes this stuff?' he asked.

'I do,' I said.

'Well, you're *certainly* on the show,' he

announced, standing beneath the large sign saying *ONLY SUCCESSFUL CANDIDATES WILL BE NOTIFIED BY LETTER*. 'You are the one thing that we look for all the time and seldom find. You're *somebody doing something different.*'

I left the hotel walking on air. The place may have looked a dump when I walked in, but now it was a palace. *They liked my stuff*! It took a bit of getting used to. These professional judges liked my stuff! I was on the programme! I needn't stop at local radio; I could be on TV! Their enthusiastic reception gave me a huge, unbelievable boost.

62

A TRIP TO THE USA

During this time, I had kept up an enthusiastic and affectionate correspondence with Leonard Strauss in Massachusetts, sending lengthy letters and daft drawings to make him laugh. We had arranged a three-week holiday together in the USA and on 1 July 1975, a familiar line-up assembled at Vandiemans Road: my brother Tony with his Ford Popular; me as the baggage-laden intrepid traveller; and Mum coming to see me off. We made our way along the circuitous route to Gatwick Airport, and I left at lunchtime in a DC8 bound for Logan Airport, Boston. The return fare cost £116.50 providing you booked up months before. I was very nervous and excited about the journey; any previous travel had been under the auspices of the WRAF, when all I had to do was turn up. I was twenty-eight, and this time I had to think for myself.

It was a cheap, packed flight but I was highly satisfied to be on it and flying to America! Looking out of the window near Newfoundland I was enchanted to see icebergs far below us. They were beautiful, motionless in the sunshine, snowy white jewels on the green sea.

It had been nearly a year since Leonard and I locked the door of the little weaver's cottage for the last time in Witney; it was priceless to be back together. One of the first things we did, as the searing hot day faded into a perfect warm evening, was to visit a local lake and swim in the silky water. Not wishing to appear unattractively pasty in my swimsuit, I had trustingly anointed myself before leaving England with an early self-tanning lotion I'd discovered in Boots. I certainly achieved my aim; I was not so much pasty as paisley-patterned. Swirls of a brownish stain ranged haphazardly up and down my legs where I had cheerfully slapped the stuff on. It wasn't a flattering look.

Interesting crops were being grown near his home in Amherst, tobacco in particular. Looking not dissimilar to cabbage, it grew in vast fields, and breezes blown through the lush leaves picked up their sweet, treacherous scent. Straight from the field, the fragrance was heady and moreish, incomparably nicer than tobacco smoke. We walked along, inhaling deeply. In another field was a ramshackle zucchini-picker, like a great winged tractor. The mattress-strewn wings lay low over the soil and, on them, half-protected by ragged sunshades, lay the face-down pickers, men and women snatching up zucchini as they came into view below.

I liked this rural, crop-growing area. It made me

feel at home. I was less happy when we reached New York. There, being used to softer landscapes, I was unnerved by the graffiti-daubed underground trains and forbidding, armoured shops. New York was notorious for crime at that time and seemed loaded with menace. People seemed hard and ruthlessly hungry for tips. We took the Staten Island ferry for a view of the Statue of Liberty, ascended the Empire State Building, admired the United Nations and were turned away at the lift of the World Trade Building by a uniformed security guard. It was unfinished, he told us; all was not ready up there in the skylobby.

We covered a lot of ground, and various scenes stand out with clarity: a baseball match at Fenway Park, Boston, between the Minnesota Twins and the Boston Red Sox. I sat with Leonard and members of his family in the bleachers while vendors strolled through the crowd calling, 'Hey! Ice-cream! Hey! Franks!' Or Harvard University, where I bought a handsome bound journal to record the trip. Leonard had studied there, so it was familiar and dear to him, but to me, who left Faringdon Secondary Modern School unqualified at the age of fifteen, this was a closed, unknowable world. At Harvard, for the first time, I felt a distance between us; I didn't know enough, I hadn't done enough. His family were professional people; they were immensely kind but I didn't have much to say. I was keenly aware of my lack of conversation.

We explored New England, and fishing-mad Maine. Outside a shack-like tackle shop I nearly suffocated with laughter at a chalked advert reading: 'Coca-Cola, Fries, Maggots.' We visited L.L. Bean, the fabled country store in Freeport, which even in 1975 was open twenty-four hours a day. I bought an expensive belt made of brown leather and plaited elastic.

Near Tunbridge, Vermont, we stopped at one of the beautiful covered bridges, roofed like little houses to deflect heavy snow. It was infinitely tactile, the wood worn silky-smooth like velvet. We toured a sugarhouse where I extravagantly bought large amounts of maple syrup in attractive containers to take home as perfect souvenirs specific to the area. Sadly, it was an area they were never destined to leave, because later when flying home I realised I had left the lot in Leonard's fridge.

Not everything was serene. We were staying in a Brattleboro motel, in a little chalet Leonard described as our dog kennel. For supper we went to Howard Jones, a popular chain of restaurants. In my Harvard-purchased journal, I described the meal: 'I had fried chicken, eating two pieces and bringing home two in "a doggy bag". Then I had a Banana Royal, made up of a halved banana, a scoop each of vanilla and strawberry ice-cream, strawberry sauce, pineapple sauce, whipped cream, nuts and a cherry on top.' Strewth.

Leaving the restaurant, we made our way out into the dark street and stopped to watch the passing of a prodigiously long freight train as it crossed the road before us. It was loaded with timber. Flatcar after flatcar emerged from the forest, clattered past and was enfolded by woodland on the other side. We were watching this strangely lonely, poignant sight when, approaching through the darkness of the trees, we saw bright, flickering lights in yellow, red and blue. A flatcar tore into view, shockingly engulfed in flames,

373

sparks streaming behind it into the blackness. Shouts of consternation and alarm went up and people ran to telephone the fire department. Eventually the train was stopped, its blazing cargo doused and the smoking lumber taken down by forklift truck. This dramatic event made the papers the next morning. Brattleboro was rocked.

Our holiday drew to a close. It had been packed with interest. As the remaining days dwindled, we talked about our future. He was something extraordinary to me, and I knew it had been my exceedingly good fortune that he was interested in English music and had happened, one summer's evening, to look in on Ducklington Folk Club. I learned such a lot from him. His generosity and thoughtfulness helped me to publish my poems. He was a fine man and I loved him dearly. We talked about me moving to America but I was English through and through and felt as if I had grown out of the very soil. I belonged where my ancestors had grown up, in Stanford, Uffington, Baulking, and in all the beautiful villages where I could look up and see the pleated slopes of White Horse Hill. I loved my big family and the great network of support, which extended out from them. The thought of permanently leaving home filled me with grief. It wasn't because we were different in terms of religion, background and education, although those things were true. I just couldn't bear to leave, particularly at that time. I had loved writing all my life and now, at home, real promising possibilities had arisen, which I found irresistible. We both knew the situation as we arrived at Logan Airport and said a heavy-hearted goodbye.

63

NEW OPPORTUNITIES

Now in the British countryside, Dutch elm disease was taking its dreadful toll. Everywhere among the vibrant summer greenness of hedges and woods stood enormous, ancient English elms brought low, their leaves rust-coloured, their grace and grandeur scorched and dying. They had sheltered the days of my childhood and I loved them. Nothing could stop their demise; the sight was terrible, terrible.

It was unbearably flat, after the long anticipation and soaring excitement of the trip to America, to go back to my job at Smiths of Witney. Parking in the same old parking spot by the chain-link fence and trudging up the same old stairs was gut-wrenchingly awful. I sat at my typewriter and gazed round the unembellished walls feeling close to despair.

I had just one bright thing to look forward to. I'd been asked to appear in a charity concert in the Oxford Playhouse. I had once seen a performance of *Dr Faustus* there, but never imagined myself on the same stage. Roy Hudd was in the show too, and this was the first time I had worked in a professional theatre. I spent a long time prowling the rich, exciting darkness backstage, the blankness from which so much may be conjured.

I was given two long spots in the show and both went well. I was very happy with the way the evening turned out. During rehearsals, I met a local journalist from a free newspaper in Oxford.

He was about my age and pleasant as he warmly congratulated me on my success. We agreed to stay in touch. A few days later, we went out for a pub lunch and he talked to me in a most interesting fashion about journalism. I was fascinated by his job of writing. I was also ludicrously green. As he seemed so friendly and trustworthy, I confided in him and told him my secret, that I had a place on *Opportunity Knocks* if I chose to take it up. I earnestly instructed this journalist that whatever he did, he mustn't tell anyone. Was that understood? Yes, he said, oh yes, he understood all right.

The following week it was all over the local paper alongside Arthur Titherington's photograph of me lifted from the cover of my booklet. 'Local Girl a Hopeful for *Opportunity Knocks*' read the headline with all the dates and information I had given him. My friends were astounded. *Opportunity Knocks*? Pam Ayres? My pipe-sucking former colleague in Mr Pettifer's office announced waspishly, 'Well, if that's the case she's gone right down in my estimation!' It was exactly what I had hoped to avoid. I had intended to go for the audition and then consider the upshot, whatever it might be, quietly on my own. My idiotic spilling of the beans taught me a short, sharp lesson about journalists and the value of keeping my mouth shut.

Because I thought the whole thing was probably going to fizzle out anyway, I had not said a great deal to Mum about the audition, and nothing at all to Dad. Now someone down the pub who had seen the newspaper told him about it, which made me feel mean. Next time I was at No. 16 Vandiemans he brought it up.

'What's this about *Opportunity Knocks* then?' he ventured.

'Oh,' I said, my heart sinking, knowing how unlikely it was going to sound: 'Yeah, well, I'm just going to give it a try . . .'

'Oh.' Dad digested this unexpected nugget of information. 'What're you gonna do for it, like?'

'Um . . .' I mumbled awkwardly, 'I . . . oh . . . well . . . I'm going to say a poem.'

'*A poem?*' Dad repeated, aghast, his former expression of polite enquiry replaced by one of incredulity and disbelief, '*A POEM? You ain't got a snowball's chance in hell!*'

He didn't mean it unkindly and I wasn't hurt at all. I knew he was just trying to save me from what seemed to him inevitable humiliation and failure. Perhaps he thought I was going to recite 'I Wandered Lonely as a Cloud', or one of those scorned poems that stood for nothing in our male, no-nonsense, hard-graft household. Poetry of any kind was an irrelevance in No. 16 Vandiemans; nobody gave it a thought, why would they? It was largely dismissed as twaddle. People had livings to earn.

I knew this, completely understood it, and had played down my moderate success with the poem pamphlet and the few bits I'd done on local radio. As for my paid folk club appearances, nobody else in the family found folk clubs appealing. They were looked on kindly as one of my eccentricities.

I did not try to explain to Dad that the poem I planned to do on *Opportunity Knocks* was a different sort of thing. I hardly understood the bizarre situation myself, how I could have believed in it as I did. Like me, Dad would just have to wait and see. I would have to find out if I could pull it off, and see if it was possible to make what worked locally work across the whole country.

*　　　*　　　*

At the end of October 1975, I was contacted by Thames Television and asked to go to the studio on 21 and 22 November to record the *Opportunity Knocks* programme. I did not know whether to accept and asked if I could think about it and ring them back. I was faced with a fork in the road. I could continue to work at Smiths and live in Mrs Harris's flat. I was earning nearly £50 a week, which was a good wage. I could muck about with writing and performing in my spare time, and relegate it to second place in my life. This would be the safe, sensible option.

On the other hand, I could give it a go. I could jump in feet first, risk the excoriating humiliation of the Clapometer and take a chance. Professional people at Radio Oxford and *Opportunity Knocks* liked my act. Lovely, ordinary, salt-of-the-earth people fell about laughing at my poems, and were quick to buy them. Those were promising signs surely.

In the end it was the lure of the unknown that did it, the thrill of a leap-in-the-dark as opposed to a life of certain grinding monotony, of growing older and duller while typing away the precious days. I rang Thames Television and said yes.

When it came to suitable clothes, I suffered from no indecision. The maxi-dress was all the rage, as championed by Laura Ashley. It was frilled, flounced and pin-tucked to oblivion. I loved the look; it was old-fashioned, chaste, figure-hugging and, like me, smacked of the country. In

Little Clarendon Street in Oxford, there was a sizeable Laura Ashley emporium, which I perused every Saturday morning. There, racks were filled with the crisp freshness of lavish cottons, crammed with full, flower-sprigged skirts, virginally white, high-collared blouses and ground-sweeping dresses. For my first television appearance, I chose a lace-trimmed blue maxi-dress, flared, belted and satisfyingly snug in the bodice.

Thames Television took my breath away. This was no village hall, folk club or Women's Institute. It was the real thing, a huge, working TV studio. I walked in through high, barn-like buildings containing innumerable wooden stage sets, domestic, sequinned, sporting palm trees. Upon their plywood backs, the names of familiar television programmes had been roughly chalked. This was where they were made, all those programmes that people watched in their homes, mesmerised; this was the source, the fount, the nub, everything came from here. I cannot emphasise enough how privileged I felt, that I was in the very heart of everything that mattered to me.

I was shown to my dressing room and walked in, revelling in the moment, absorbing every detail. Pink-painted, it had a curious powdery smell that never dispersed. It was just as I had envisaged it, with every vital ingredient: a wardrobe and washbasin, a chair drawn up to a worktop and, most evocative of all, a mirror surrounded by lights.

The two days at Thames TV were spent rehearsing. There were six acts, groups and individuals who had passed the audition as I had done. All contestants were given a specially designed 'set', an area that it was hoped would

379

enhance their performance and show them off to advantage. A young man was on the programme, a singer performing a ballad in the style of Gene Pitney. I was mightily impressed by the set designed for him; to me it was the epitome of showbiz glamour. The backdrop was a slash curtain, made of thin, brightly coloured lengths of aluminium foil turning and twinkling in the lights, suggestive of tawdry nightclubs. At the singer's feet, unseen by viewers at home, was a squatting stagehand operating a large bellows connected to a rusting cylinder. This puffed dry ice around the performer's feet, giving him a look of misty mysteriousness. I was entranced and hoped against hope that when it was my turn, I would be cloaked in misty mysteriousness as well.

Life is full of disappointments and this was one of them. When it was time for my rehearsal the floor manager took me across to a little collection of furniture that I had seen but disregarded, thinking it was where the stage crew gathered for a fag and a sit-down. 'This is your set Pam,' he announced cheerily.

I looked at it with contempt. My set? There was just an exhausted-looking wing-type armchair. Placed beside it was a little round table on which a group of comfy-looking objects had been assembled. These included a small bunch of flowers, an old-fashioned lamp and a teapot *with a knitted tea cosy.* I was horrified. Leaving aside the uncool, folksy, spinsterish look, I *never* sat down for a performance; I liked to stand up, be expressive and wave my arms about.

'I don't like that very much,' I said doubtfully. 'Couldn't I have the slash curtain and the dry ice?'

He shook his head with finality. ' 'Fraid not

Pam,' he replied. 'We feel that this reflects your homely personality.' There was no room for negotiation. I was lumbered with the comfy corner.

During rehearsals, it was suggested that my poems might work better if spoken to music. I immediately detested the idea. They weren't written as songs. The comic effect depends on a certain elasticity in the delivery, a pregnant pause here and a rush of words there. To apply it to a regular musical rhythm would be like putting a straitjacket on it, forcing regularity on something meant to be erratic. I did my best. As an example for me to follow, they played some Betjeman poems set to vague pastoral music. I obligingly tried to chant 'I Wish I'd Looked After me Teeth' to some bland tune like 'English Country Garden', but it was cringingly awful. I could not use my natural timing. Thankfully, everyone agreed and I was left to my own devices.

The evening came on and the audience started to arrive. Each act taking part received an allocation of tickets; Hughie had rung me on 10 November to say I could have thirty. My family had loyally organised a busload from the village, the coach being supplied by a local company, Crappers Coaches. The rest of the audience arrived in minibuses and dignified saloon cars; my party turned up in a large coach bearing *Crappers* in ornate script along the side.

At last, the audience was installed, everything was in place and the huge studio doors were closed in readiness for the recording. A warm-up man went out to tell jokes to the audience. It was an agonising wait for the contestants. I don't remember much about my fellow performers, as I was wrapped up in myself and my own fears. When

381

my turn came, I was shown out and installed in the comfy armchair. Next, a supporter, someone you had nominated as your sponsor, appeared and told Hughie a little bit about you by way of introduction. When asked for a sponsor, I had originally suggested Bill Govier, since I was only there because of his persistence. Doris Barry did not think much of this, and was abrupt. 'What does he do, dear?' she asked. 'What's interesting about him? What could he talk to Hughie about?'

'Well,' I faltered, 'he does a lot of charity work . . .'

'*Masses of people* do charity work,' snapped Doris, 'leave it with us.'

A delightful lady from East Anglia introduced me. Her name was Mrs Crook and she was ninety-five years old. I had not previously met her, which I found slightly perplexing, but she was a dear, lovable old lady. She was hard of hearing and exceedingly nervous. The introduction went something like this:

Hughie: And tell us again, how old are you, dear?

Mrs Crook: What?

Hughie: Ninety-five years young, isn't that right?

Mrs Crook: Miss Pam Ayres.

Hughie: And is this who you are introducing us to tonight?

Mrs Crook: A poem she wrote herself.

Hughie: Absolutely. Mrs Crook would like you to give a really warm welcome to our next contestant, who is a *poet*, ladies and gennelmen, tonight, for Miss Pam Ayres, Opportunity Knocks!

Mrs Crook: Stanford in the Vale.

This was it. A big black television camera spun across the studio floor towards me. Alongside it in the gloom ran a man, an assistant who whipped the thick, snaking cable clear of obstructions. The floor manager appeared in front of me counting down the seconds with big, deliberate fingers: three, two, one! He made a huge 'over to you' gesture, the red light on the camera lit up and I was on.

My immediate concern was that people at home could see my heart beating. I was so terrified that my whole body shook with every thumping beat. Hindered by the restrictive chair, I took a huge breath and launched off into the lengthy 'Pam Ayres and the Embarrassing Experience with the Parrot'.

I just remember that I got through it and did not make any mistakes. At the end, each act took their place beside the hated Clapometer as a range of expressions, including hope, fear, humiliation and devil-may-care nonchalance, flashed fleetingly across their faces. I was placed second behind a good group named Pendulum. I then collected my belongings from the smart dressing room, got on the Crappers coach and went home.

The show was broadcast in early December. When I saw myself on television, I was appalled. I had cherished an image of myself as sprightly and mischievous, brimful of fun and youth. Instead, on the screen I looked ponderous and slow-witted, declaiming in a heavily accented voice and immobilised by a chair. It was deeply disappointing. Anyway, that was it; there was nothing more I could do about it. The show had gone out and the whole country had seen it.

The routine was that after the programme was broadcast at prime time on Saturday night, the postal vote was counted and the winner notified by teatime on the following Thursday. The Thursday came. At work in Ernie Skinner's office, I was nervous and fluttery. I couldn't imagine how I'd done, or whether the day would culminate in success or humiliation. The hours seemed long and I couldn't settle to anything.

My small office was adjacent to Ernie's big one. Outside there was a huge general office where people sat in lines doing paperwork, or discussing credit control on the telephone. An aura of cigarette smoke and suffocating boredom hung over the place. A large, constantly watched clock was fixed to the wall.

Teatime came and I had heard nothing. Somebody else must have won. I was an also-ran. The feeling of suspense, which had been with me for weeks, dispersed and a leaden feeling seeped into its place. I hadn't made the grade.

Somebody knocked on my office door. 'Phone call for you Pam,' they said, 'out in the general office.'

I knew this had to be it, because nobody would normally ring me out there. I made my way to the phone and picked it up. Everyone knew I had gone in for the programme and that today was the day. An unaccustomed hush fell over the whole office.

'Hello?' I ventured.

It was Keith Beckett, the producer.

'You've won darling!' he cried in his flamboyant fashion. 'You've *won*.'

I don't know what else he said after that, but the call ended and I put the phone down. Everybody was looking. In a small voice almost to myself, I

384

said, 'I've won.'

A huge, joyful whoop went up. I was astonished. A great, spontaneous cheer ripped across the office, normally so dead and sterile. It was such a heart-stoppingly touching reaction to my success. I never forgot the electrifying sound. I think it was because one of us had managed to escape.

64

CHANGE ON ALL FRONTS

Now there came a very odd time, a period of limbo, of being neither one thing nor the other. There was a sense of tremendous expectancy. The word on everyone's lips was *made*. 'You're made!' rang in my ears and 'You've made it!', and I could feel people's great pleasure all around me. No. 16 Vandiemans was bursting with excitement. Mum congratulated me, her face beaming with happiness, 'Well old gal, you've made it! You're made now, that you are! You've put Stanford on the map!'

It was the talk of the local pubs. 'They be all on about it down the Lion,' said Dad, pleased, and taking a wicked delight in impersonating some upper-crust type person who had come up to him and asked, 'Har you the father of the celebrated poet?'

Celebrated or not, I was still employed as Ernie's secretary and expected to fetch and carry as usual. A certain tension crept into the atmosphere between us now because, increasingly, when the phone rang, the call would be for me.

Ernie would appear in the doorway, holding out the receiver and wearing a long-suffering expression. 'It's for you,' he would say, grimly.

I appeared on the next *Opportunity Knocks* programme and tied for first place with an Australian singer named Tony Monopoly. On the third programme I was placed second, and that was the end of any competitive appearances, although I was a guest on two more programmes, one a round-up of winners, and the second a satellite link-up with Australia, which was innovative and far-reaching for its day.

Keith Beckett recommended an agent based in London. I did not know the city at all, so he arranged to meet me in the doorway of Waring & Gillow, a furniture shop near Oxford Circus, and he took me to their office. The agents took over everything, including my book, which was now going to be produced on a much larger scale. This was unbelievably exciting, but I missed being involved with it very much. Previously I had done everything, the writing, typing up and illustrating of my original material, as well as negotiating with the printers and bookshops. It had been my own project, which I had nurtured with affection and a rising joy. The process had built up my own confidence, and part of me felt bereft when an illustrator was peremptorily brought in and the presses rolled in some far-off factory.

A few job offers trickled in via the agent including a panto season in Jersey for £200. I didn't see myself in panto and still needed to pay my rent to Mrs Harris so I turned that down. I did misguidedly accept an excruciatingly and toe-curlingly awful engagement at a place in Birmingham called Tubes and Extrusions. The

386

company were having a knees-up in the works canteen and as the manager's wife had been 'charmed' when she saw me on TV, I was booked to give a short surprise performance. I suspect it was more along the lines of a shock. A highly appropriate professional band with female singer had been booked and was on stage. Halfway through the evening I was introduced and clattered up to the microphone in my Scholl sandals and long *Opportunity Knocks* frock. After the band and good gutsy singer, my poems sounded thin and timid. Fresh from Ducklington Folk Club, I was painfully nervous. Hardly anybody laughed, except my current boyfriend, standing loyally at the back and faking it.

Mercifully after a short time the compere walked on, arm extended in the time-honoured fashion to bring something painful to an end. 'Ladies and gentlemen, will you give a big hand for Pam Ayres!' he bellowed. Gratefully, I clumped off. A few people clapped. Clearly, I was no cabaret act. The money was nice. The job satisfaction was zero. The humiliation was fathomless.

This odd situation continued for some weeks, with people slapping me on the back exclaiming 'You're made!', while a few offers came in for things like Tubes and Extrusions, which I didn't want to do. Mercifully, something very significant then happened and I was offered a television commercial for a dairy company named Eden Vale. The product was a full-fat cream cheese, which was marketed like an oversized sausage encased in white plastic. The prospect of advertising a cheese likely to clog up people's arteries wasn't that overwhelming, but I was amazed by the fee my agent had serenely secured from the client. I had to write a little complimentary verse about the product and say it to the camera. This is what I wrote:

I always choose Eden Vale
It's natural and it's nice,
There's one thing better than having it once

(pregnant pause, raise left eyebrow in suggestive manner)

And that is . . . having it twice!

Making the advert was enjoyable. The company provided, and then gave me as a gift, a beautiful woollen maxi-skirt in a burnt orange colour. It was luxuriously, silkily lined and of far better quality than anything I had ever owned before. The recording was made amid much laughter, and the advert was well received. I could not believe the fee. At the time, I was earning about £50 a week from Smiths, but for the advert I was paid £600. It was unbelievable. I had never dreamed of having such a vast amount of money. To celebrate, I finally gave up cigarettes.

Other, more exciting work was coming in by this time, which was reassuring. My agent was even talking about an offer of a TV series from no less gilded a figure than Michael Grade! Now, with these fascinating possibilities appearing, and £600 to my previously impoverished name, I could support myself and pay the rent to Mrs Harris for many weeks. This enabled me to consider the possibility of a life beyond Smiths, which was timely because the situation at work was becoming intolerable. Ernie's phone was red hot, and all the calls were for me. His mouth had formed itself into a permanent, tight line. The situation could not go on.

It seemed to me that I was being offered one chance to break away. An unexpected path had opened up and though I did not know where it might lead, I could see that it looked more tantalising than the grinding, routine-filled days that made up my life, and which I loathed.

I handed in my notice. One lunchtime I went with a group of my friends for a strangely unsatisfactory farewell drink at The White Hart pub in Minster Lovell. Ernie presented me with a leather-bound book of outdated road maps and, on Friday 13 February 1976, I screwed up my courage and walked out of Smiths Industries of Witney for the last time. I intended to try to make my way as some sort of writer and performer for as long as the £600 lasted. Although it was truly frightening to be detached from the company, to be cut off from the security and a regular income, it was still the best decision I ever made.

My poems and verses, which I wrote purely for the fun of it, brought me more money in royalties than I had ever dreamed of. This enabled me to do lovely things, not only for myself, but also to help my family and friends with things they had always wanted: a new car, a garden shed, the final payment of a mortgage. I knew that much of my parents' life had been a long, hard struggle and that cash had been desperately short. At last, I could do something significant for them, something that had always been so out of the question it hadn't even been discussed. I helped them to buy our council house at No. 16 Vandiemans. Some time afterwards, I was over there on a visit and Dad said, 'You come just right. Me and Mother always sits here by the window on a Thursday morning.'

'On a Thursday morning?' I said. 'Why?'

His blue eyes were alight with mischief: 'Why?' he repeated with mock surprise. 'Well, so we can watch the rent man walk straight past the gate!'

AFTERWORD

I have loved writing this book, and have tried to describe, with tenderness, affection, humour and detail, an era that has now passed. I want to acknowledge the village as I knew it, as a self-sufficient place bustling with businesses and peopled with those who, in their various ways, helped to shape me into the person I became.

As this book is published, it is 2011 and I am sixty-four years old. It is thirty-five years since I walked with such trepidation out of Smiths Industries to try to make a go of things on my own. What happened afterwards is still difficult to believe.

Two books of my poems were published in the year after *Opportunity Knocks*. The first one remained in the *Sunday Times* Top Ten bestseller charts for a period of forty-six weeks from April 1976 to February 1977, and the second one stayed in the same chart for seventeen weeks from November 1976 to March 1977. This reaction to the verses that I penned on my ironing-board desk in Mrs Harris's flat was heart-warming and beyond anything I had ever imagined.

Tongue-tied and on alien territory, I remember seeking the advice of a local accountant. When I nervously enquired about the possibility of buying a house, he assured me it would be a sensible step. Thunderstruck, I ventured into an estate agent for the first time in my life and bought a little terraced house for £11,500. It was in Standlake not far from Ducklington, and situated opposite a pub named The Golden Balls. When I moved in, the only furniture I had was a wicker stool in the shape of a lobster pot. It looked a bit lost. The thing that stands out to me, then and now, is the feeling I had when I went into that house and closed the front door behind me. I can still hear the click of it, and feel the atmosphere of the house settling around me as I stood there quietly breathing it in. I actually introduced myself to it, politely. My own house. I could hang things on the wall, invite friends, and do anything I wanted. It was mine. After the cheerful overcrowding of my childhood, the WRAF barracks, the doleful bedsitters and all the accommodation I had lived in where owners could wag their finger and tell you what you could and couldn't do, this was it. It was my own darling little house by The Golden Balls. Incredibly, my poems had enabled me to buy it.

Not long afterwards, it was my good fortune to meet Dudley Russell who would become my dear husband and the father of our two much-loved sons. He rescued me from the appalling contracts I had signed, and ever since has steered the ship of our family with vision and good sense. He has always believed in me and made me feel I could carry something off, even when I was filled with doubt myself. I would not have achieved the same things without him.

I loved writing from the first moment I sat down in Stanford school with a new ruled exercise book in front of me. The mystery of where it comes from, how humour, sadness and pathos can be conjured up from a blank sheet with a pen and an idea. The challenge of finding the perfect word or phrase to fit a subject snugly and describe it exactly. How it can be possible to write a couple of lines which, when correctly delivered, cause an audience to shake with laughter.

I was hooked on performing by the age of seven when, in my lavish curtain robes, I played the haughty queen opposite King Marmaduke on stage in Stanford in the Vale Village Institute while waving my balsa-wood lorgnette. After that, I did it whenever I had the chance.

What was so unbelievably fortunate was that I was able to harness my two abilities and use them to make a living. I could write the material and perform it in a way that made people laugh. Furthermore, I absolutely loved doing it. It knocked spots off all the miserable, boring, repetitious clerk jobs I'd had previously. And I felt I was doing something eminently worthwhile. People came up to me at the end of shows and said, 'I have not laughed like that for years.' One lady gave me the best compliment I have ever had. She said, 'I have never seen my mother laugh like that *ever.*' My audiences have been fantastic, friendly and supportive.

I have had spectacular failures of course, and made awful, toe-curling mistakes. Then I was unutterably thankful that I had my family to come home to. They thought I was as good as ever.

It has been and continues to be a richly varied life of writing and performing. From the humblest of beginnings, for example the Young Farmers' evening in Windrush Village Hall where I and my fellow minstrels were lucky to escape without being impaled on pitchforks, I went on to play astonishingly prestigious places: the London Palladium, Sydney Opera House, St James's Palace and Sandringham where I performed on my own for the Queen and had the pleasure of seeing our sons present her with flowers and champagne. In

393

2004, I wonderingly unfolded a piece of thick cream notepaper informing me that I had been awarded an MBE for services to literature and entertainment.

I toured Australia thirteen times and I am just about to embark on the fourteenth tour. I fell in love with the country and the warm, welcoming audiences from Darwin to Hobart, from Wollongong to Perth. I have worked often in the clear, crystal spaces of New Zealand, travelled its pristine countryside with my husband and stared in admiration at the jaggedly spectacular Remarkables, my favourite range of mountains in the world. These lovely countries inspired me to write pieces that became gloriously popular. In Australia I wrote 'How God Built the Duck-Billed Platypus' and in New Zealand, 'The Akaroa Cannon', and others.

As a family, we have seen unforgettable sights: the whales of New Zealand, the sea turtles of Ascension Island and the still, intoxicating beauty of the Australian bush. At the very start of the new millennium, we were in Cape Town harbour watching a laser clock projected on to the slopes of Table Mountain. As the hand flicked over into the first second of the year 2000, every vessel large and small sounded its siren in a deafening, galvanising wail that shocked and thrilled us all. We have visited the little chapel at the base of Christ the Redeemer high above Rio de Janeiro, teetered on the edge of the Grand Canyon and been thoughtfully studied by trackside bears as we spun through the Rocky Mountains in a glass-roofed train. We flew at unbelievable speed in the pencil-like Concorde, and from the tiny flight deck, I watched the nose-cone drop before our landing at

Heathrow. In Hong Kong, we made our way along pavements crowded with blossom-laden revellers going home to celebrate Chinese New Year; in Kenya saw our sons catch, tag and release gigantic sailfish; and in New York, we stared into the unspeakable crater that was the World Trade Center. I met good people; I met thieves and liars.

All my life I have been interested in animals and in our Cotswold home I make room for as many as I can. We have let our hedges grow thick and tall; they are alive with birds. From the window of my office, I can see my bird feeders, nest boxes and a stone birdbath all in daily use. Scores of swallows flick and swoop over the field and a green woodpecker undulates away to feed her young. In our pond tiny newts scull about, intent on their hard-to-quantify business, dragonflies wait for their wings to dry and froggy eyes watch for insects with infinite patience. Among the trees, hidden from view, are piles of old logs gently rotting down. Beneath their sheltering presence are perfect little grass snakes with yellow collars, large muscular beetles that stand no nonsense and small, busy, mousy types.

Thirteen cows live in the fields surrounding our house, nine Cotswold sheep obligingly mow the grass of awkward, hard-to-reach corners and, in the copse, three piglets drive their snouts into the leaf litter and crunch snails. Like my dad and beautiful grandmother Ada, I keep a hive of bees, and my brother Tony, an ace beekeeper, helps me when I am baffled. There are two dogs, eight laying hens and seventeen guinea fowl that remind me of my childhood in Stanford. How could I ever have dreamed, when I was the girl from Mrs Harris's flat driving a Morris 1000 engulfed in smoke, that the things I wrote for pleasure would bring such a reward? It has been simply staggering.

I am sad that Dad never achieved the smallholding he dreamed of and deserved, and that Mum had no chance to take up her scholarship and shine, as she surely would have done. I regret that I never thanked her for deflecting me away from the job as a washer-up girl, which I was intent upon, and into the Civil Service, which gave me opportunities to develop and improve my education. I am glad that Mum and Dad found an eventual harmony. I am sorry I was mean to Paddy the horse and for innumerable other unkindnesses. I regret them all.

I thank my terrific and invaluable agent Vivien Green of Sheil Land Associates for believing in me over a very long period, for encouraging me to write this book and for instilling confidence whenever I didn't have much.

I want to thank my husband Dudley and our two sons Will and James for always being on my side. They mean everything to me. I am pleased that we were able to provide our boys with the confidence-builder of a good education, so that unlike me they were never limited by the feeling that they weren't good enough, or in some way did not measure up. I am sorry that while I have been writing my book I have not cooked any decent meals and my husband has lived on fishcakes.

I also thank my brilliant brothers Tony, Jeff, Roger and Allan, their families and friends, my cousin Marcella who farms on White Horse Hill, and Valerie Bendall and her family, all of whom I have pestered for their memories over many months. They have been unfailingly helpful and patient towards my project, and where, despite my best efforts, I have got my facts wrong, I apologise and welcome correction.

It was my great good fortune to have a sister. Though as children we were keen to beat each other up and did so whenever the chance arose, as adults we have been close through thick and thin. She is my dearest friend and, without her, my life would have been infinitely poorer. I thank Jean, her husband Ginge and their kind, beautiful daughters Stella and Tanya.

I am still friends with Leonard Strauss, and now with his delightful wife, Janet. Dudley and I are hoping to visit them in Massachusetts in 2012 and to take a holiday among the blazing autumn colour of New England.

You see, I was hopeless at being an accounts clerk, punched-card operator or draughtswoman. I couldn't plot, had no hope of being an air quartermaster, wasn't much of a typist and couldn't get fired up about being aide to the Hydraulics Buyers or right-hand woman to the Works Engineer. But I think I made a pretty good job of being Pam Ayres. I was so lucky. The things I wrote, and the way I said them, made people laugh. It wasn't that difficult. You could probably do something similar using your own abilities, if you wanted to. It's all a matter of having the necessary aptitude.

Pam Ayres
June 2011